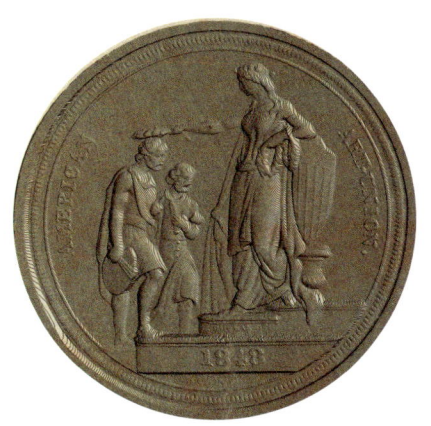

Perfectly American

THE ART-UNION & ITS ARTISTS

Amanda Lett | Patricia Hills | Peter John Brownlee | Randy Ramer | Foreword by Duane H. King

GILCREASE MUSEUM | TULSA OKLAHOMA

PUBLISHED

BY THE

AMERICAN ART-UNION

FOR THE

SUBSCRIBERS

OF

1848

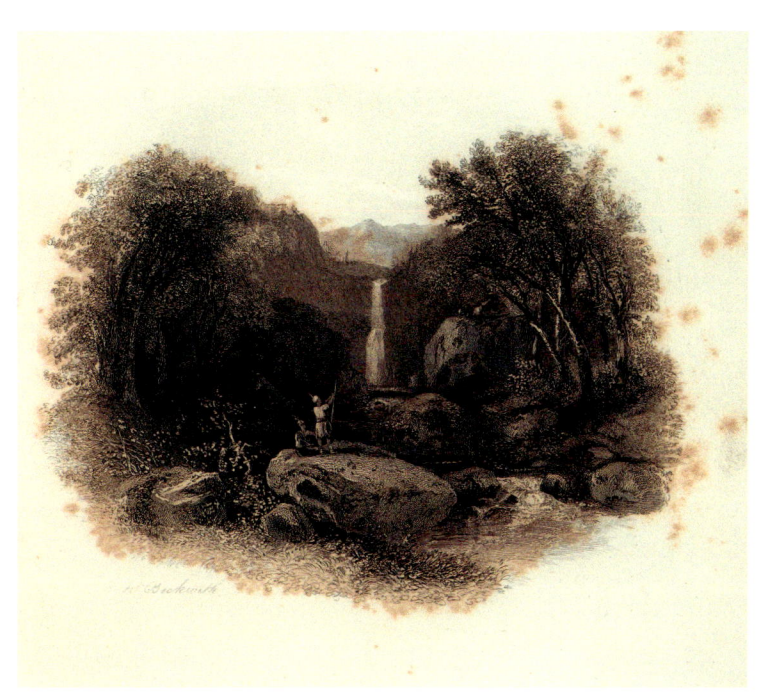

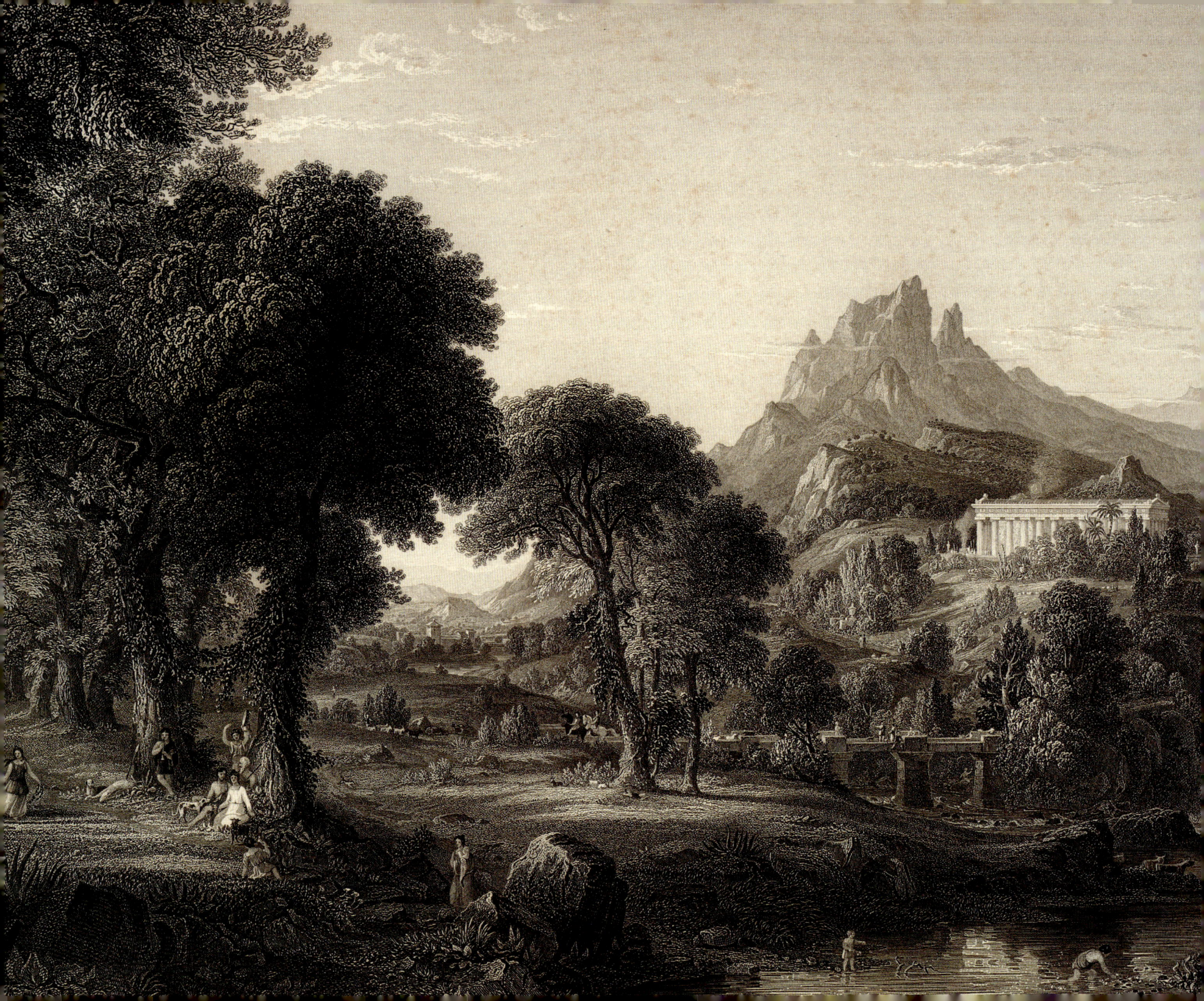

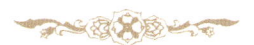

Design, editing, and production:

CAROL HARALSON DESIGN

Gilcrease photography:

ROBERT S. CROSS

Gilcrease publication assistants:

BRITNI PELTON

AND COURTNEY TAYLOR

PHOTOS: Page one: P. P. Duggan and C. C. Wright, John Trumbull medal, American Art-Union, bronze, 1849, GM 08.219; Page three: H. Beckwith after John Frederick Kensett, *Catskill Mountain Scenery,* American Art-Union, engraving, 1851, GM 5126.1061.101; Page nine: Bobbett and Edmonds after Jasper Cropsey, *Temple of the Sibyl at Tivoli,* American Art-Union, engraving, 1851, GM 5126.1061.5

This publication, like so many worthwhile endeavors at Gilcrease Museum, has been made possible by members of The Gilcrease Council.

THE GILCREASE COUNCIL

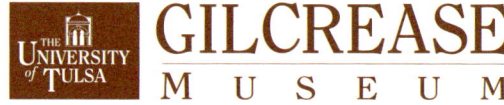

1400 NORTH GILCREASE MUSEUM ROAD

TULSA, OKLAHOMA 74127-2100

Gilcrease Museum is a University of Tulsa/City of Tulsa partnership.

The University of Tulsa is an EEO/AA institution.

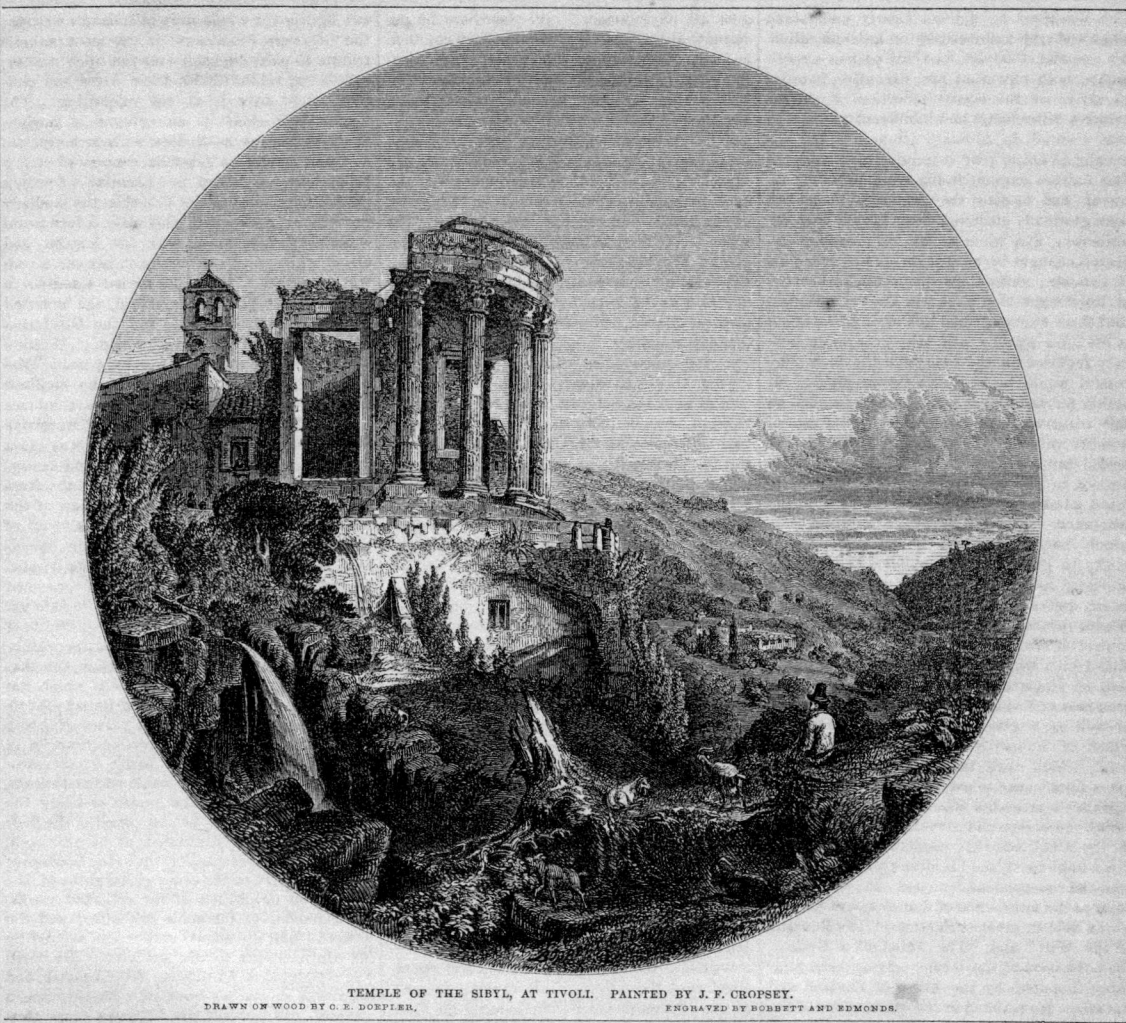

TEMPLE OF THE SIBYL, AT TIVOLI.　PAINTED BY J. F. CROPSEY.

DRAWN ON WOOD BY C. E. DOEPLER.　　　　　ENGRAVED BY BOBBETT AND EDMONDS.

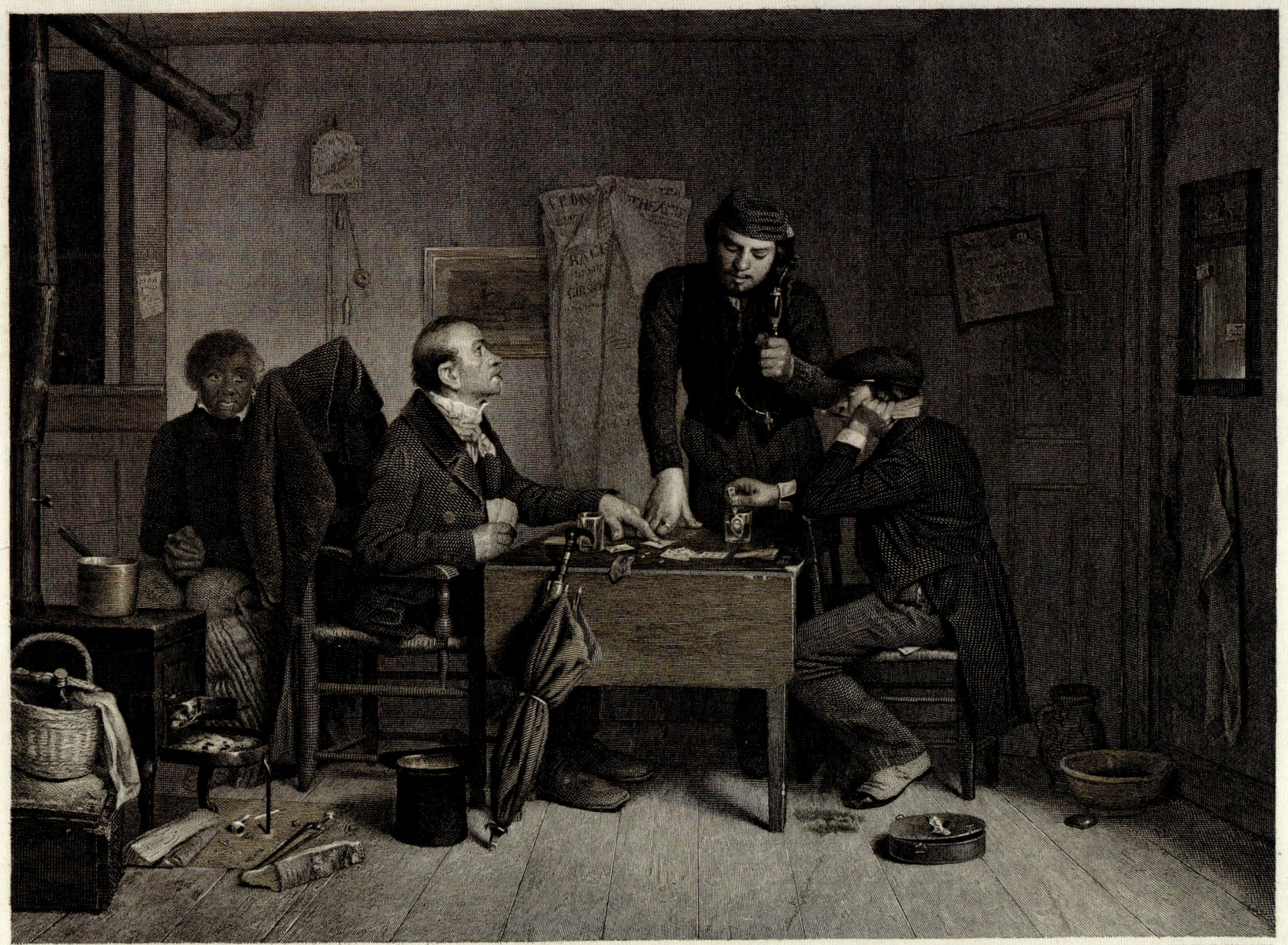

PRINTED BY R.C.WOODVILLE.   ENGRAVED BY CHARLES BURT

THE CARD PLAYERS.

Engraved from the Original Picture in the possession of William F. Hoppin Esq.

American Art Union, 1850

A 19TH=CENTURY Experiment

Every object in the Gilcrease Museum has a story. Occasionally, the stories of very disparate items intersect in ways to create a collective history that eclipses the provenance and documentation of the items individually. Such is the case with some masterful mid 19th-century oil paintings, some inexpensive prints, two illustrated novels, and memorabilia of an organization defunct for more than a century and a half. All of these items were created by or for the American Art-Union, a successful but short-lived experiment with subscription art founded in 1840. The paintings and prints created for the American Art-Union were thoroughly contemporary but are today counted among the most historically significant art in the United States, providing visual representations of our collective memory. This body of work offers an "unspoiled" view

FACING: Charles Burt after Richard Caton Woodville, *The Card Players*, American Art-Union, engraving, 1850, GM 15.1138

1 For a list of items in the Gilcrease collection that are related to the history of the Art-Union, see page 128 of this volume.

2 The engravings in George Catlin's Indian Portfolio (GM 4576.92-93) were displayed in the AAU gallery in 1847.

3 See the Constitution of "The Apollo Association for the promotion of the Fine Arts in the United States" as it appears in Mary Bartlett Cowdrey, *American Academy of Fine Arts and American Art-Union: Introduction* (New York: New York Historical Society, 1953), 101.

of America with a clear sense of place, history and/or cultural identity. It helped the public connect with the frontier spirit and the idea of Manifest Destiny, although the primary audience lived in metropolitan areas far from the frontier.

The prominent display at the Gilcrease Museum of oil paintings by famous artists such as Alfred Jacob Miller, Seth Eastman, Charles Deas, and William Tylee Ranney belies their origins as prizes for the lucky winners of the annual lottery held by the American Art-Union to promote American art, artists, and visual ideals to the general public.[1] Prints in the collection by accomplished engravers such as James Smillie, Charles Burt, and Alfred Jones were distributed by the thousands to subscribers who paid a modest fee to be patrons of the arts. The most respected and generous patrons were acknowledged with a bronze medal cast with their likeness, such as the John Trumbull medal of 1849 (see page 87). Visitors to the Art-Union Gallery saw individual pieces as well as collected art, including George Catlin's Indian Portfolio.[2]

Chartered on May 7, 1840, the American Art-Union followed the path of successful European models. Tasks for the new organization were first to enlighten and educate an American public about its national art and secondly to provide a venue for the exhibition and sale of art from contemporary and emerging American artists. For a subscription fee of five dollars, members received a copy of the minutes from the annual meeting, at least one engraving, and the chance to win an oil painting at the end of the year.[3] The Art-Union's gallery, supported by subscription fees, was free to the public. With each passing year, the endeavor grew in popularity. With increased support, however, came increased scrutiny, and by 1852 the New York Supreme Court declared the American Art-Union an illegal lottery, closing the doors on this experiment forever.

Books on the American Art-Union are rare and have not kept up with recent scholarship. It is a subject often overlooked by art historians, yet one that illuminates an important chapter in antebellum American culture, reflecting, as it does, a time of growing regional political differences and the belief held by some that art could bring people together around a shared heritage and identity. The following essays, by Dr. Patricia Hills, Professor of Art History at Boston University, Dr. Peter John

Brownlee, Associate Curator of Art at the Terra Foundation of American Art, and Randy Ramer and Amanda Lett of Gilcrease Museum, examine the history, patronage, and economics of the Art-Union and its revolutionary Perpetual Free Gallery. These writings place the Art-Union back in its proper context and illustrate the continuing influence of the organization.

In retrospect, the popularity of the American Art-Union may, in part, be attributed to timing. Eastern cities had a growing middle class, literate and bombarded with written descriptions about the frontier. Photography was in its infancy, and visual imagery of the expansive West was scarce. The American Art-Union created for its audience tangible pictures of the visions already created in the mind's eye. The Union helped shape the tastes of a rising constituency of American art aficionados for nationalistic art with cultural and historical themes. As America attempted to define itself through grandiose themes such as Manifest Destiny, so too did the American Art-Union attempt to define what American Art should be—adventuresome, risk-taking, defiant, independent, optimistic and "all-American." Works of art that did not exude the right qualities were not accepted. The choices made by the committee reflected its members' own values and helped shape public thinking about the collective identity of Americans. Thomas Gilcrease shared those values and ideals as evidenced by his own choices in collecting one hundred years later.

Although the existence of the American Art-Union was short, its influence has endured. The art choices made by the Union have been validated by history. Today, many works created as a result of the American Art-Union now hang in the most respected institutions in this country, including the Halls of Congress, the White House, and Gilcrease Museum.

DUANE H. KING, PH.D.

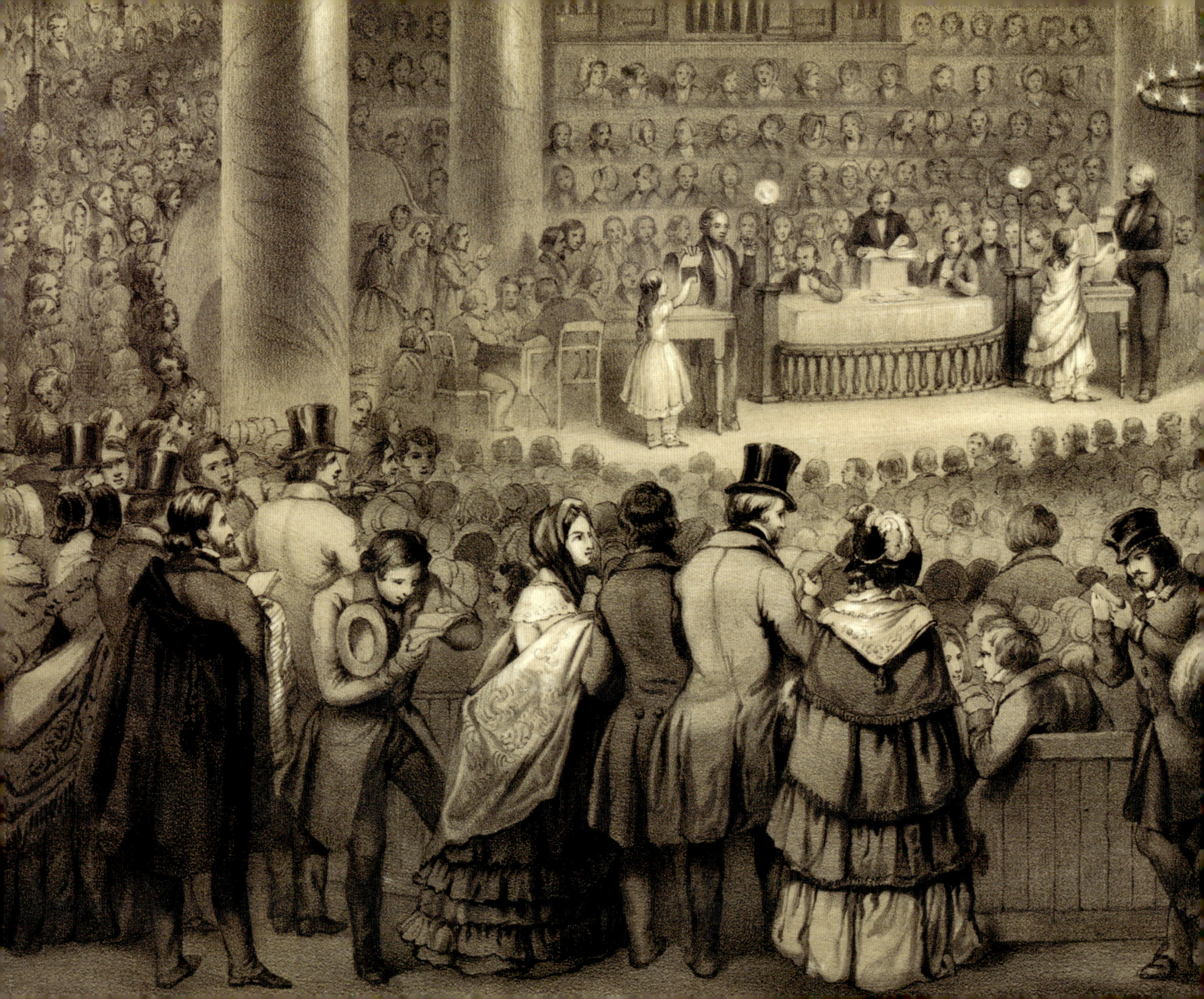

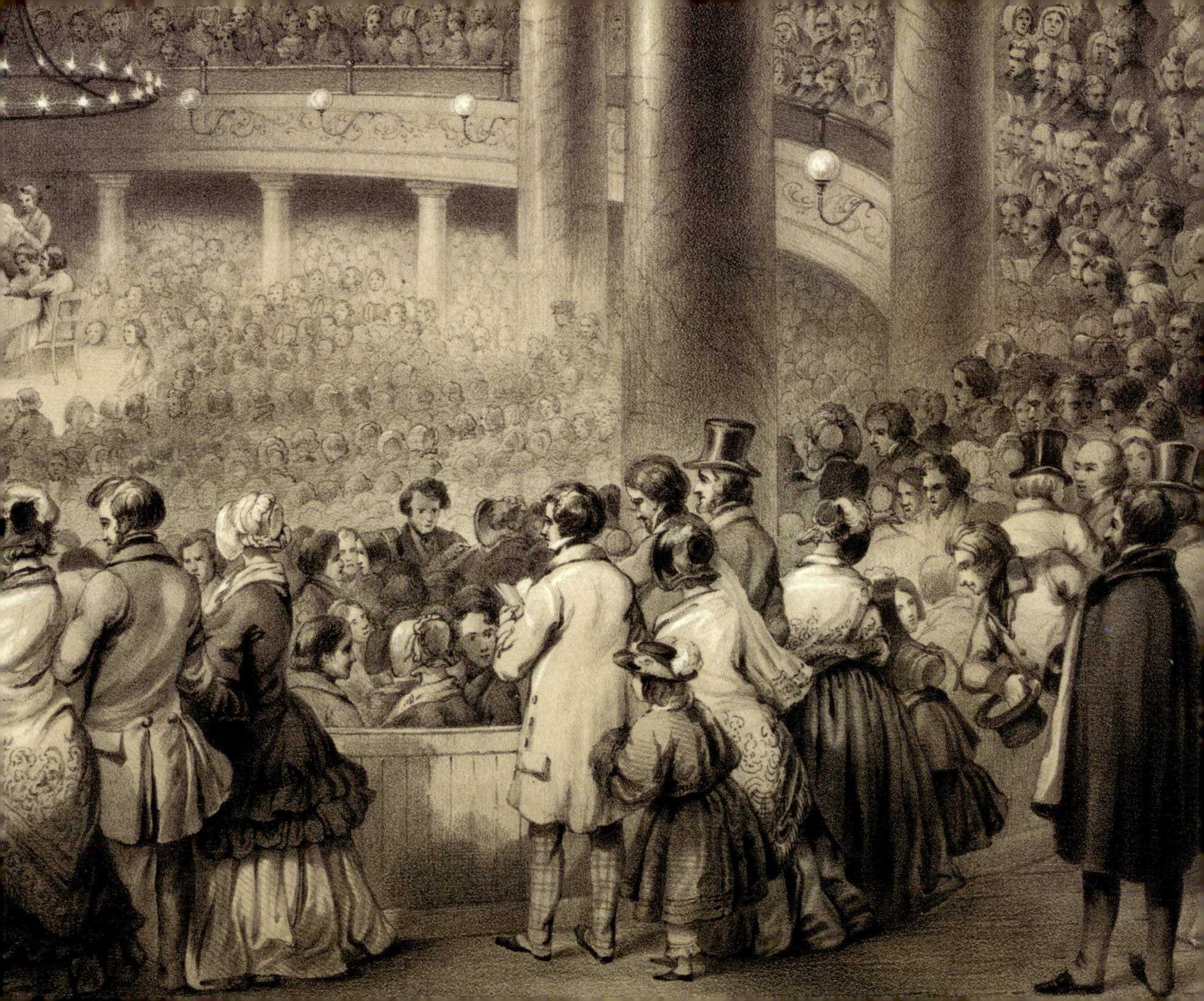

ILLUSTRATIONS

OF

RIP VAN WINKLE

DESIGNED AND ETCHED

BY

FELIX O C DARLEY

FOR THE MEMBERS OF

THE AMERICAN ART-UNION

MDCCCXLVIII.

Pictures ARE MORE POWERFUL THAN SPEECHES

As the United States left its Revolutionary generation of 1776 behind, the youthful country began to develop its own sense of identity, separating itself from its heritage of European philosophers, writers, and politicians and embracing its seemingly limitless possibilities for the future. John O'Sullivan, the disputed originator of the phrase "Manifest Destiny," expressed his hopeful vision in an 1839 editorial for the *United States Magazine and Democratic Review:* "Our national birth was the beginning of a new history, the formation and progress of an untried political system, which separates us from the past and connects us with the future only."[1] In the decade after O'Sullivan's pronouncement, the country would change rapidly. Unprecedented expansion, improvements in communication and transportation, and a growing interest in the betterment of all Americans resulted in an optimistic nation full of potential. And yet these very elements that held such promise also created a rift that would not begin to heal until after the Civil War.

FACING: Washington Irving and Felix O. C. Darley, Illustrator. *Rip Van Winkle,* American Art-Union, book, 1848, GM 5026.4403

1 Sarah Burns and John Davis, *American Art to 1900: A Documentary Reader* (Berkeley: University of California Press, 2009), 425.

2 Daniel Walker Howe, *What Hath God Wrought: The Transformation of America, 1815-1848* (London: Oxford University Press, 2007), 583. Walker explores the way technology changed the United States in the first half of the 19th century and magnified the divisions between Americans before the Civil War.

3 Howe, *What Hath God Wrought: The Transformation of America, 1815-1848*, 583. The impact of Whig economic policy is explored further in Peter John Brownlee's chapter in this book.

As the country moved closer to division and economic instability, the Apollo Association, later the American Art-Union, emerged in 1839, trumpeting the noble cause of national unity through a common art and creating a much-hoped-for beacon for new artists with few other resources. This uplifting goal, to create not only a national art but also a cultured and attuned audience for that art, fell well short of expectations. Accusations of sectionalism, lack of perceived artistic value, and the vocal criticism of artists from outside the organization doomed the American Art-Union to a short life. Despite its brief window of influence, however, the organization fostered an interest in American art that would grow throughout the remainder of the 19th century, and its distribution of prints whetted the appetite of a growing middle class who looked for idealistic scenes to decorate their parlors.

Although development in the American art world lagged behind that of Europe, the country at large experienced rapid physical and social growth throughout the 1840s and 1850s. As the United States expanded west and acquired lands through both treaties and war, the political outlook of these territories occupied the thoughts of leaders in the East. At the very root of this division, argues historian Daniel Walker Howe, was a fundamental difference in worldview espoused by the two main political parties—from economics to morals—that threatened to pull the nation apart.[2] Whigs, for example, while valuing the traditional role of agriculture in American economic life, sought to diversify the nation through industry and banking, while stressing the need for the nation to unify around its shared cultural heritage. Democrats, on the other hand, supported traditional, agrarian lifestyles in the mold of Thomas Jefferson's vision for the country and viewed with suspicion attempts "to impose cultural homogeneity" by their Whig counterparts.[3] Improvements in communication and transportation only served to enhance these differences. By the 1840s, mass printing became economical, and the number of newspapers, magazines, and books available to the public increased rapidly. It could also cater to niche audiences—Whig or Democrat, men or women. Howe notes that "By the 1840s, the United States possessed the largest literate public of any nation in world history. The reading public extended well beyond the urban middle class. Many farmers and mechanics

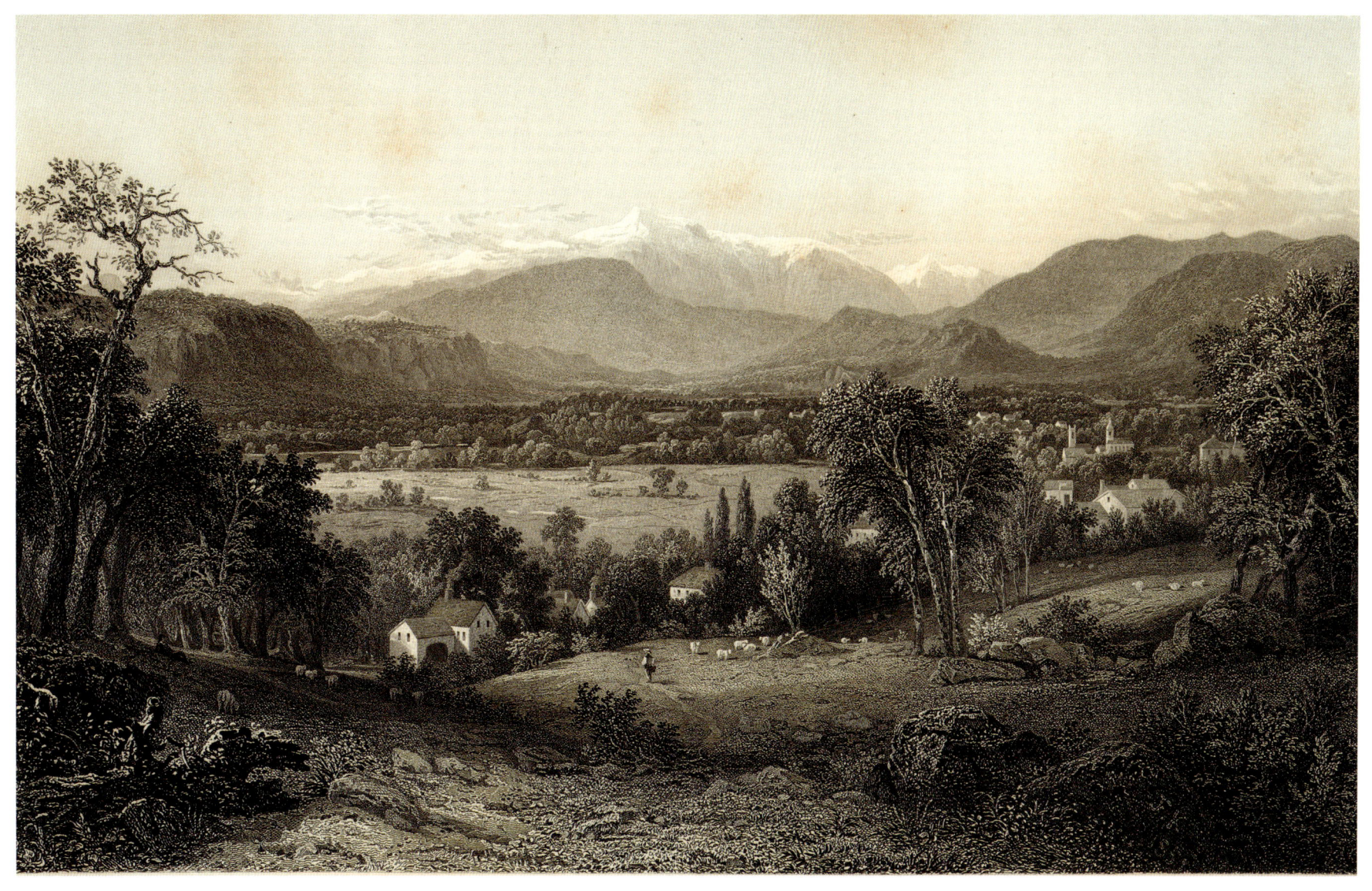

James Smillie after John F. Kensett, *Mount Washington From the Valley of Conway*, American Art-Union, engraving, 1851, GM 15.1139

4 Howe, *What Hath God Wrought,* 627.

5 Mary Bartlett Cowdrey, *American Academy of Fine Arts and American Art-Union: Introduction* (New York: New York Historical Society, 1953), v. Cowdrey's book is one of the most extensive written on the American Art-Union, examining the Art-Union's relationship to both the American Academy and the National Academy of Design. Cowdrey and her co-authors relate the story of these art organizations by drawing extensively from their minutes and bulletins.

6 Theodore Sizer, "A History of the American Academy," in Mary Bartlett Cowdrey, *American Academy of Fine Arts and American Art-Union: Introduction* (New York: New York Historical Society, 1953), 20. Sizer explains that Trumbull's reign "was due to the force of his personality."

7 Cowdrey, *American Academy of Fine Arts and American Art-Union: Introduction,* 21, 48. In traditional European academies, art was divided into hierarchies, with historical paintings more highly valued, and genre scenes less so. As artists broke away from the academy system in the mid-19th century, these categories became less important.

found time to read; even some factory operatives did."[4] Newly available journals supported causes ranging from expansionist policies to the abolition of slavery. These partisan rifts served to separate Americans and forge regional alliances based on common beliefs that would harden throughout the 1850s. Territorial gains resulting from the Mexican War gave Americans new lands in which to pursue their future, while politicians in Washington, D. C., battled to shape these new lands for their constituents. In the face of this heightened division, the country's cultural critics argued for unity through literature and through the visual arts.

Strict hierarchy and closed ranks marked the art world in the United States prior to the 1840s. Few opportunities existed for artists to exhibit their work, and once a patron purchased a work of art it generally disappeared from public view.[5] The American Academy of Fine Arts, founded in New York City in 1802, hoped to encourage the arts in the United States, providing exhibition space and the chance to study art. The fledgling organization struggled in its first few years, but in 1816 the Academy nominated John Trumbull, well known in the United States for his paintings documenting the Revolutionary War, to be its president. Trumbull, at the helm of the American Academy almost until the end of its existence, proved a strong, if not always popular, leader. Under Trumbull, the group sought to replicate the success of similar academies in Europe despite the lack of royal or political patronage. The Academy purchased plaster casts of famous classical sculptures for the instruction of students, borrowed works of art by old European masters for exhibitions, and supported the hierarchy of art, with history painting at the pinnacle, prevalent in Europe until the late 19th century.[7] The Academy's reliance on a European model, coupled with a board made up of businessmen rather than artists, led to discontent among its "student," or artist, members. In 1825, under the leadership of Samuel F. B. Morse, a group of artists decided to break from the American Academy. Organizing themselves as the National Academy of Design, these artists aimed to correct the problems they encountered at the American Academy—namely limited working hours for artists and exhibition selections that favored both President Trumbull's own work and that of prominent members of the board.[8] Despite a few attempts at reconciliation, the two competing arts organizations remained at odds. In his 1833 address to a delegation from the National Academy of Design, Trumbull expressed the Academy's sentiment that "we of the American Academy of Fine Arts, have the satisfaction of knowing that the separation did not originate with us. We did not secede, we were seceded from."[9] This hard line proved unfruitful. Soon an ailing Trumbull, two disastrous fires, and lack of interest from both stockholders and the general public brought the institution to an end.[10] It would not be long until another organization with similar goals took its place.

Out of the ashes of the American Academy the Apollo Association emerged. Willing to provide artists a venue to display their work and spurred on by cultural critics who clamored for art that depicted American scenes for an American audience, James Herring opened his Apollo Gallery in 1838.[11] Herring, an artist, publisher, and engraver, offered a space for revolving exhibitions throughout the year, where both the visitor and patron could see new works of art, and, perhaps, purchase a painting. Charging 25 cents for general admission, Herring believed, would make the gallery self-sufficient. A little over a year later, however, mounting debt forced Herring to call on other art enthusiasts to keep the doors open.[12] Working under the name "The Apollo Association," the group petitioned the New York legislature for incorporation. Its organizing constitution reflected the ideas that the American Art-Union would also adopt, namely using revenues to purchase art and a board primarily consisting of art enthusiasts, with very few artists represented.[13] In 1844, the Apollo Association formally changed its name to the American Art-Union. With the change in name came a renewed sense of purpose. Subscriptions—five dollars per year—not only encouraged subscribers to visit the gallery, where that year's artwork was displayed, but also guaranteed that each subscriber would receive at least a print of a prominent work of art annually and a chance to win a larger painting each December. Herring based his organization on similar art unions that sprang up in Europe throughout the 1820s and 1830s, in particular "one that proved highly beneficial to the Arts in Scotland," espousing that "it is known that in London, Paris, Munich, and other continental cities, where Associations had been formed, they had given an impulse

8 Sizer, "The History of the American Academy," 36

9 Sizer, 55.

10 Sizer, 59-60.

11 Rachel N. Klein, "Art and Authority in Antebellum New York City: The Rise and Fall of the American Art-Union," *The Journal of American History,* (1995), 1536.

12 Klein, 1537.

13 Charles E. Baker, "The American Art-Union," in Cowdrey, *American Academy of Fine Arts and American Art-Union: Introduction,* 101-102.

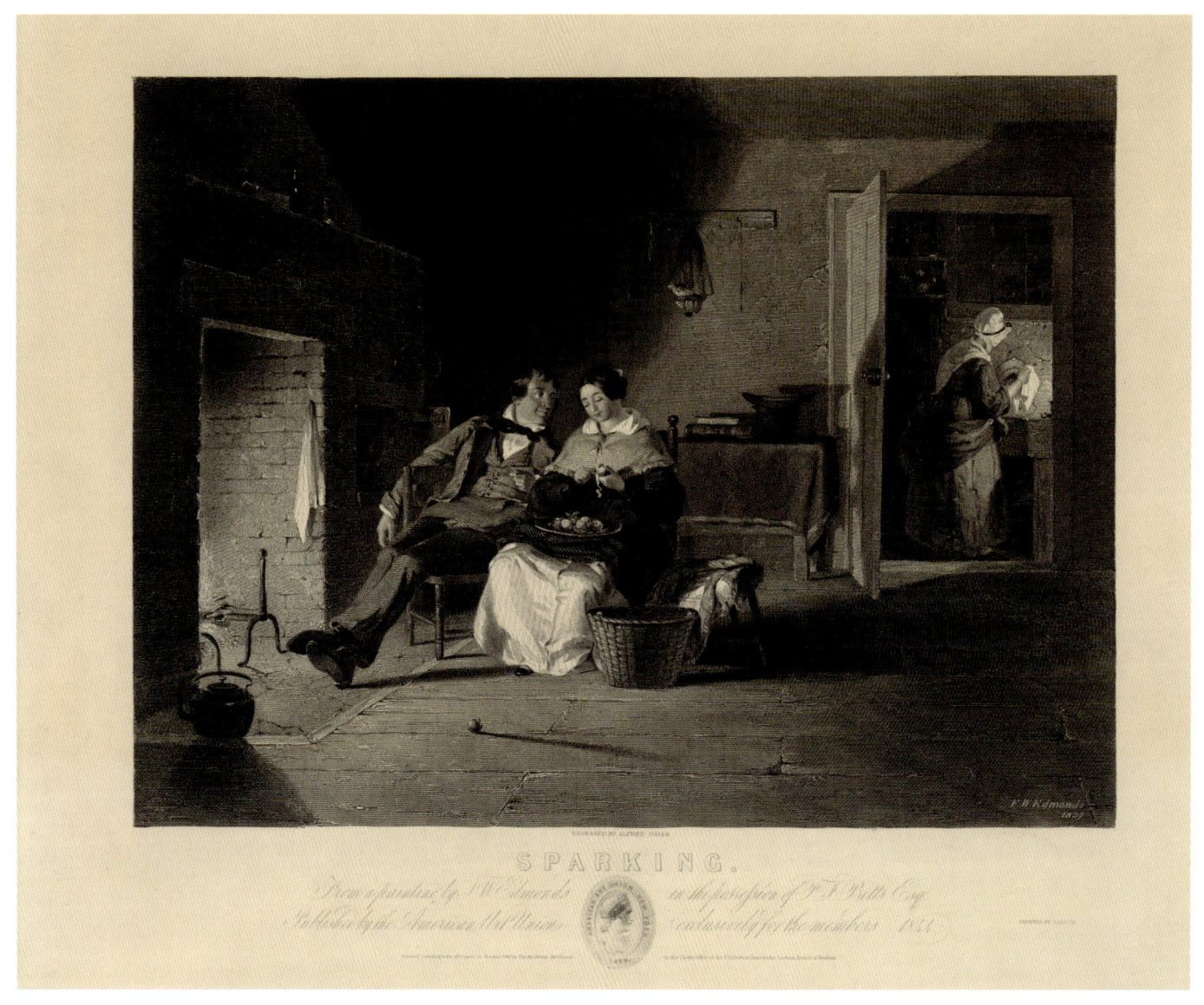

Alfred Jones after Francis W. Edmonds, *Sparking,* American Art-Union, engraving, 1845

to the Arts."[14] By linking the American Art-Union with its European cousins, the managers implied that this model for the promotion of the arts could succeed and foster an interest in art that went beyond traditional wealthy patrons. With a relatively modest subscription fee, the directors of the Art-Union could reach an elusive, but increasingly influential group—the American middle class. In addition, by opening their galleries to the public free of charge, they could expose more viewers to the work created by American artists. Over time, these men became the arbiters of taste for thousands of subscribers throughout the United States.

The directors of the American Art-Union included luminaries such as William Cullen Bryant, editor of the *New York Evening Post,* merchant and civic leader Prosper Wetmore, and Francis Edmonds—who, while working as an artist in his free time, brought his banking skills to the group. The group shared a strong belief in the power of the visual image. In President Wetmore's 1849 address to the managing committee, he spoke of how art had a power words did not. "Every great national painting of a battlefield, or great composition illustrating some event in our history—every engraving, lithograph, and woodcut appealing to national feeling and rousing national sentiment—is the work of art," he stated, "and who can calculate the effect of all these on the minds of our youth? Pictures are more powerful than speeches."[15]

Educating a nation to appreciate art meant, of course, that the committee had to select images carefully. Although the Art-Union was based in New York, its reach was far-flung—there were subscribers in cities such as Savannah, Detroit, and Portland, Maine.[16]

In an effort to appeal to all regions and political sensibilities, the directors selected works that, as art historian Elizabeth Johns points out, satisfied three requirements: "they were arguably national in implication, they were easily readable by a minimally experienced audience, and they appeared at least to be high-toned in content."[17] To fulfill these three requirements, the officers of the Art-Union faced a public that had little knowledge of fine art, yet were well versed in low quality and satirical prints.

14 Baker, "The American Art-Union," in Cowdrey, *American Academy of Fine Arts and American Art-Union: Introduction,* 132. Baker and others, including Rachel N. Klein, have discussed the influences of European art unions on the American Art-Union.

15 Cowdrey, *American Academy of Fine Arts and the American Art-Union: Introduction,* 153. In 1850, the committee once again announced its dedication to subjects of "national character, history, or scenery."

16 Elizabeth Johns, *American Genre Painting: The Politics of Everyday Life* (New Haven: Yale University Press), 76.

17 Johns, *American Genre Painting,* 76.

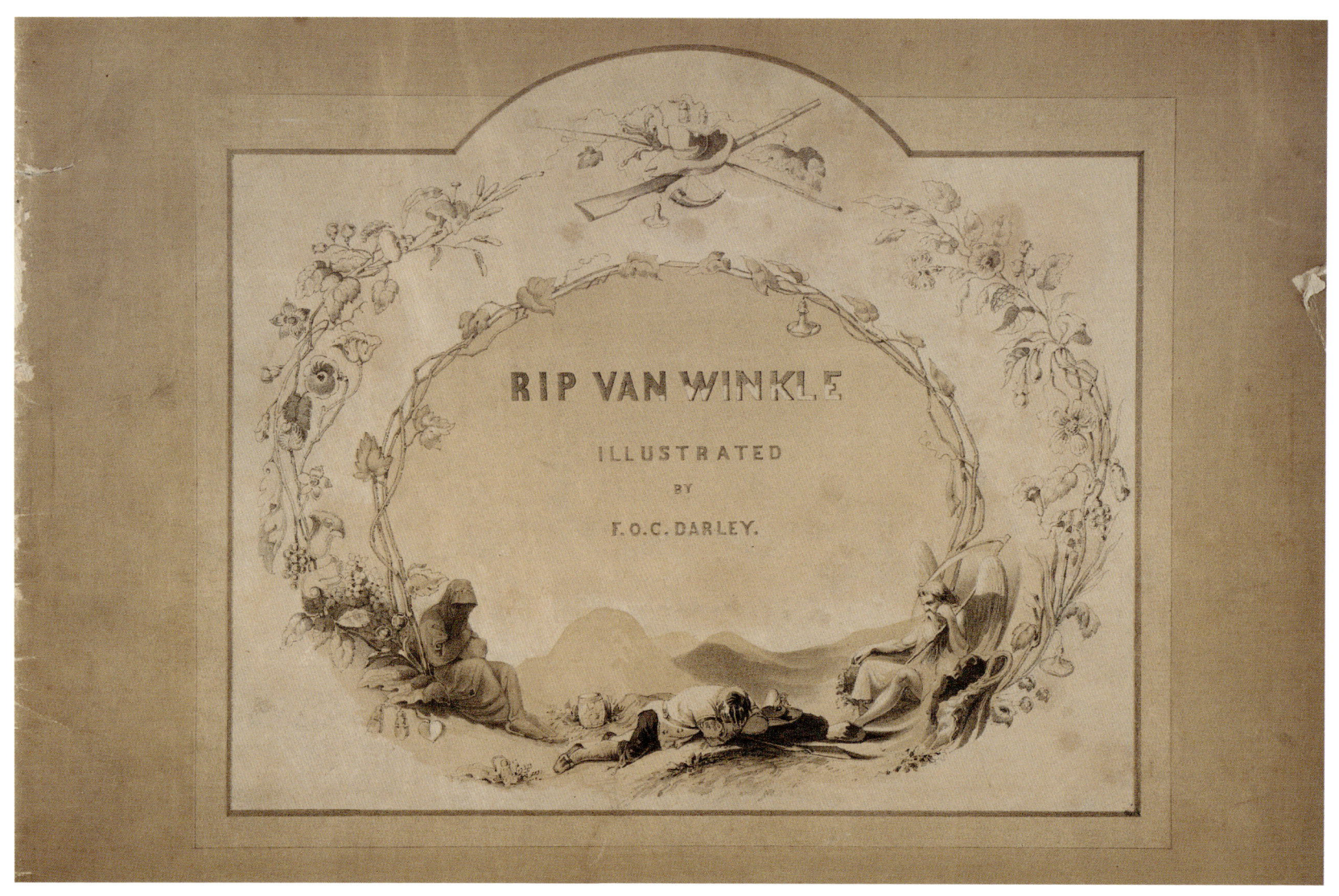

ABOVE AND FACING: Washington Irving and Felix OC Darley, Illustrator. Cover and illlustrations from *Rip Van Winkle,*
American Art-Union, engraving, 1848, GM 5026.4403

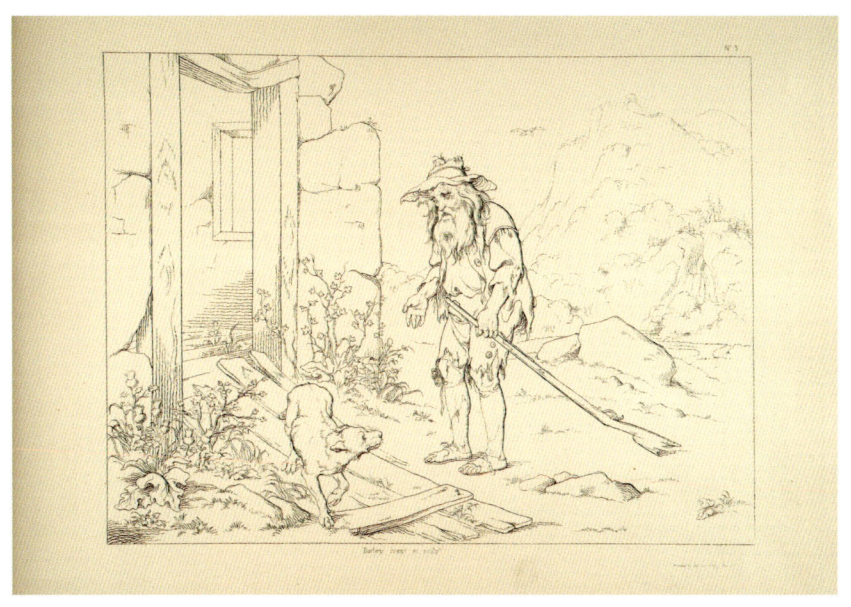

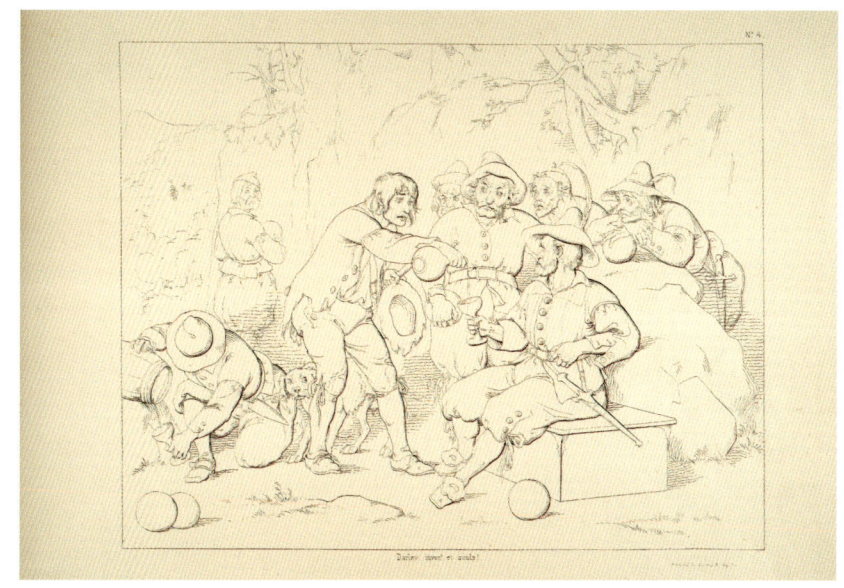

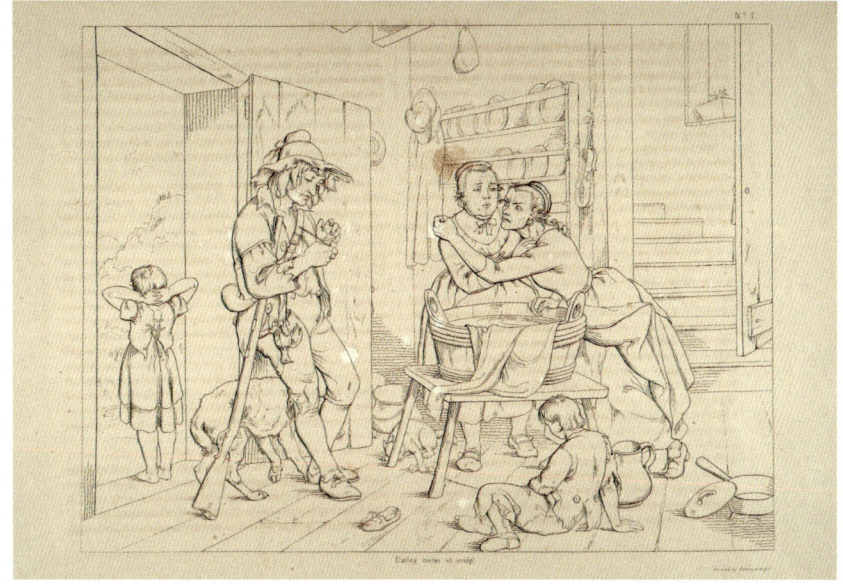

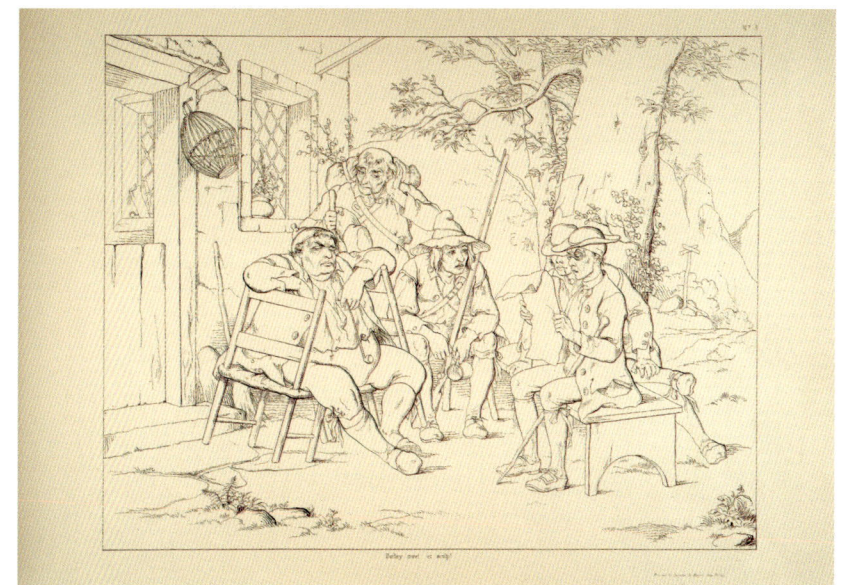

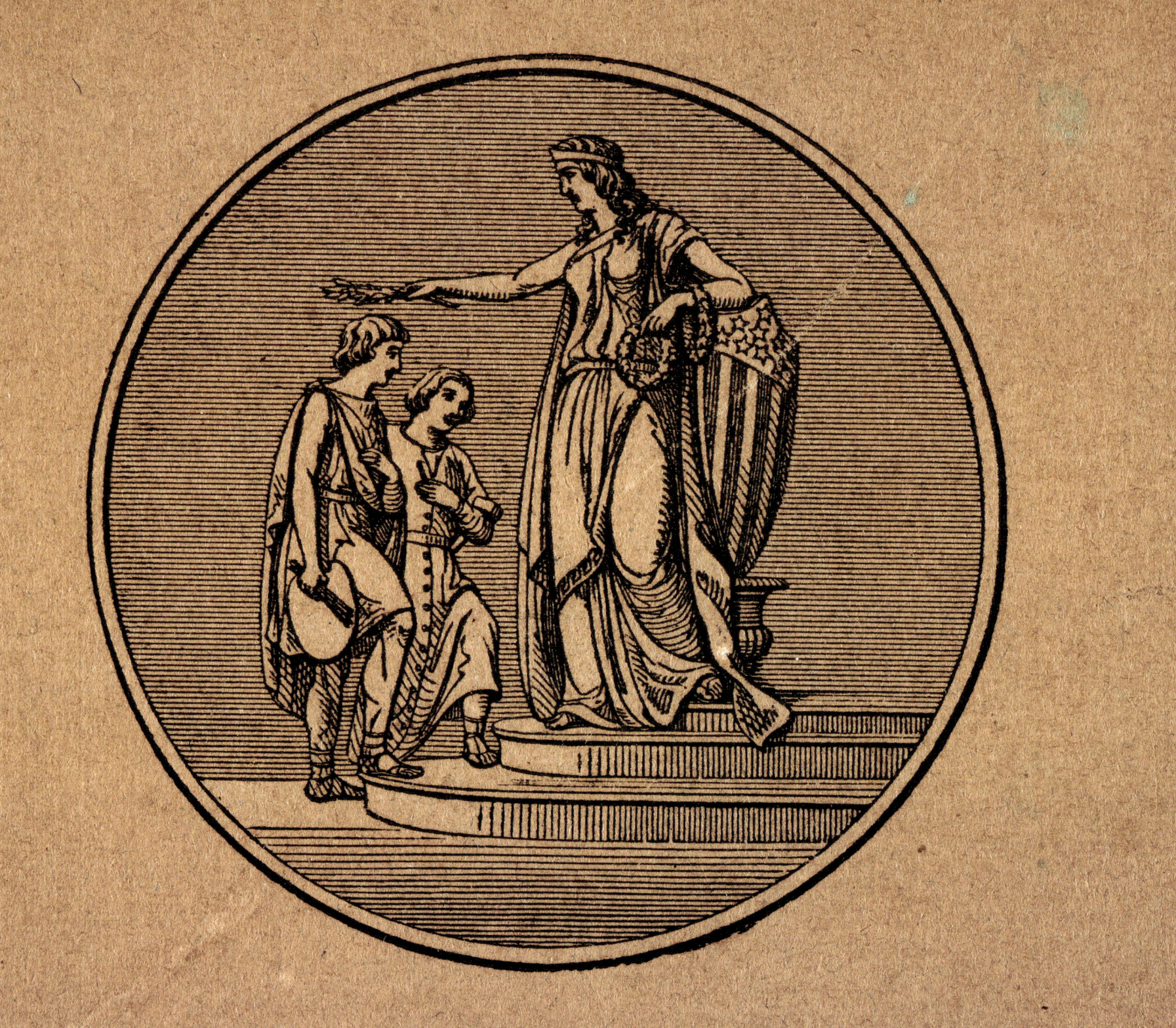

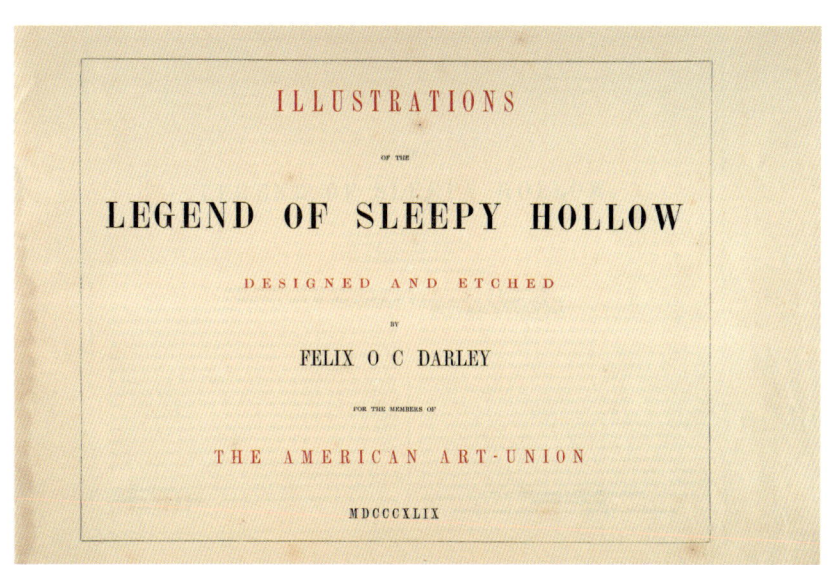

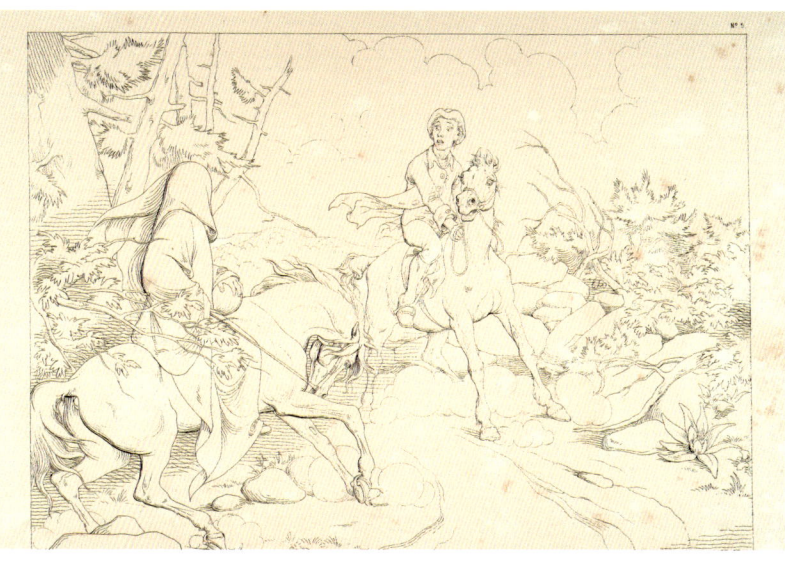

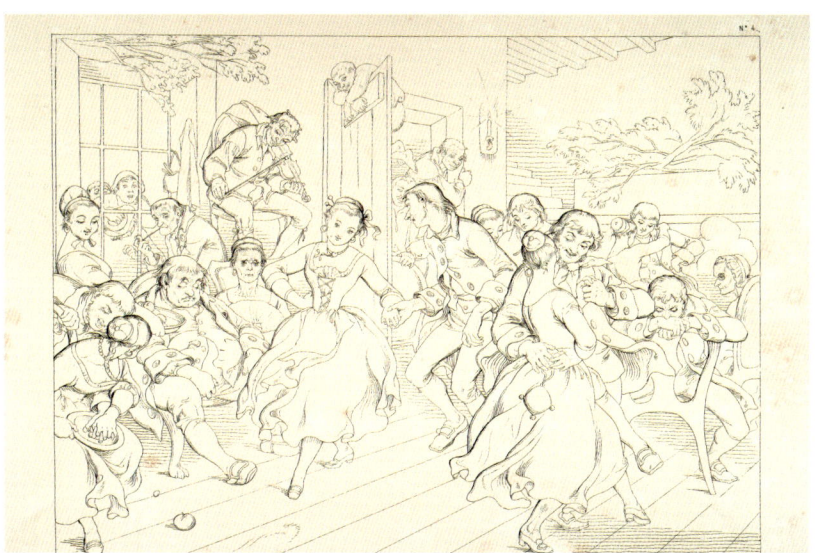

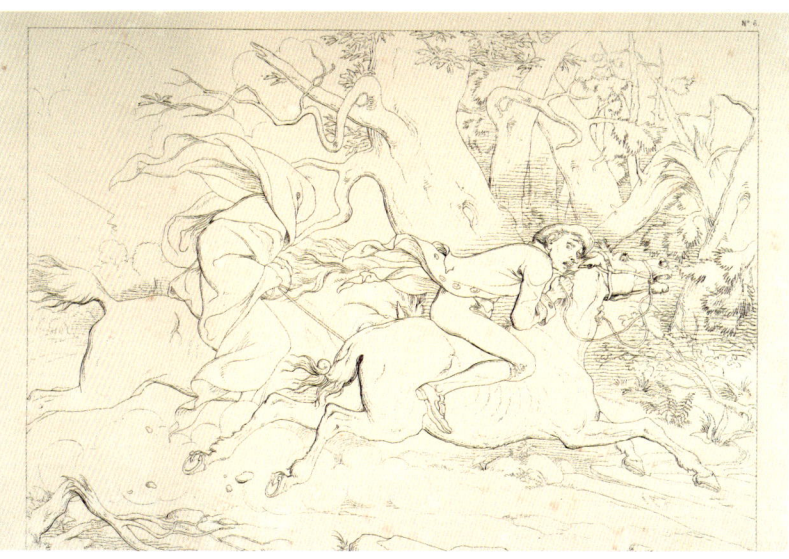

ABOVE AND FACING: Washington Irving and Felix O. C. Darley, Illustrator. Back cover and illustrations from *The Legend of Sleepy Hollow,* American Art-Union, engraving, 1848, GM 5026.4404

18 "American Art," *The New York Quarterly* (1852), Burns and Davis, *American Art to 1900,* 403-404.

19 Burns and Davis, *American Art to 1900,* 403-404.

20 Burns and Davis, *American Art to 1900,* 403-404. The authors go on to note that Mount will be seen as a great American artist even after his contemporary fame has passed.

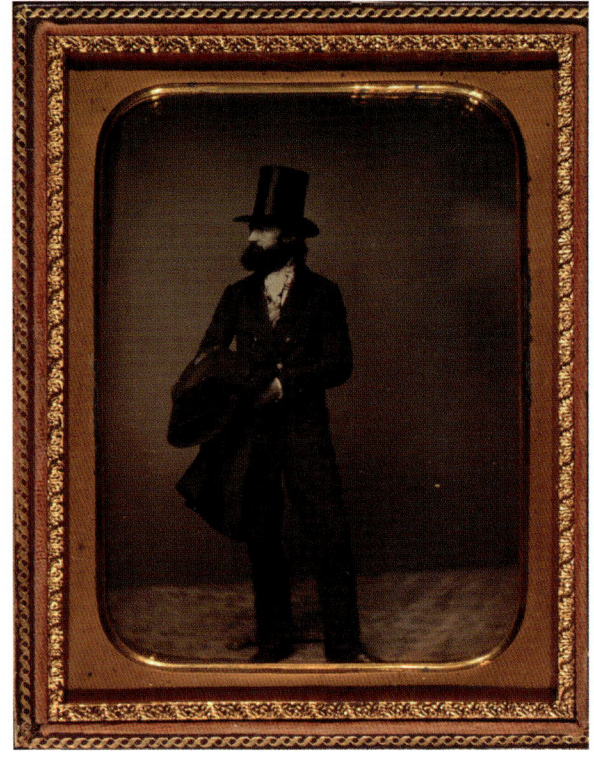

Mathew Brady, *William Sidney Mount,* daguerreotype, ca. 1853

In 1852, the *New York Quarterly* decried the American public's taste in art as too often uninformed and leaning toward sentimentality.[18] Yet, it also noted certain contemporary artists who found both critical and popular acclaim not by imitating the Europeans but by examining the American character in their paintings.[19] The works deemed by the Art-Union to be most successful unabashedly celebrated this character. Images featuring the rugged beauty of the West or the heroics of the battlefield were likely to make the Art-Union's yearly list.

Art depicting scenes of everyday American life quickly became popular with the Art-Union's directors, as well as with the public. This coincided with the *New York Quarterly*'s favorable reviews of the work of William Sidney Mount, a New York artist. Mount, the editors said, "has been met by the approval of both high and low. His art is earnest and vital. His men are not only exponents of his story, but they are "representative men," each typifying his section of the country as well as his class and nature."[20] Mount and artists like George Caleb Bingham, of Missouri explored the popular stereotypes of the "Yankee," "yeomen," and the

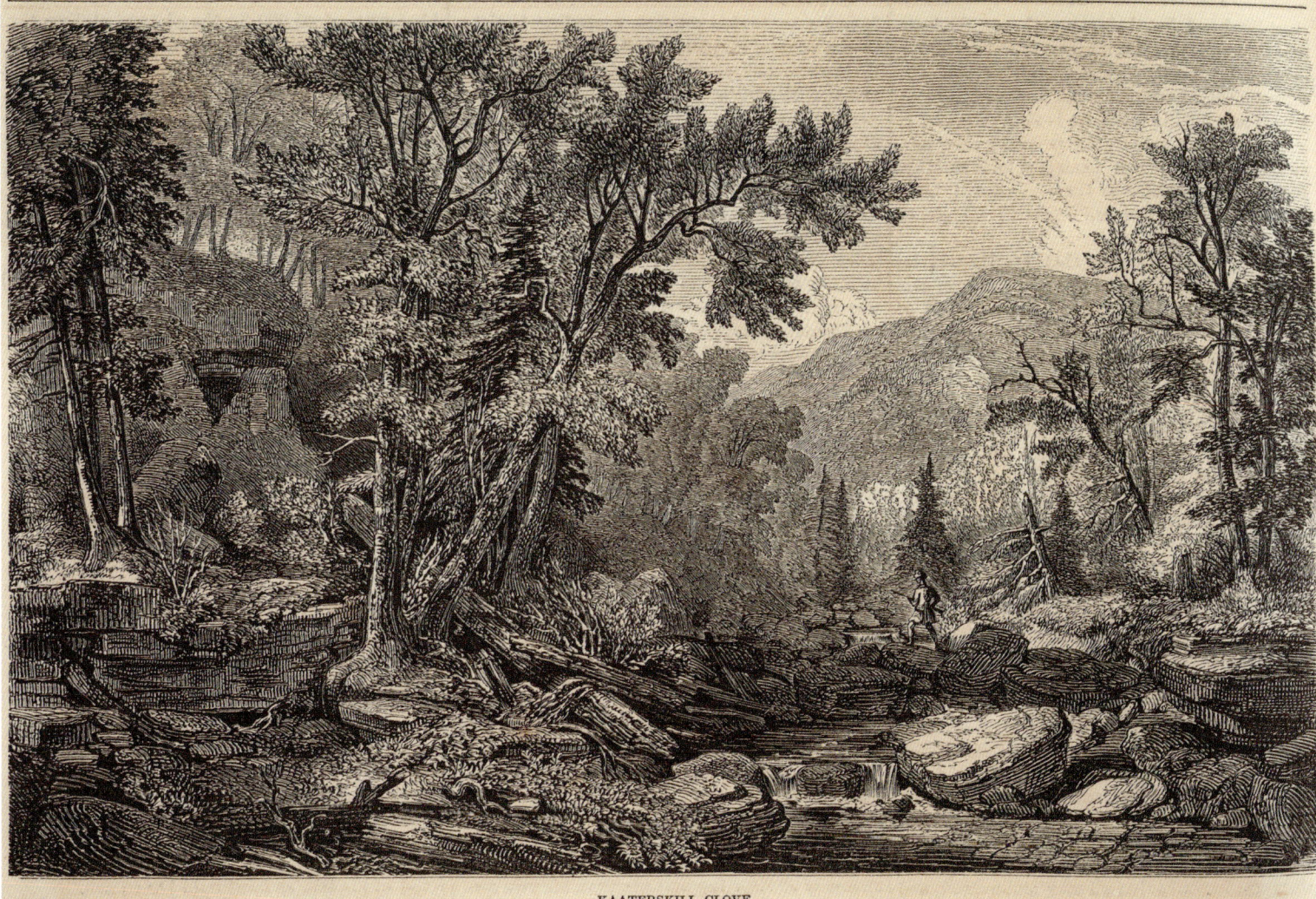

KAATERSKILL CLOVE.

Engraved by BOBBETT & EDMONDS, from a Painting by A. B. DURAND, P. N. A., in the Exhibition of the National Academy of Design.

Bobbett and Edmonds after Asher B. Durand, *Kaaterskill Cove*, American Art-Union, engraving, 1851, GM 5126.1061.40

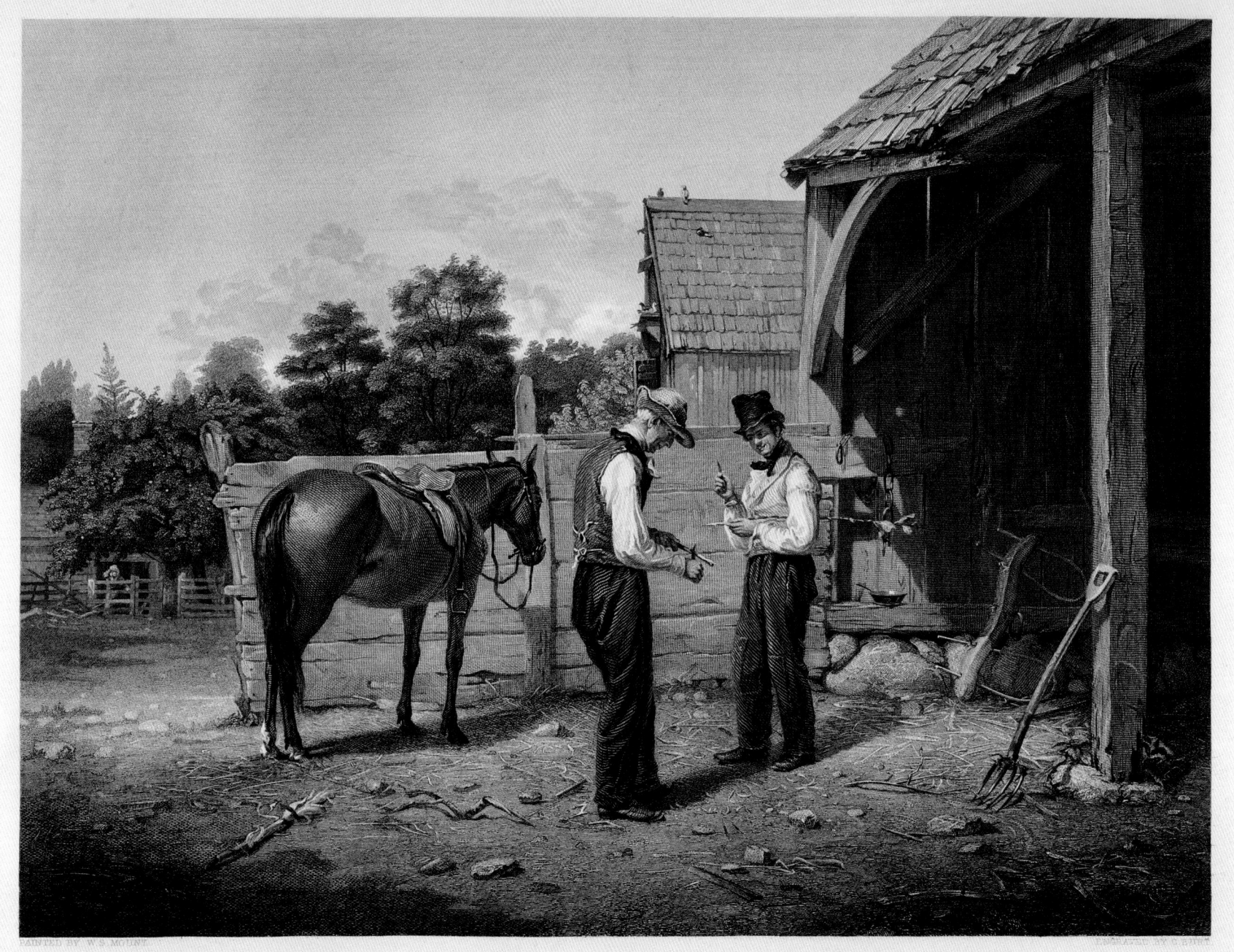

BARGAINING FOR A HORSE.

PAINTED BY W.S.MOUNT.   ENGRAVED BY C. BURT.

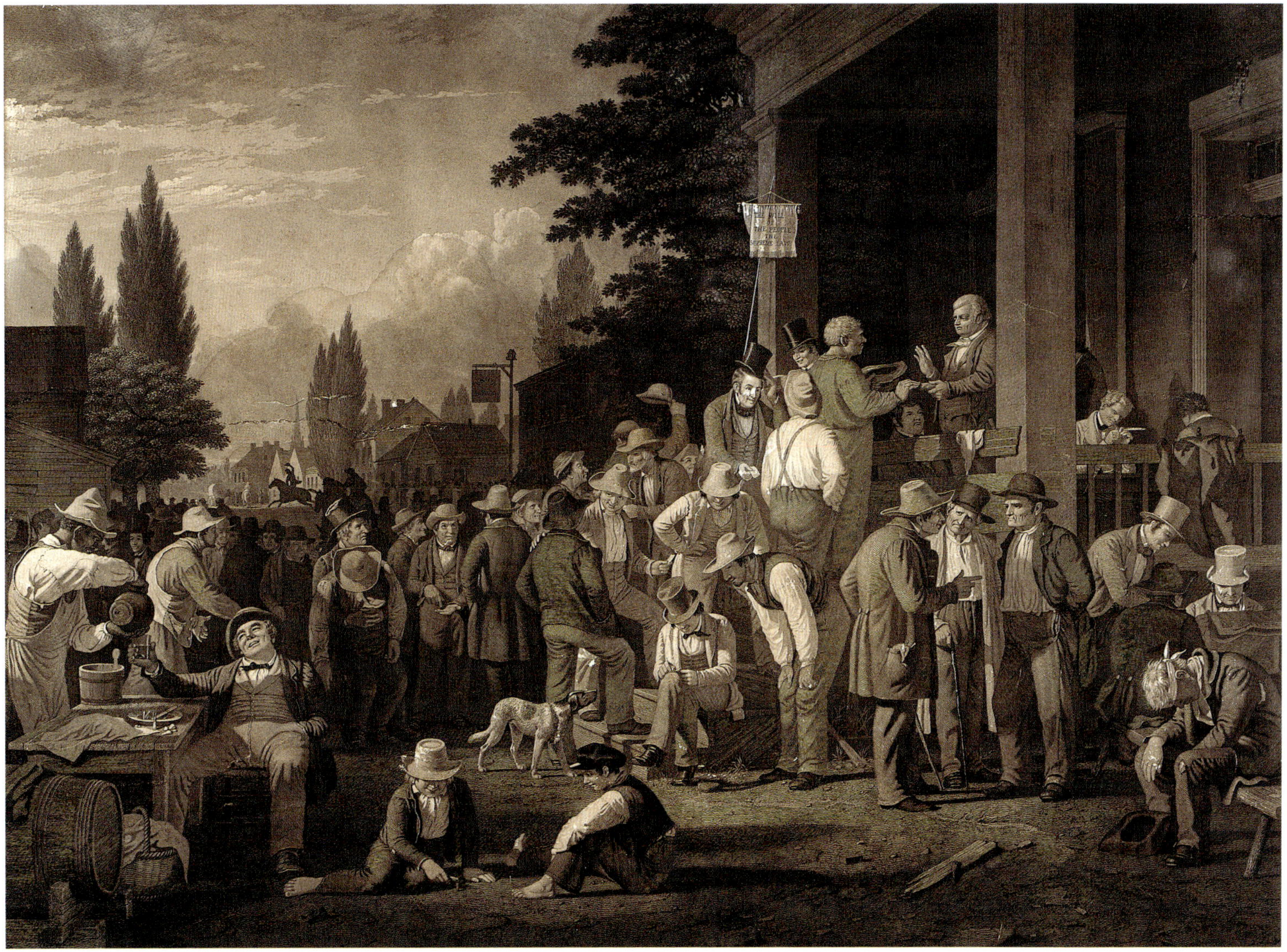

George Caleb Bingham, *The County Election*, engraving, 1852, GM 1526.569

FACING: Charles Burt after William Sidney Mount, *Bargaining for a Horse*, American Art-Union, engraving, 1851, GM 15.1140

21 Johns, *American Genre Painting*, 98.

22 In the last edition of the American Art-Union's *Bulletin* (1851), the editors reference the oil version of this print, exclaiming "Persons of highly cultivated taste in the fine arts, and critics in general, will accord to it a remarkable degree of genius and merit. The political scenes are original and bold, and present a class of subject entirely new," 151.

23 "Paintings," *Daily Missouri Republican*, April 21, 1847, in Burns and Davis, *American Art to 1900*, 457.

24 Cowdrey, *What Hath God Wrought*, 705.

25 Johns, *American Genre Painting*, 60.

26 Angela Miller, *The Empire of the Eye: Landscape Representation and American Cultural Politics, 1825-1875* (Ithaca: Cornell University Press, 1993), 13.

27 Miller, *The Empire of the Eye: Landscape Representation and American Cultural Politics, 1825-1875*, 13.

western "rivermen," and allowed their audiences to chuckle knowingly at the rough characters making up the new America while maintaining their distance from them.[21] Mount's scenes of New England Yankees and Bingham's representations of Missouri traders confirmed viewer's regional assumptions, reaffirming visually the jokes and stereotypes of American life in the 1840s.[22] Bingham, in particular, was singled out for his ability to take "the simplest, most frequent and common occurrence on our rivers—such as every boatman will encounter in a season—such as would seem, even to the casual and careless observer, of very ordinary moment, but which are precisely those in which the full and undisguised character of the boatman is displayed."[23] Genre scenes like those of Bingham and Mount were displayed regularly at the Art-Union's gallery and accounted for nine of the thirty-one prints distributed over the ten-year history of the organization.[24] It would be another genre, however, that would get a boost from the American Art-Union.

Depictions of the West became a popular subject for Art-Union pieces as the region came to dominate the national discussion. The West prom-ised new opportunities, but was also an arena of political and social uncertainty.[25] While the prairies could be seen as "gardens of the desert" simply awaiting new husbandmen, as they were described by William Cullen Bryant, they could equally represent, as Washington Irving wrote, "something [that is] inexpressibly lonely."[26]

Expansion in the West brought the debate over slavery to the fore, and each new territory and state added to the Union threatened to tip the balance between Democrats and Whigs. As newspaper editors encouraged westward expansion, especially during the Mexican War, the Art-Union displayed works like Alfred Jacob Miller's romanticized Native American vignettes, painted as he traveled west, William Tylee Ranney's expansionist scenes celebrating the exploration of the country, and Charles Deas's depictions of the difficulties of frontier life.

Landscapes, too, revealed the uniqueness of the American situation. As citizens of a new nation with a limited history yet rich in natural wonders, viewers of landscape paintings could marvel at the vastness and beauty of their country in a controlled environment.[27]

FACING: Alfred Jones after Francis Edmonds, *The New Scholar*, American Art-Union, engraving, 1850, GM 15.1141

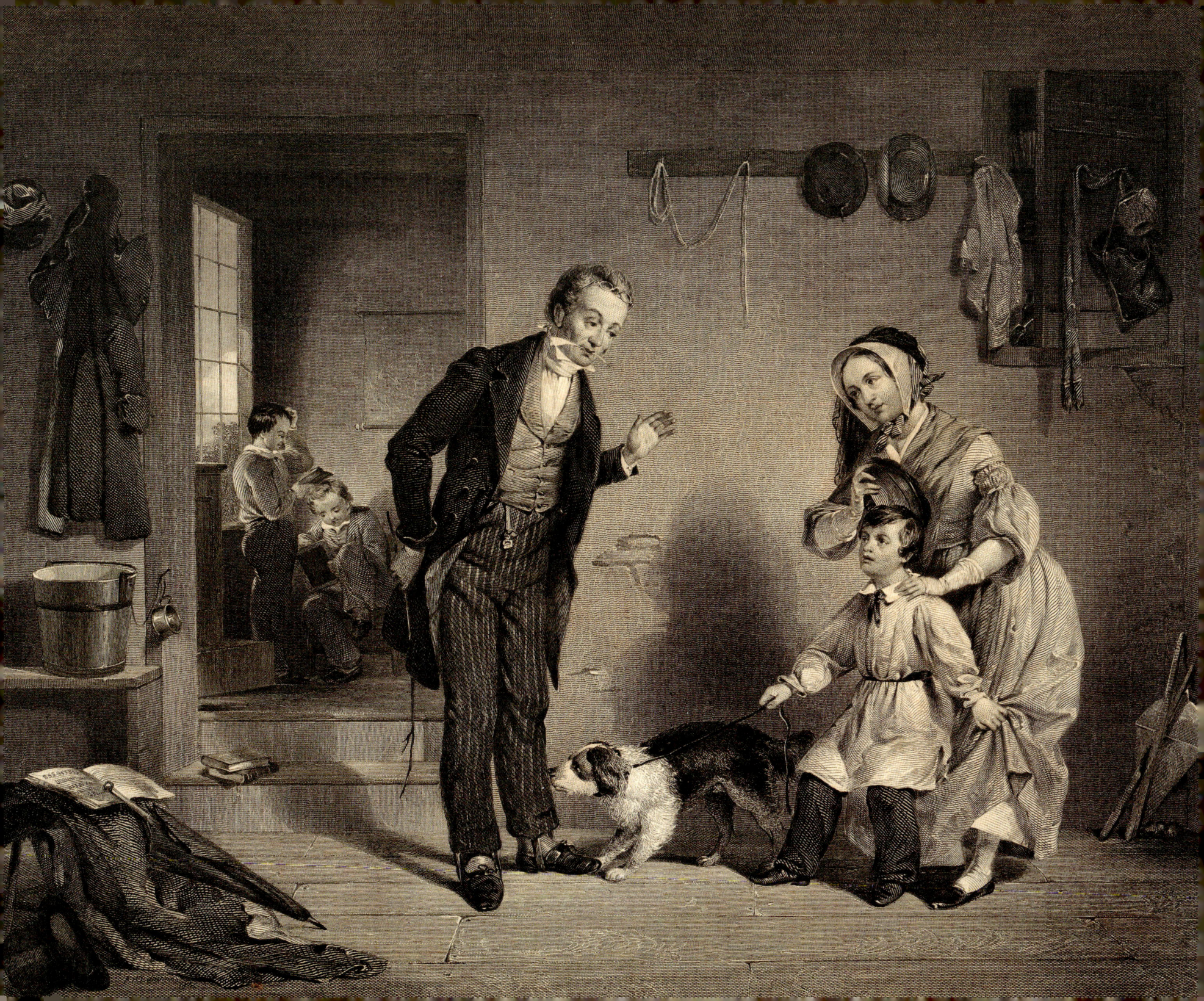

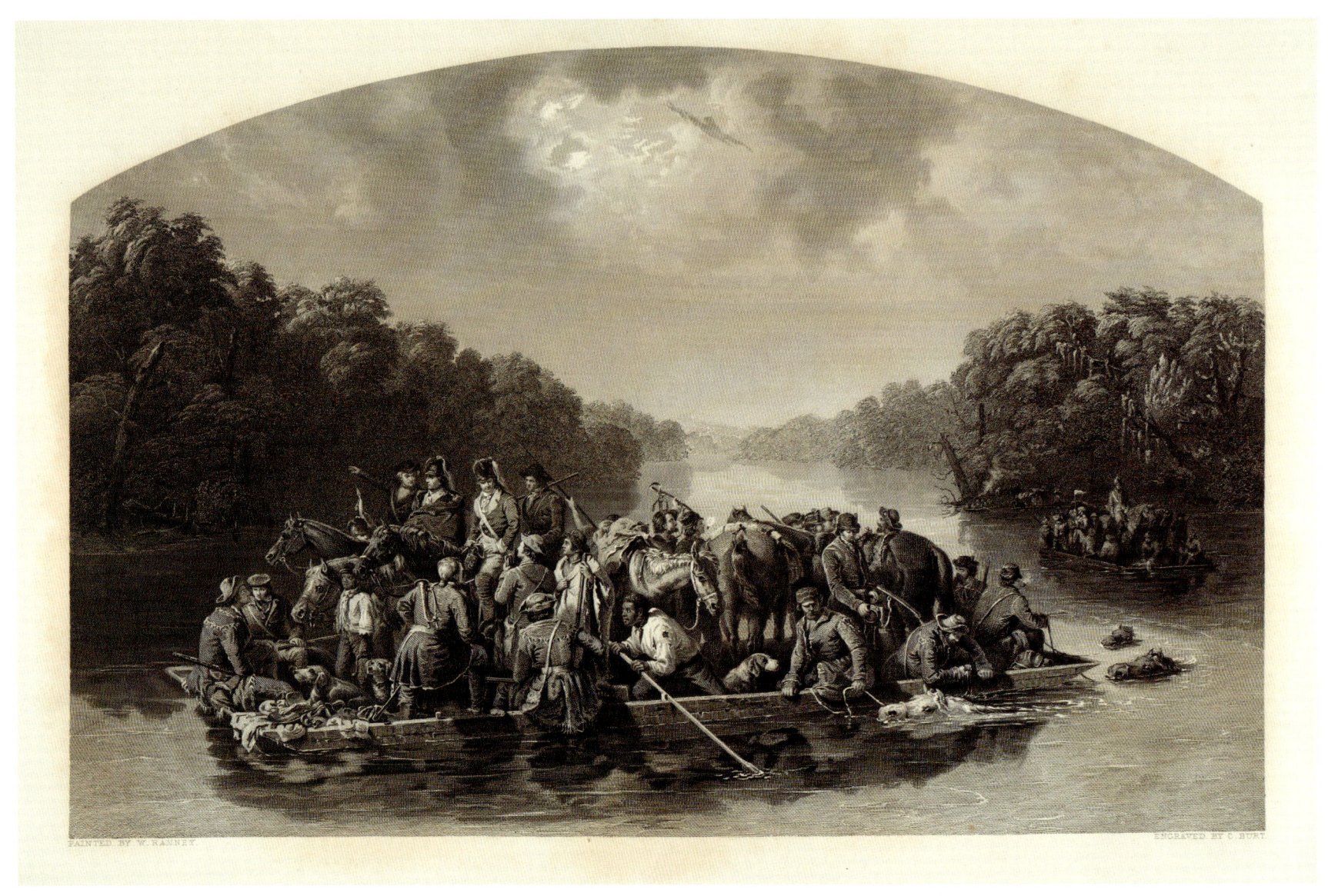

Charles Burt after William Tylee Ranney, *Marion Crossing the Pedee,* American Art-Union, engraving, 1851, GM 15.1142

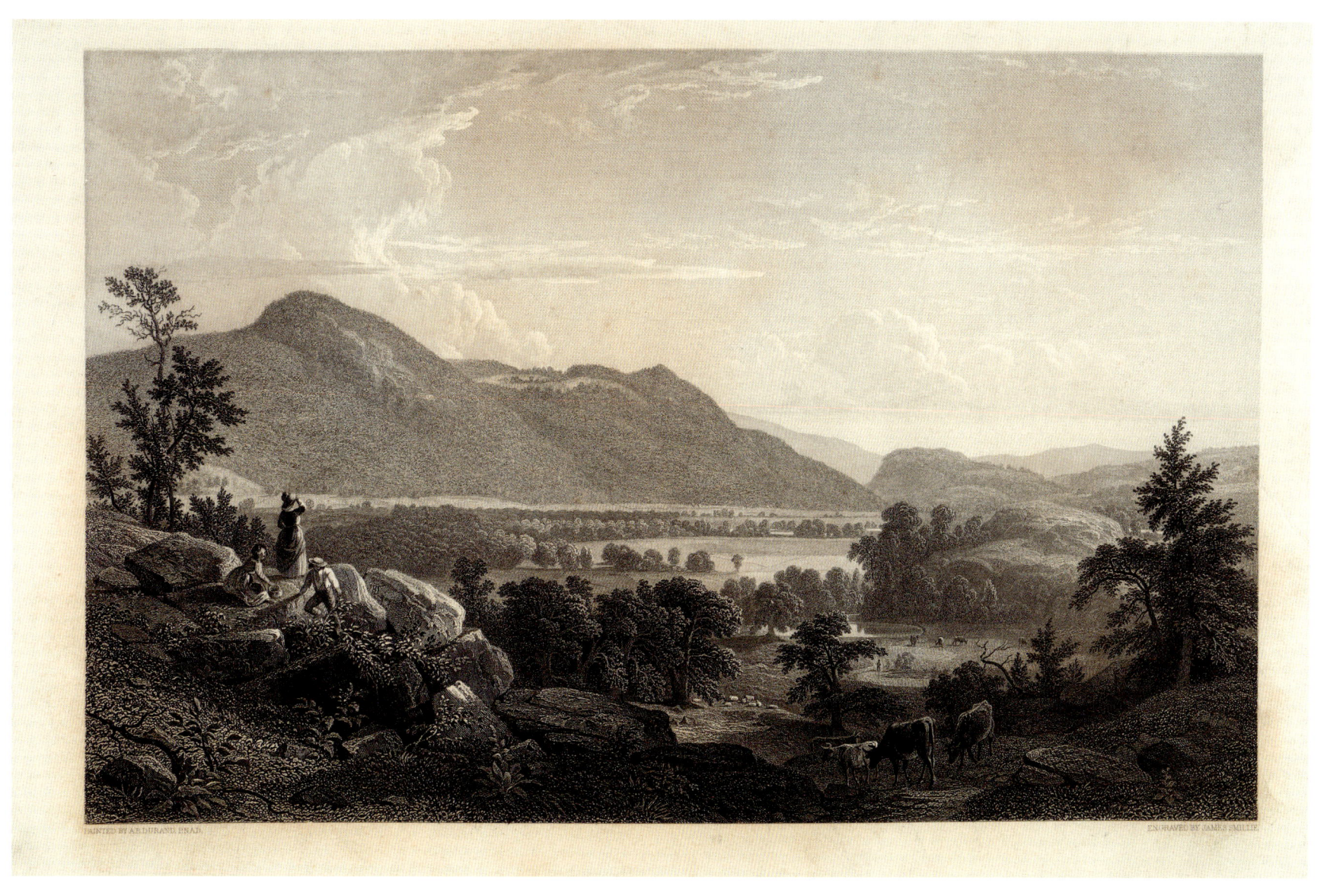

James Smillie after Asher B. Durand, *Dover Plains*, American Art-Union, engraving, 1850, GM 15.1143

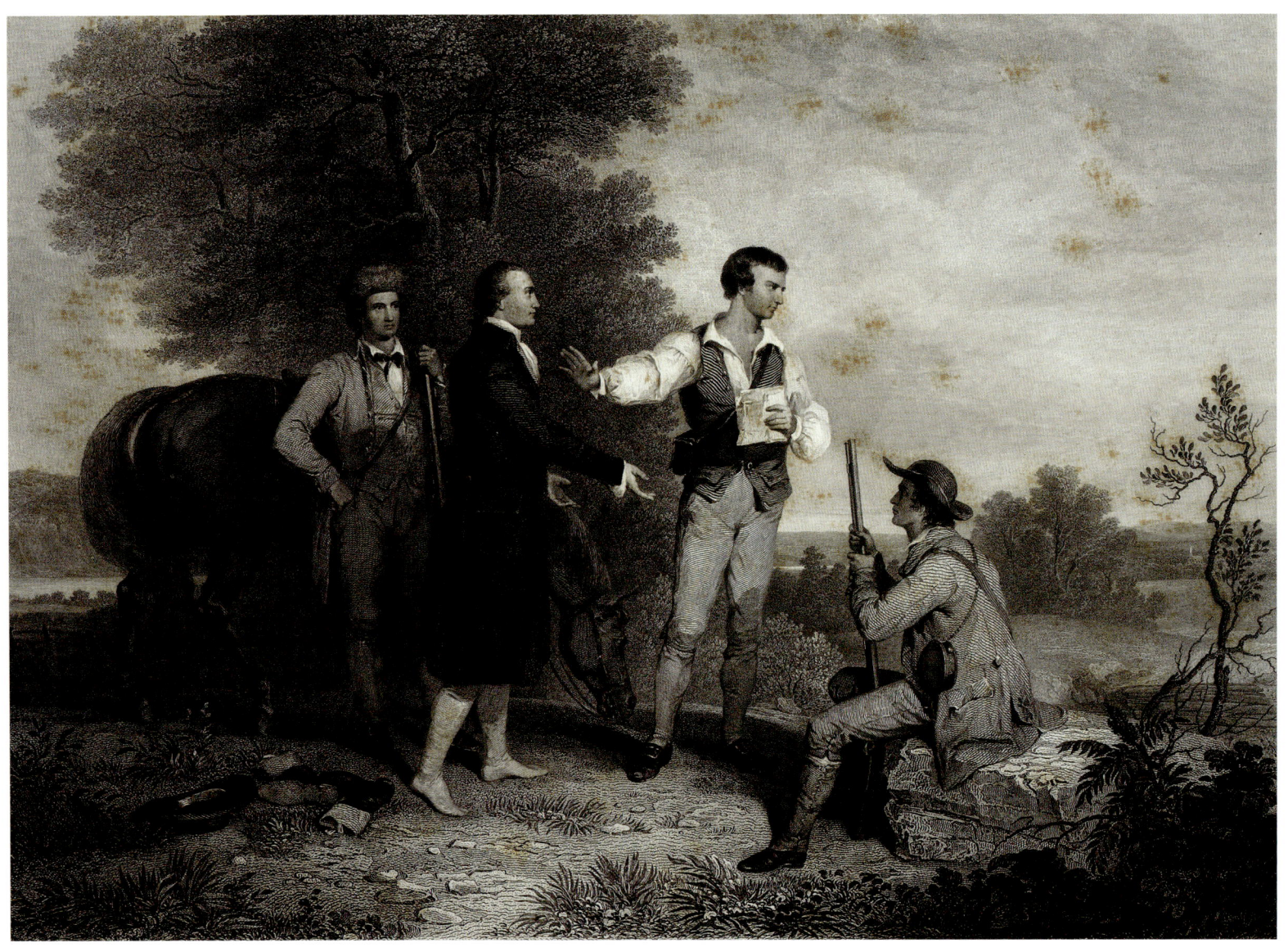

Alfred Jones, Smillie & Hinshelwood after Asher B. Durand, *The Capture of Major Andre*, American Art-Union, engraving, 1845, GM 15.1145

The artists Asher B. Durand, Thomas Cole, and others removed the uncertainty and danger of the wilderness to represent nature in an idealized state. Their works reinforced a providential way of thinking for most Americans at the time. The figures in many of Ranney's and Deas's paintings celebrate self-reliance, the triumph of planning over nature, and the creation of useful land, all aspirations that many in the East had for lands in the West. While the paintings by Miller reminded viewers that this newly acquired territory was not uninhabited, his romantic scenes with their soft brushstrokes read more like novels than like sharp-edged documentaries. Because the West in the 1840s held such unknown potential, western genre scenes and landscapes appealed to the Art-Union managers, especially when purchasing pieces for the gallery. These scenes crossed all regional divisions, supporting the organization's nationalist claims.[28]

While scenes of everyday life proved popular with Art-Union judges, of equal importance was the discipline of history painting. As historian Rachel N. Klein has noted, a look at the roster of distributed prints over the life span of the Art-Union stresses the importance of history painting to the directors. Nine of the works distributed between 1840 and 1851 featured historical themes, taken primarily from the Revolutionary War but also including British historical vignettes such as *The Signing of the Death Warrant for Lady Jane Gray* and scenes from Shakespeare, Washington Irving, and other authors.[29]

Emanuel Leutze, a German-trained artist who emigrated to the United States as a child, received a warm reception from the Art-Union for his historical scenes, including his most well known work, *Washington Crossing the Delaware* (see page 70). The paintings of Leutze married the nationalistic and inspirational goals of the Art-Union.

In the Art-Union's 1851 *Bulletin*, an unidentified author wrote,

How tame the descriptions in Marshall [a Washington biographer] and other writers appear beside this canvas, so full of life and motion! How much more powerful and lasting will be the impression made by even a brief inspection of it than by a careful reading of any treatise or history! It gives a body and

28 Johns, *American Genre Painting*, 76.

29 Klein, "Art and Authority in Antebellum New York City: The Rise and Fall of the American Art-Union," 1542. Klein goes on to note that these choices for engravings, primarily of men on the battlefield, feature a "tendency to locate significant moral action in a masculine sphere of public virtue rather than in the domestic sphere that was claimed and largely constructed by bourgeois women."

30 "The Chronicle: Art and Artists of America," *Bulletin of the American Art-Union* (1851), in Burns and Davis, *American Art to 1900*, 436.

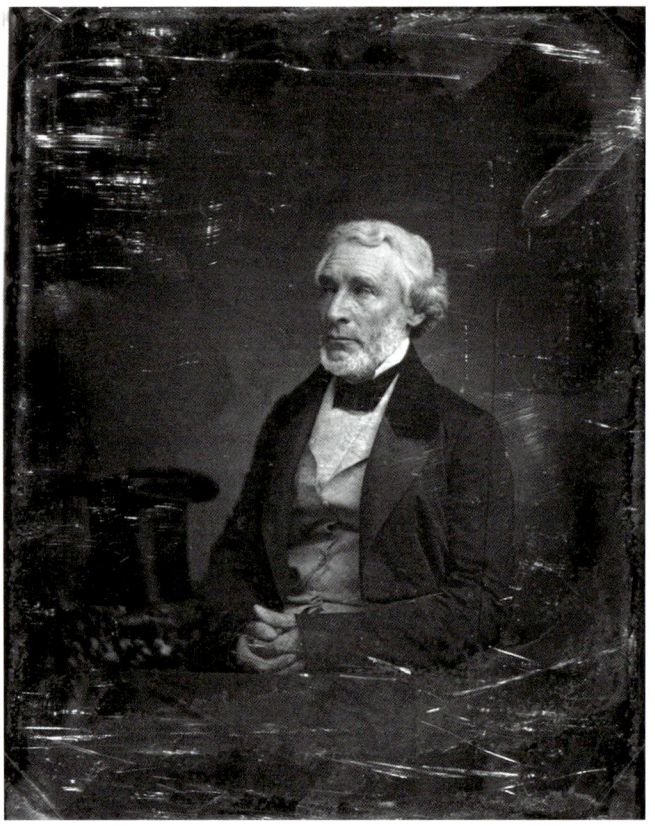

Mathew Brady, *James Gordon Bennett, Esq.*, photograph, 1851

substance to our ideas; and hereafter, when we think of Washington, in connection with the passage of the Delaware, the image in our minds will be complete and glowing, and not that vague and confused one, which is all we have gained from books. Half an hour's sight of this painting will infuse into a boy's bosom a clearer notion of the great exploit, and a more intelligent and durable admiration of the men who performed it, than the study of books for years.[30]

Effusive praise aside, these artists generated interest in the Art-Union and propelled it to nearly 19,000 subscribers by 1849, its most successful year.[31] The Union gave away nearly 1,000 paintings in the drawing that Christmas. Influenced by contemporary events, the selections made by the group's managers attempted to straddle the divide between North and South, East and West, Whig and Democrat. Yet the effort to appeal to all created hard feelings among rejected artists and political opponents. Still, the Art-Union threw its support behind artists who benefited greatly from their increased profile in the art world.

FACING: Charles Burt after CR Leslie, Anne Page, *Slender and Shallow, A Scene from the Merry Wives of Windsor*, engraving, 1850, GM 15.1146

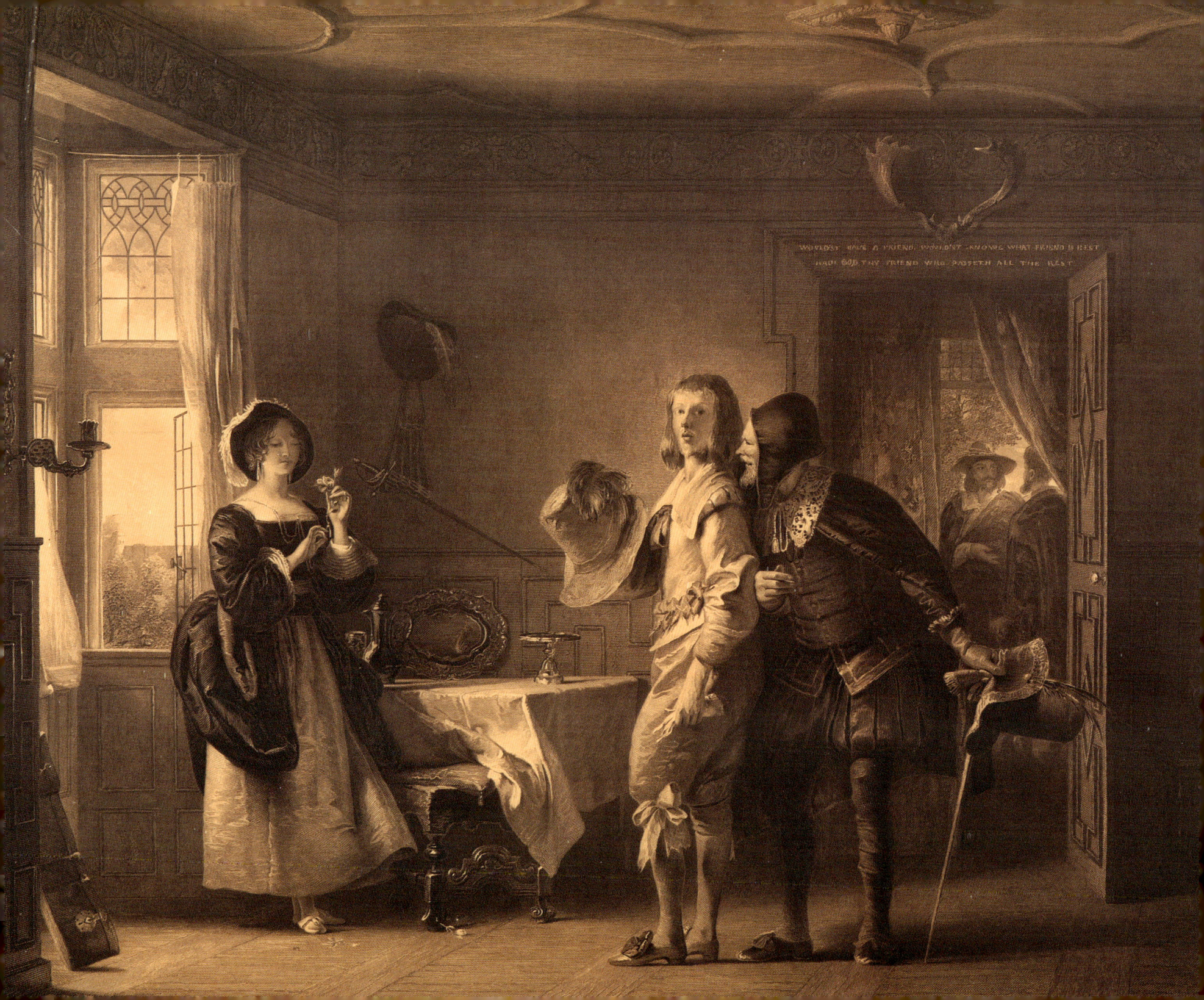

31 Baker, "The American Art-Union, " in Cowdrey, *The American Academy of Fine Arts and American Art-Union: Introduction,* 252.

32 Patricia Hills, "The American Art-Union as Patron of Expansionist Ideology in the 1840s," in Andrew Hemingway and Will Vaugn, eds., *Art in Bourgeois Society, 1790-1850* (New York: Cambridge University Press, 1998), 317, 322.

33 Klein, "Art and Authority in Antebellum New York City," 1557. Klein quotes an editorial in the *New York Herald* that refers to the Art-Union as an "abolition clique," and a newspaper called the *Police Gazette,* which refer to the Art-Union as a "swindle" designed to "pamper the pockets of the few who secretly control it." These sentiments are also echoed in Miner K. Kellogg's editorial in the *International Monthly Magazine* from January 1851 entitled "Art-Unions: Their True Character Revealed."

As the Art-Union's popularity grew, criticism from both artists and outside parties increased. James Bennett, editor of the *New York Herald,* and cultural critics argued about the political and financial motivations of the Art-Union, complaining about the quality of the works accepted and the treatment of the artists who submitted art. Initially amenable to the goals of the Union, Bennett grew displeased with the support the managers threw behind the *New York Times,* the *Herald*'s rival both politically and for readership.[32] At the heart of the debate were accusations that the managers allowed their political views, mainly Whig and abolitionist in nature, to influence the art selected for exhibition and distribution to subscribers. The *Herald* also accused the Art-Union managers of using surplus money generated from subscriptions to fund pet political projects, as well as their pockets.[33] This would prove particularly damning to the organization, which prided itself on its nationalist views. Seizing upon the complaints of artists like Thomas Doughty, who, while he did sell pieces to the Art-Union, was dissatisfied with its lack of constancy in purchasing and its unwillingness to pay top dollar, the *New York Herald* and other members of the

press published their complaints, alleging that the Art-Union behaved unscrupulously towards both artists and subscribers. Anonymous letters to the editor began to appear as early as 1846, alleging that the Art-Union undercut participating artists by buying their pieces second-hand, or not at all. A letter to the *Courier and Enquirer* stated that "Mr. Doughty, by publishing the fact that the Art-Union has purchased some of his pictures at second hand, has, I think, done manfully what he could to expose one of the abuses which have crept into that institution."[34] The letter writer also alleged favoritism with his closing remark: "I will not go farther in the present notice of the Art-Union than to observe that of one artist, eleven pictures were purchased (Harvey); while the names of some of our distinguished painters are not on the catalogue at all!"[35] While the *Herald* and other journals questioned the American Art-Union's transparency and integrity, other criticisms went after the art and its patrons.

Attacks on the organization could be subtle as well. In its review of the 1850 distribution of prizes, the *New York Weekly Herald* described the scene thus: "The building was filled throughout with a respectable, but by no means fashionable, audience. The "upper-ten" do not appear to have come forward as patrons of the fine arts on this occasion; but their place was well filled by the middle classes."[36] This idea of providing art to the masses caused many to question the quality of the art produced and purchased. In a scathing 1851 editorial, Miner K. Kellogg, writing for the *International Monthly Magazine*, explained, "numbers rather than quality seem to govern the Art-Union in their purchases of works, that they may give to subscribers a greater number of chances to draw something for their money."[37] Nathaniel Parker Willis, editor of the *Home Journal*, explained that the Art-Union's operating system could not help but encourage mediocre artists and discourage top artists. Describing the quality of the prizes as low, Willis argued that the Art-Union's selections did nothing to encourage artists to work harder, nor would it foster an appreciation for good art among subscribers.[38] Although the managers attempted to counter these arguments in their own publications, such as the *Transactions* for 1847, their statements fell on deaf ears. "It would appear from the criticism of these persons that masterpieces were 'Thick as

autumnal leaves that strow the brooks of Vallombrosa,'" wrote William J. Hoppin in his address to members of the Committee of Management, "and that the Committee were only embarrassed by the richness and variety of the stock from which they made their selection. The inquiry should be, not whether the gallery may not contain several inferior works, but whether it does not represent fairly the present condition of American Art."[39]

Arguments railed on concerning the quality of the work, the quality of the patrons, and the use of funds. But it would not be these disputes that would force the group to close its doors. Instead it was New York state law and the Art-Union's lack of growth. The year 1851 was hard for the Union. Subscriptions were down, without apparent reason. The annual distribution of prizes was postponed until there were enough subscribers in good standing to pay for expenses. There had been rumblings of problems previously. Several letters sent by field agents, or "Honorary Secretaries" as they were called, in smaller cities wrote to the New York office complaining that the engravings subscribers were guaranteed each year were delayed or missing.[40] In the closing decades of the 1840s, the hon-

34 "Letter to the Editor," *New York Courier and Enquirer*, ca. 1846. Newspaper Clippings, Reel 3, Vol. 1-2, BV American Art-Union, New York Historical Society.

35 "Letter to the Editor."

36 "The Annual Distribution of Prizes," *The Weekly Herald*, December 28, 1850, New York, New York, 415.

37 Miner K. Kellogg, "Art-Unions: Their True Character Considered," *International Monthly Magazine* (1851), quoted in Burns and Davis, *American Art to 1900*, 232.

38 Klein, "Art and Authority in Antebellum New York," 1551.

39 William J. Hoppin, "Report to the Committee of Management," American Art-Union, *Transactions for 1847*, 23.

40 Letter from C. F. J. Lorks to the Art-Union, June 2, 1848, and letter from Henry Sexton to the Art-Union, June 26, 1848, BV American Art-Union Reel #16, Letters Received, New York Historical Society.

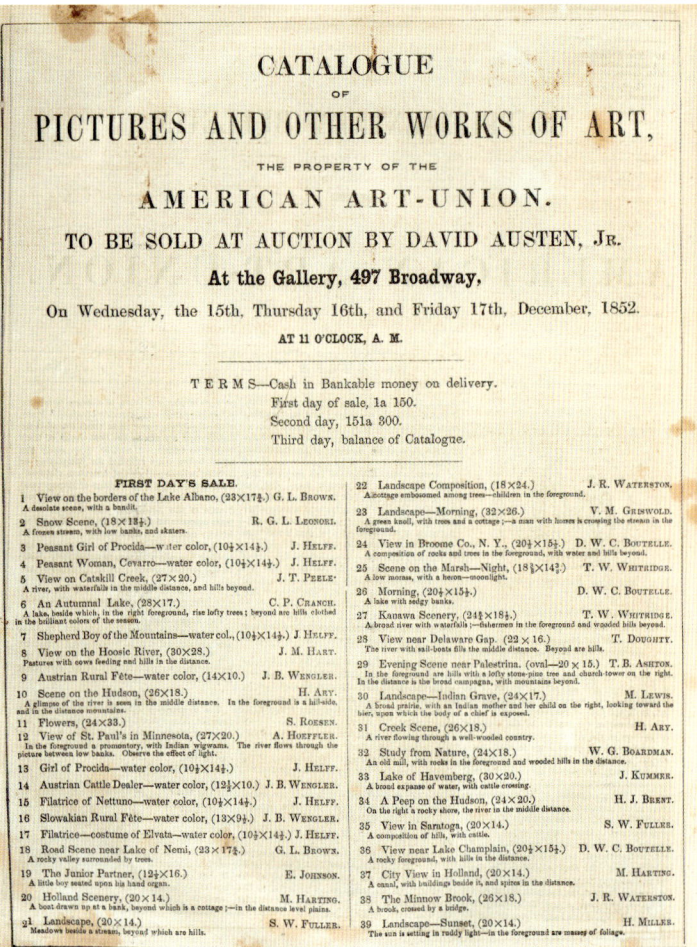

Advertisement for the Liquidation of the American Art-Union, 1852,

GM 5126.1061.156

orary secretaries, as well as members of the New York office, were pleading with subscribers to pledge early, rather than wait until the end of the year to send in their money.

The constant stream of criticism, especially from Bennett and the *New York Herald,* increased scrutiny on the group. Accused of running an illegal lottery and therefore morally suspect, the Art-Union's directors unsuccessfully sued the *Herald* for libel. When the case was dismissed in the spring of 1852, Bennett applied for an injunction against the Art-Union to stop the previously postponed 1851 distribution.[42] The Supreme Court of New York heard arguments in May and decided that, indeed, the American Art-Union had operated as an illegal lottery. Despite an appeal, the Art-Union officially ceased operation on October 22, 1852. There would be one final sale, to liquidate all holdings in order to pay off debts owed by the group. In the Art-Union's last *Bulletin,* the editor recorded the event: "The sale accordingly took place by public auction, in the Galleries of the American Art-Union, on the 15th, 16th, and 17th December and went off with great éclat."[43] Despite his disappointment, the editor still believed that the auction helped fulfill the Art-Union's mission. The auction, he wrote "distributed the paintings and sculpture which were designed to be scattered over the United States as lessons and examples of national progress in the Fine Arts, to diffuse refining influences, develop the love of the beautiful, and enkindle youthful genius."[44]

The American Art-Union experiment was over. The group had provided crucial support to fledgling American genre art and art of the American West. But in the end, its attempt to appeal to a wide audience, regardless of erudition, political affiliation, or region, limited its selections and gave fuel to its critics. Hoppin said this in his 1847 presentation to the Committee of Management:

> It [the American Art-Union] will soon possess the power to do more good or harm to the cause of Art in America than any other society or body whatsoever. It is no longer a feeble club of individuals of slender resources and questionable permanency. It is something else than a mere lottery. Neither is it an asylum for broken down picture makers. Instead of occupying this insignificant position, it is fast becoming one

of those great institutions which influence the character and manners of the whole nation.[45]

Overreach and political and artistic infighting may have silenced the American Art-Union, yet its selections speak volumes about the values and culture of antebellum America through the legacy of art it left behind.

41 Baker, "The American Art-Union" in Cowdrey, *The American Academy of Fine Arts and American Art-Union: Introduction,* 224-225.

42 Baker, "The American Art-Union," 228.

43 Baker, "The American Art-Union," 233.

44 Baker, "The American Art-Union," 233.

45 Hoppin, *Transactions for 1847,* 24-25.

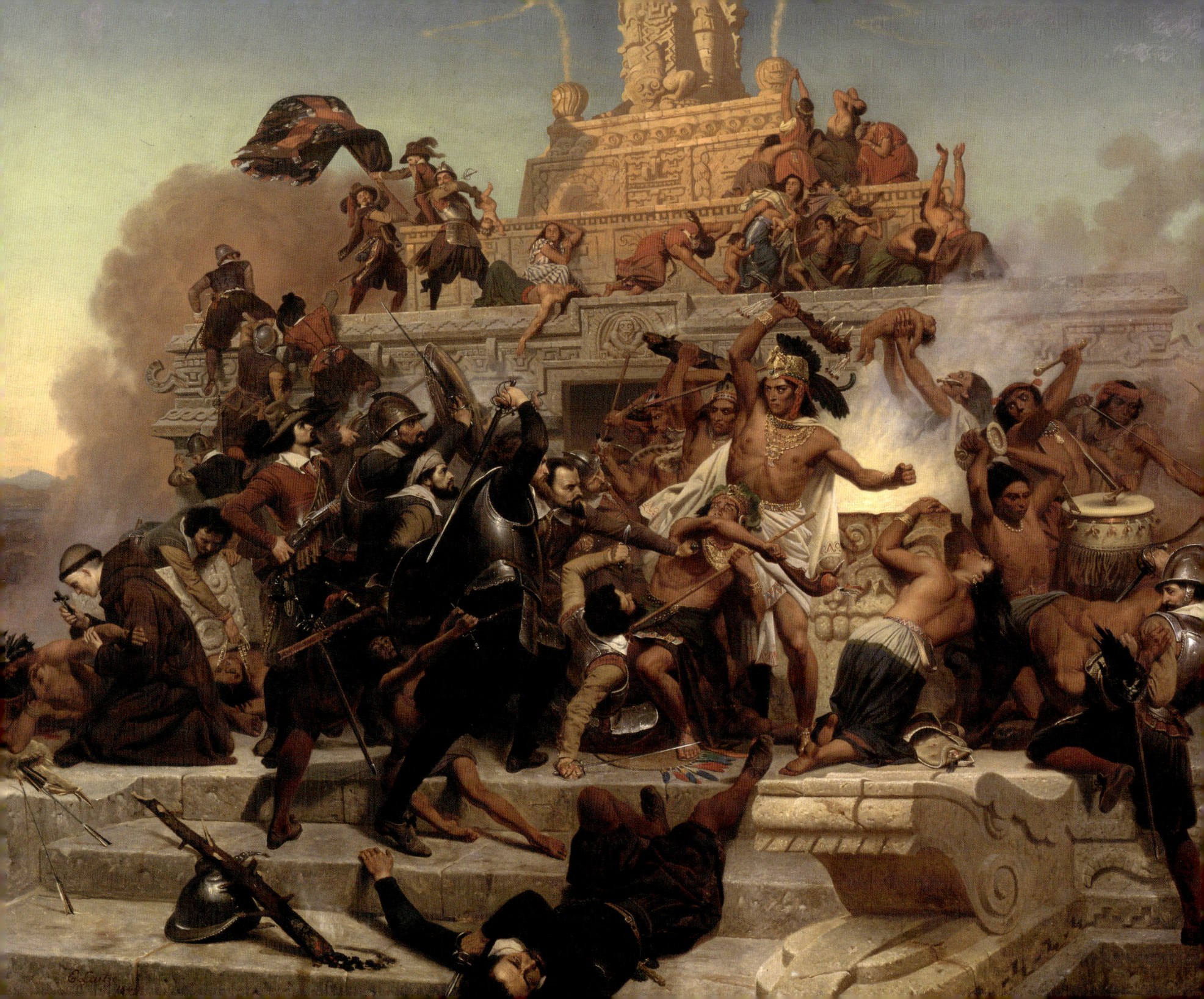

THE ART=UNION AND THE Ideology OF EMPIRE

The American Art-Union emerged in the 1840s as the most daring institution ever organized by private patrons to foster the fine arts in the United States.[1] The brilliant scheme was hatched in 1838 by portrait painter James Herring. He had been running the Apollo Gallery in New York City, which welcomed artists excluded from the prestigious annual exhibitions held at the National Academy of Design. Some 96 artists had assigned 260 works to his gallery, but poor sales threatened the gallery's existence.[2] When Herring received a copy of a report from the Edinburgh Association for the Promotion of the Fine Arts in Scotland, an art union celebrating its successful first two years of operation, he was inspired to organize a similar institution for New York. He invited a group of prominent and wealthy New Yorkers to

FACING: Emanuel Leutze, *The Storming of the Teocalli by Cortez and His Troops*, oil on canvas, 1848, Wadsworth Antheneum Museum of Art, The Ella Gallup Sumner and Mary Catlin Sumner Collection Fund, 1985.7

1 See author's note at the end of this chapter for full citations of Mann, Nichols, Klein, Baker, and Bloch.

2 According to Maybelle Mann, *American Art-Union*, 1: "Failure of the show was due, in part, to the country's severe financial depression as well as the fact that the major portions of the exhibit consisted of portraits and copies of Old Masters." Nichols, "Merchants and Artists," 194-224, describes at length the 1838 exhibition and Herring's relations with artists. Herring no doubt saw the loan exhibition held at the Stuyvesant Institute, November-December 1838; the committee included artists Robert W. Weir, Henry Inman, Thomas Cole, Asher B. Durand, and Charles C. Ingham and New York notables Philip Hone, William Cullen Bryant, and Prosper Wetmore. The exhibition was held for the benefit of William Dunlap; see *Catalogue, Descriptive, Biographical and Historical, of the Exhibition of Select Paintings by Modern Artists... at the Stuyvesant Institute* (New York: G. P. Scott, 1838), James R. Lambdin Collection, Pennsylvania Academy of the Fine Arts; my thanks to Maura Lyons for providing a photocopy. See also her *William Dunlap and the Construction of an American Art History* (Amherst: University of Massachusetts Press, 2005).

a meeting on January 8, 1839, and volunteered to operate such an art union that would assist artists through purchases and, even more, promote future patronage of the arts in America. He received an enthusiastic response; by January 16 a fifteen-member Committee of Management plus a treasurer, recording secretary and corresponding secretary (Herring himself) were in place, and thus was launched "The Apollo Association for the Promotion of the Fine Arts in the United States."[3] In 1844 the managers officially renamed the organization the American Art-Union (AAU), a name change that underscored the group's ambitions.

NATIONALISM AND EMPIRE IN THE 1840s

The organization played itself out on the stage of 1840s American history. The AAU managers wanted it to be a national institution, representing all areas of the country, but sectional strife over the issue of slavery contested the notion of national unity. Linked to the sectional debates was the issue of westward expansion: would new states entering the Union be free states or slave? In the early 1840s, even with the slavery issue, public support for expansion gained strength, in large part through enthusiasms expressed by the print media. One newspaper promoting expansionism was the New York *Herald*. The editor James Gordon Bennett, a Democrat, wrote in March 19, 1844:

It is now assumed as being the destiny of this republic, that her power will be incomplete and civilization restricted, until her institutions of all kinds be spread from the Isthmus of Panama at the South to Hudson Bay at the North, and from the shores of the Pacific to the shores of the Atlantic—thus embracing the whole of North America and forming the North American Republic, comprehending within its wide-extended arms the British Possessions in the North and all of the Texian [sic] and Mexican territories in the South, as far as the isthmus. This is believed to be the ultimate destiny of this republic.[4]

The reality of expansionism, fueled by the rhetoric of Manifest Destiny—such as that promoted by Bennett—intensified throughout the 1840s; from 1845 through 1848 the country acquired almost 1,205,000 square miles of new territory.[5] At the same time, to preserve the Union the North continued to make concessions to the South, culminating, as the decade turned, with the Compromise of 1850.[6] Such historical circumstances led the AAU managers to tend to favor "national" pictures that would appeal equally to southern and northern interests as well as pictures projecting an image of westward expansion and empire.[7]

THE AMERICAN ART-UNION AS STEWARD OF TASTE IN THE FINE ARTS

The ostensible rationale for the organization was not political but aesthetic: to support fine artists through purchases of their art and to raise the level of cultural taste in America. During its first year the AAU purchased 36 paintings from artists of New York, Washington, and Philadelphia, using funds collected from the early subscribers. Included in the first group of paintings to be distributed by lottery were *Cupid with a Dove* by the

3 See Baker, "The American Art-Union," 100. Although 82 men served as Managers during its existence, Baker has noted, p. 104, that only a handful were consistently involved, and that "in actuality the Committee of Management was a self-perpetuating body of New York merchants and professional men."

4 James L. Crouthamel, *Bennett's New York Herald and the Rise of the Popular Press* (Syracuse, NY: Syracuse University Press, 1989), 58. The first use of the phrase "manifest destiny" is credited to John L. O'Sullivan, in his unsigned editorial for the July-August 1845 issue of the *Democratic Review*. For a discussion of the rhetoric of progress, see Patricia Hills, "Picturing Progress in the Era of Westward Expansion," in William H. Truettner, *The West as America*, Exh. Cat. (Washington, D. C.: Smithsonian Institution Press, 1991).

5 According to William Appleman Williams, "Expansion," in Eric Foner and John A. Garraty, eds., *The Reader's Companion to American History*, (Boston: Houghton Mifflin Company, 1991), 368, during 1845 the United States annexed Texas, thereby acquiring 390,143 square miles of new territory, including parts of present-day New Mexico and Colorado. In 1846 the United States made a treaty with Great Britain and acquired Oregon territory, thereby adding 285,580 more square miles of land, including Washington and Idaho; in 1848, as the result of a successful war with Mexico, the US gained California, New Mexico, Arizona, Utah and Nevada, another 529,017 square miles of land.

6 The Compromise of 1850 "enabled Congress to avoid sectional and slavery issues for several years" by enacting laws bringing parity to the slave and free states; see Foner and Garraty, eds., "Compromise of

1850," *The Reader's Companion to American History*, 209-10. Ruling elites became ideologically polarized according to the two political economies that the North and South represented—growing industrialization and "free soil" farming in the North and agricultural slavery in the South. However, the threat of secession by the South in the late 1840s disturbed the notion of an expanding empire, more than ever necessary because thousands of European immigrants were then pouring into the ports of the East. Hence, party politics were exceedingly complicated with new special interest parties forming and the old parties—Whig and Democrat—constantly realigning. The Compromise of 1850 hardly helped. In the presidential election of 1852 both Whigs and Democrats split over the issue of slavery.

7 The art union movement was not uniquely American, for art unions had sprung up in Edinburgh, Liverpool, and London, as well as in Switzerland, Germany and Italy. All sought to help young artists by facilitating purchases of their works and to extend art patronage to the rising middle classes through various schemes—primarily lotteries—whereby paintings (acknowledged as luxury goods) could be obtained at a fraction of their cost. Although the American Art-Union shared with many of the art unions of Europe a desire to educate the middle classes in art appreciation, it also differed in fundamental ways: first, in the professional composition of its Committee of Management—merchants, lawyers, bankers, and newspaper editors rather than artists; second, in the tight control it exercised over its artists; third, in its favoring of specifically "American" subjects over generalized genre scenes. The European art unions varied in a number of ways; see Lynda Joy Sperling, "Northern European links to nineteenth century American landscape painting: the study of American artists in Duesseldorf" (Ph.D. thesis, University of California, Santa Barbara, 1985) and Lyndel Irene S. King, "The Art-Union of London: 1837-1912" (Ph.D. thesis, University of Minnesota, 1982).

talented 23-year-old Emanuel Leutze, genre scenes by Christian Mayr and J. D. O. Browere, and landscapes by Thomas Doughty and Thomas Birch. For five dollars subscribers received a ticket for the annual lottery of the pictures the AAU had purchased, held the third Monday in December, and a high quality engraving of an American painting.

At the first annual meeting, held in December 1839, the AAU managers congratulated themselves for their public spiritedness in advancing art, and they passed the following resolutions:

Resolved, That the success which has attended the efforts of this Association during the past year, gives the best encouragement for perseverance; therefore, . . . Resolved, That we will not hesitate in our course, but will press forward to . . . the establishment of a permanent Institution for the encouragement of the Fine Arts, and the gradual acquisition of a property in works of Art, for the cultivation of a pure taste, that the productions of genius in our own country may be justly appreciated.[8]

In May 1840, when the organization incorporated as a charitable organization in the State of New York, the AAU stepped up its efforts. It had two rocky years, but a core of managers soldiered on to make the AAU an astounding success from 1842 to the late 1840s.[9]

The AAU can thus be understood as historically situated within those democratic endeavors to make the fine arts available to a wide, middle-class public. By making possible the distribution of artworks to those who could not afford luxury items, the Committee of Management hoped to broaden the "cultivation of a pure taste" among not just those lucky enough to win a picture at the lottery but the subscribers receiving the fine arts engraving. In the *Transactions* of 1844, they reported:

The artist must have purchasers, and the people must have works of art, before the quiet lessons of the ideal and the beautiful can produce their proper effect. But the purchase of works of Fine Art is an expensive luxury. How can the artist have patronage without a patron, or the people have works of Art which are not confined to the wealthy and high-born? The plan of the Art-Union seems to be the only one to meet these wants and cultivate the general taste.[10]

The public responded by subscribing as members. One admirer, T. J. Nevins, wrote the AAU on August 19, 1846, to praise the organization's plan "to make every member a *connoisseur*, and to excite an interest in behalf of the fine arts among the people."[11]

After 1842, the Art-Union began to enjoy popular success, with increasing numbers of paintings bought from artists as a result of the growth in membership. From 1839 through 1851, the AAU purchased a total of 2,161 paintings from American artists; all but the 1851 purchases were distributed at the December lotteries. The organization issued at least one or two fine arts engravings each year to all members, for a total of 13 single engravings, 12 illustrations of stories by James Fenimore Cooper and Washington Irving, three medals, and two portfolios of five smaller engravings each for the dozen years of the AAU's existence. Subscribers also received an annual report, called *Transactions*, identifying the artworks for the lottery and listing the names of the subscribers. By April 1848 members began receiving a semi-monthly *Bulletin*, which became a first-rate journal with essays about the visual arts and that highlighted the AAU's favorite artists.[12]

Equally impressive were the increased numbers of subscribers, which grew from 829 in 1839, when the AAU distributed 36 paintings; then dipped in 1840 and 1841, but grew again to 3,233 subscribers in 1845, when it distributed 123 paintings; and then to 18,960 subscribers in 1849, the year of its greatest influence, when it offered through its lottery 460 paintings, 400 medals, 100 sets of engravings after sketches by Washington Allston, and 20 bronze statuettes. By 1851, 1000 regional secretaries were selling AAU subscriptions throughout the country, but unfortunately by that time the AAU numbers of paid-up subscribers had fallen precipitously.[13]

This growth of the AAU depended upon modern methods of promotion and development, and James Herring, the original organizer, carried on his mission with a shrewd public relations talent. During the fall of 1840 he traveled through Pennsylvania, Maryland, and Virginia, signing up

8 *Transactions of the American Art-Union* (1839), 11.

9 See Nichols, "Merchants and Artists," 313-14. Beginning in January 1842 Herring had left, but Prosper Wetmore, John Ridner, and John Austen stayed on to lead the organization. Nichols, 130-65, discusses at length Herring and his role in the AAU.

10 *Transactions of the American Art-Union* (1844), 44.

11 "Letters Received," Microfilm Reel 8, American Art-Union Archives, New-York Historical Society.

12 In 1848, the Bulletin consisted of 17 issues put out between April and December and had a print run of 80,000 plus; in 1849 (when it had 9 issues and two supplements) 150,567 were printed; during 1850 there were 113,500; and in 1851, 130,000.

13 Subscribers were down to 16,310 in 1850 and 13,450 in 1851.

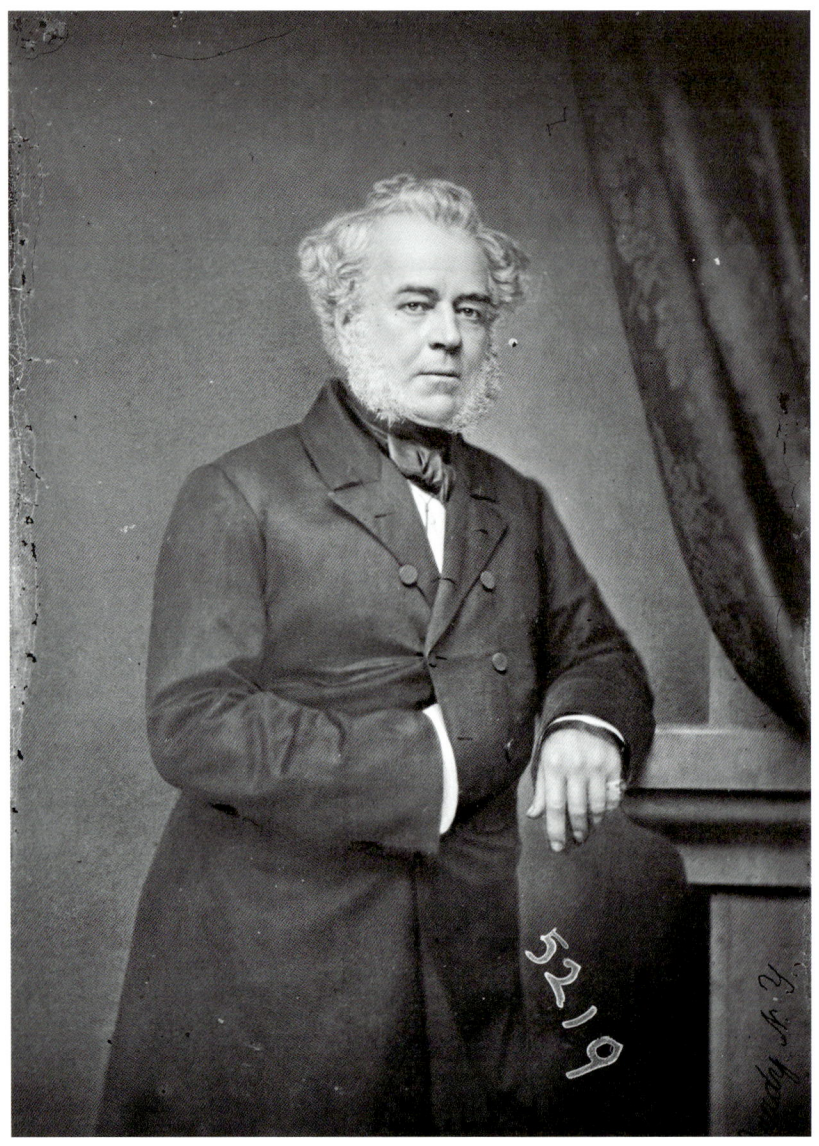

Unknown photographer, *James Watson Webb*, photograph, ca. 1855

subscribers, recruiting assistance with subscription lists and visiting artists. Letters written during his travels to John P. Ridner, a mahogany merchant serving as AAU superintendent, reveal his strategies. Herring knew the value of winning newspaper editors to the cause, even those writing for the mass-circulated "penny-press" newspapers that catered to a non-elite audience. On August 27, 1840, Herring urged Ridner:

> You must patronize *The Herald*. It is the only paper from N.Y. I meet *everywhere*, and Bennet [sic] has always favored us, and should be kept in a good humour. I sincerely hope New York will be true to itself in sustaining the Institution. When you see anything good in any of your papers, it would do good to send a copy to me and to the Hon. Secretaries. I scarcely meet any person now who does not know of the Apollo, but I have had the newspapers at work.[14]

Endorsements from Bennett, Herring realized, would stimulate interest in the AAU, even among the working classes.

At the start, the Art-Union's Committee of Management included only one newspaperman, James Watson Webb, editor of the *New York Courier and Enquirer*. In 1842 the AAU recruited other journalists to the committee: William Cullen Bryant, the famous poet and editor of the *New York Evening Post*, who would serve as AAU president from 1844 through 1846,[15] and Charles F. Briggs, a journalist who started the *Broadway Journal* in 1844.[16] Evert A. Duyckinck, who joined the AAU managers in 1848, had been a contributor to the *New York Review* before he assumed the editorship of the *Literary World* in 1847.[17] Henry J. Raymond, who joined in 1847, had worked for Horace Greeley's *New York Tribune* for two years before moving on to Webb's *Courier and Enquirer* in 1843, and finally founded his own anti-slavery paper, the *New York Daily Times*, in 1851.[18] The *Literary World*, the *Courier and Enquirer*, and the *Times* would later rally to the defense of the AAU when James Bennett of the *Herald* launched a campaign to bring it down.

THE THEME OF NATIONAL UNITY AND EXPANSION

A close examination of the institution's history and its managers reveals that the agenda of the AAU managers was not just to provide funds for artists and develop cultural taste among the rising middle classes, but to promote national unity and, as a corollary to that, empire building. In his letters from the field, for example, Herring continued to express his conviction that art had the power to inspire national unity. On October 1, 1840, he wrote to Ridner from Baltimore:

It [the AAU] is viewed here as the *only Institution* in the country which ever has been devised to unite the people of the whole land in Brotherly community free from sectional, party or sectarian strifes or jealousies. I wish my dear Ridner, you would press home these arguments upon our friends at home. If New Yorkers will do their duty, it will be the great Institution we have dreamed and thought & talked about...[19]

14 "Letters Received," Microfilm Reel 8, American Art-Union Archives, New-York Historical Society.

15 See Charles H. Brown, *William Cullen Bryant* (New York: Charles Scribner's Sons, 1971).

16 See obituary, *New York Times*, 22 June 1877, 5. In 1853 Briggs went to work for *Putnam's Magazine*, and later the *New York Daily Times*.

17 See Duyckinck's obituary in the *New York Times* (August 15, 1878), 2.

18 See Raymond's obituary in the *New York Times* (June 19, 1869), 4.

19 "Letters Received," Microfilm Reel 8, American Art-Union Archives, New-York Historical Society. Part of this passage is quoted in Klein, "Art and Authority," 1540.

20 "Letters Received"; the postscript is dated Oct. 3.

21 Walter Benjamin's seminal essay "The Work of Art in the Age of Mechanical Reproduction" is relevant here.

22 See William R. Taylor, *Cavalier and Yankee: The Old South and American National Character* (New York: George Braziller, 1961), 264-66. Herring had been closely involved in the selection of White's work for the first engraving; see Nichols, "Merchants and Artists," 309-312.

23 "Letters Received."

In a postscript, Herring comments on the eagerness people in cities outside New York had for lectures on art: "What does it matter where they [the lectures] are delivered if they have their effect on the federal interests of the body corporate in their delivery and publication."[20] In other words, persuasive lectures about pictures could serve to consolidate a national outlook—a federal as opposed to a states-rights' point of view.

Herring realized that the fine arts engravings—those images selected by the AAU, engraved by master engravers, and distributed to all the subscribers—had important cultural work to do. He grasped the importance of the mechanical reproduction of art as a tool for unifying mass culture.[21] Hence, Herring consistently urged the AAU to choose *national subjects* for its engravings. On April 21, 1841, he reported to Daniel Elliot of the Committee of Management that Washington, D. C., subscribers liked the first engraving distributed by the AAU, a subject focusing on the South Carolina general in the Revolutionary War, *General Marion in His Swamp Encampment Inviting a British Officer to Dinner* by the South Carolina artist John B. White. To Herring and the New York managers, the American Revolution recalled the time when North and South were united in their fight against a common enemy. In the 1840s the South, on the other hand, looked back at the Revolution as the era when local government boldly rebelled against an oppressive government situated elsewhere.[22]

Herring urged that the AAU act upon subscribers' desires for appealing historical and national subjects, such as the General Marion engraving:

Now I must remark that our members abroad [outside New York] feel themselves just as much members as we do ourselves, and the interest they take in the Institution quite as lively, therefore it is the more important that their views should be taken into account. They say that the second engraving should be a companion to the first; almost every body will want a pair; and the subject should be *historical* and of no trivial incident, but *national*.[23]

As it happened, the Committee of Management ignored Herring's plea, for they did *not* choose a national subject for the second engraving; rather, they

FACING: John Sartain after John B. White, *General Marion in His Swamp Encampment Inviting a British Officer to Dinner*, Apollo Association, engraving, 1840

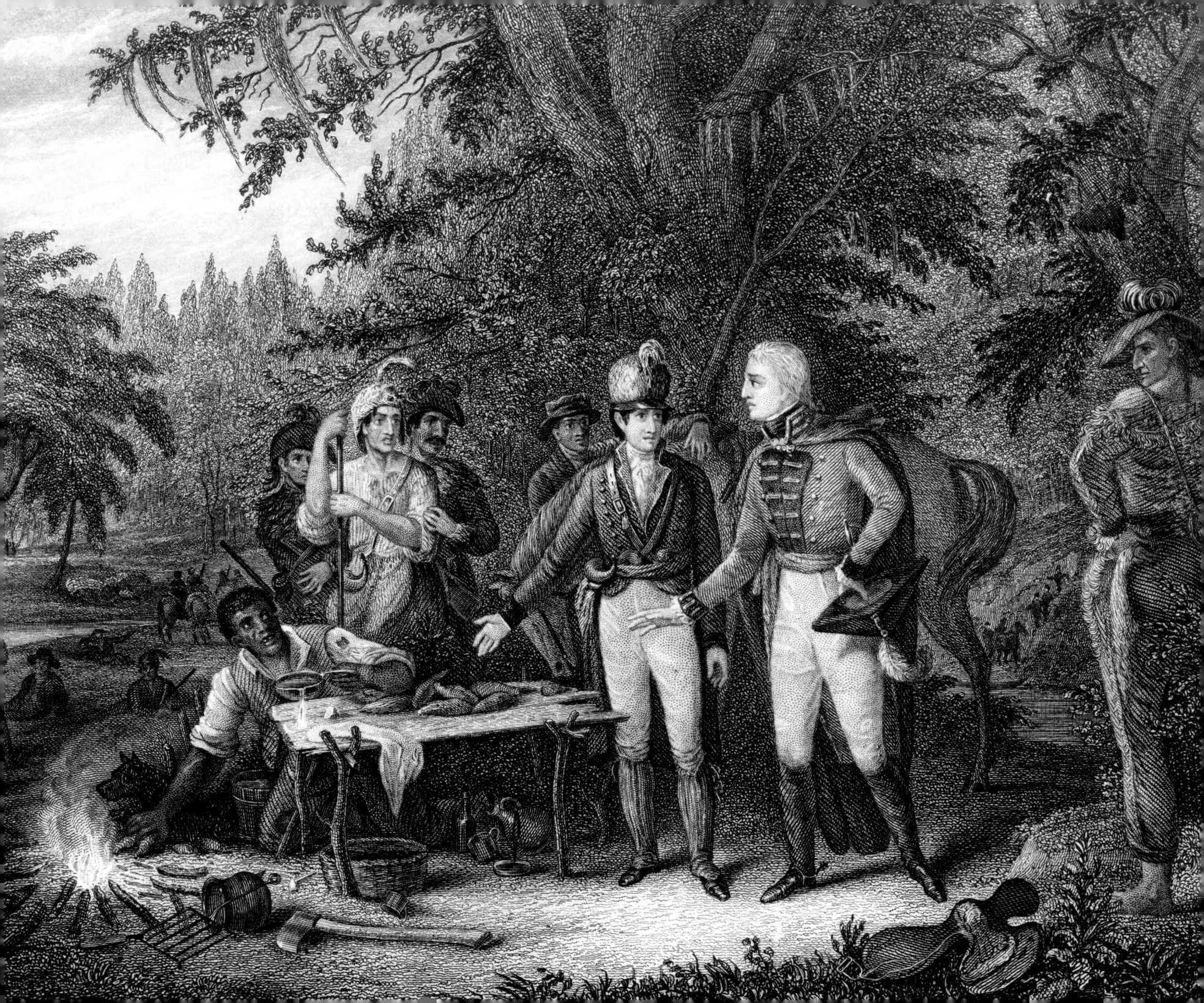

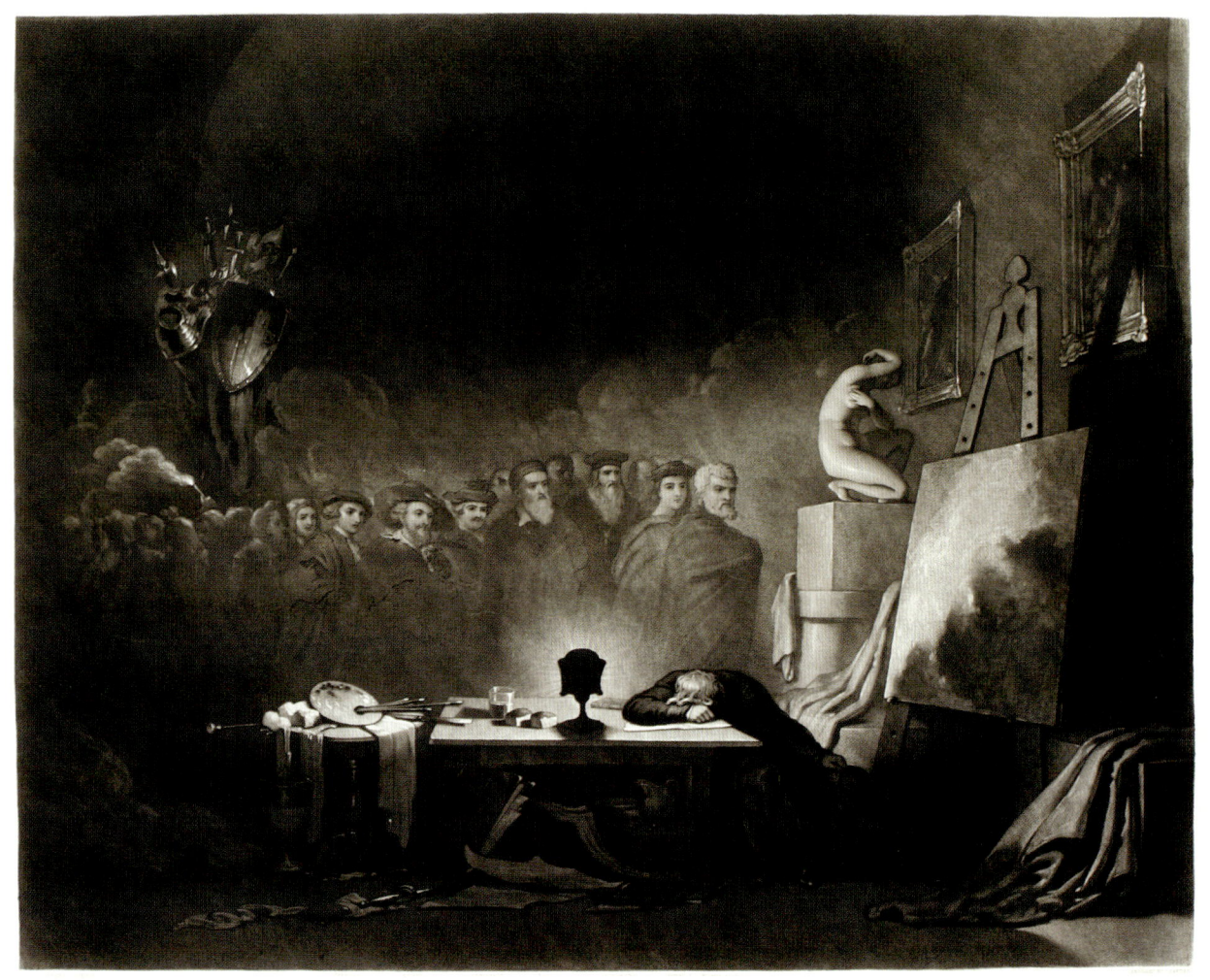

John Sartain after George H. Comegys, *The Artist's Dream*, Apollo Association, engraving, 1840

PERFECTLY AMERICAN

selected the mezzotint after George H. Comegys's *The Artist's Dream* to be engraved. Deploring this decision, Herring wrote from Norfolk, Virginia, on May 3, 1841: "The subject of the 1st engraving pleases everyone, but the subject proposed for the next I have not dared to mention to a single person, and hope that some historical illustration will be adopted instead." Herring suggested substitutes: Robert Weir's *Landing of Hendrick Hudson*, the same artist's *Columbus Disputing with the Doctors upon the Spherical Form of the Earth* or John Gadsby Chapman's *The Rescue of Captain Smith by Pocahontas*. Herring knew that both artists were not only well known for their Capitol rotunda murals but capable of doing compelling historical subjects.[24]

For the third engraving, issued in 1842, the managers again chose to ignore Herring's suggestions. They did not choose an American subject, but, rather, John Vanderlyn's *Caius Marius on the Ruins of Carthage*. They rationalized their decision on the grounds of aesthetics by admitting that the first two engravings "were not in a style of art calculated either to gratify or create a correct and refined taste."

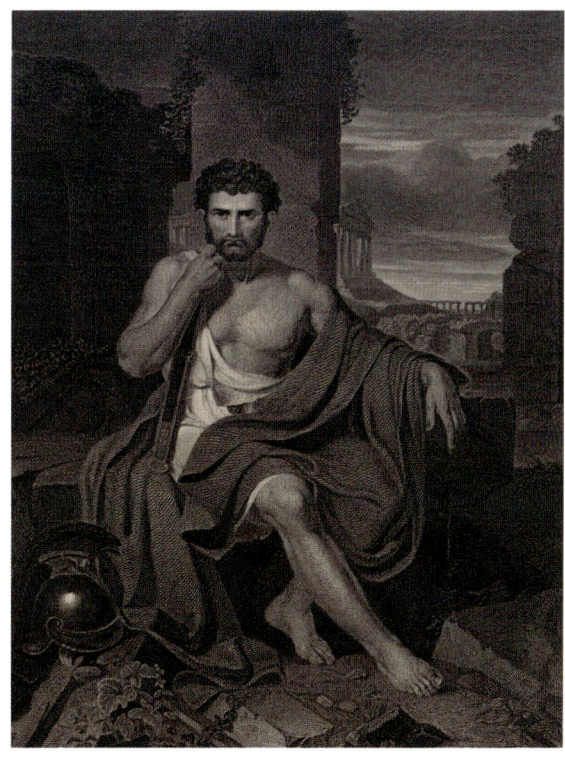

S. A. Schoff after John Vanderlyn, *Caius Marius on the Ruins of Carthage*, Apollo Association, engraving, 1842

24 "Letters Received." Chapman would be well known to a Washington area audience, since the year before he had completed his large history painting, *Baptism of Pocahontas*, for the Rotunda of the United States Capitol. Weir was finishing up his own Rotunda commission, *The Embarkation of the Pilgrims.*

25 *Transactions of the American Art-Union* (1842), 4.

26 Southerners and their allies could chuckle at the tam-o'-shanter on the white boy's head as a symbol for abolitionist groups, particularly Scottish abolitionist groups at that time attempting to awaken anti-slavery sentiment; Elizabeth Johns, *American Genre Painting: The Politics of Everyday Life* (New Haven, CT: Yale University Press, 1991), 34, makes a convincing argument for the abolitionist symbolism of the tam-o'-shanter. A contemporary of Mount's, W. Alfred Jones, who did the engraving, wrote that "one field still remains open to [Mount] which he could worthily occupy—the Southern negro, plantation life, corn shuckings, &c. He would find open-handed patrons among the cultivated and opulent planters." See *American Whig Review* 14 (Aug. 1851), 124, quoted in David Cassedy and Gail Shrott, *William Sidney Mount: Works in the Collection of The Museums at Stony Brook* (Stony Brook, NY: The Museums at Stony Brook, 1983), 53.

27 *Transactions of the American Art-Union* (1843), 8.

28 *Transactions of the American Art-Union* (1848), 42.

They therefore decided to appropriate one thousand dollars (an enormous sum for that time) and to choose a picture that "identified with the history of Art in this country, and which has been subjected to a severer test than any painting ever executed by an American Artist," namely, that it won a gold medal from the French when exhibited at the Louvre. "The subject is in itself one of high poetic interest; but the Committee would have preferred one of a national character, if a suitable picture could have been obtained."[25] In this instance aesthetics trumped politics, but not without regrets.

The next year, 1843, the AAU did at last find a suitable picture that expressed national character for its fourth engraving—William Sidney Mount's *Farmers Nooning* of 1838, owned by AAU manager Jonathan Sturgis. This picture of farmers on their lunch break would have pleased both sides. Northerners would recognize a free black working on a New York farm; however, the figure is reduced in status, presented as a plaything of children, not yet awake to his power.[26]

In its annual report issued at the end of the year, the AAU could also boast of its choices for lottery pictures: "the largest part of these works [46 paintings and 5 plaster casts] are illustrative of American scenery and American manners. The Committee would be happy to distribute none others." However, in a nod to artists' individuality—their aesthetic freedom from prescribed subjects—the report added, "but Genius loves a wide field for its exercise, and overleaps all conventional boundaries."[27] In other words, the managers would not insist on American subjects, but made it clear that such subjects would most please them.

Throughout the 1840s the managers continued to remind their growing audience that the AAU was indeed a national institution. The *Transactions* for 1848 proclaimed:

The American Art-Union has only arrived at its present eminence, by a constant adaptation of its every change and feature to the peculiar characteristics and wants, not of a *single city*, but of *the whole republic*—it has pursued a course independent alike of alien influences, or home dictation. Created for "the greatest good of the greatest number," it has been modeled after naught but the demands of the age and of the land we love.[28]

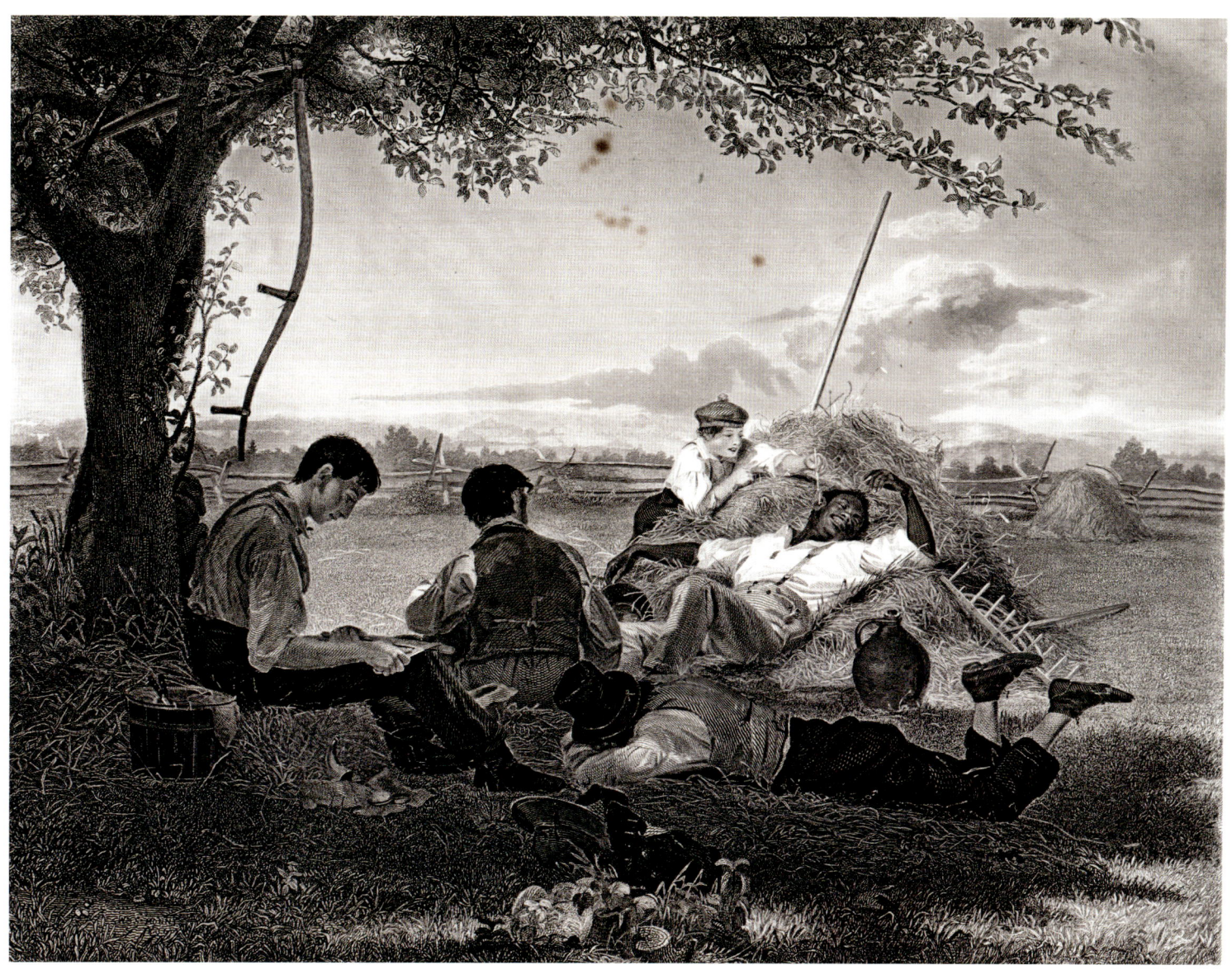

Alfred Jones after William Sidney Mount, *Farmers Nooning*, Apollo Association, engraving, 1843

29 Quoted in Baker, "The American Art-Union," 150-151.

30 Volume two of Cowdrey, *American Academy of Fine Arts and American Art-Union,* lists all of the works submitted.

31 *Transactions of the American Art-Union* (1845), 14-15.

32 *Circular of the American Art-Union: Containing the Plan of the Institution, List of Its Officers, and Catalogue of Paintings, and other works of Art, Now to Be Seen Gratis at their Rooms, 322 Broadway, New-York"* [1847].

33 The free gallery was a source of friction with the National Academy of Design. For a discussion of the relationship between the AAU and NAD, see Baker, "The American Art-Union," 176-201.

34 See, for example, *Circular of the American Art-Union…* [1847]. Twenty-nine paintings on exhibition were listed "as the property of private citizens," including works by Charles Deas, Thomas Birch, John Kensett, Jasper Cropsey, and James Clonney. Daniel Huntington's painting *A Sybil,* owned by the AAU and then being engraved, was also on view along with copies of eight engravings already sent for distribution and some

Even as the AAU was ending its tenure as a cultural institution, the president reiterated that "One of the most promising features of the American Art-Union was its *national* character. It has no sectional views, no local interests. It seeks to encourage genius and talent wherever they may be found."[29] A few southern artists had in fact sent in works for the lottery, although artists from New York, New Jersey, Pennsylvania, and New England were clearly the majority.[30]

At a time when the notion of art's "enobling mission" went undisputed, the AAU managers not only believed that art might forge a national consensus, but went further. J. T. Headley, at the annual meeting of 1845, asserted that the control of culture by the state paved the way for political control:

> Some one has said, give me the writing of the *songs* of a country, and you may make its laws. I had almost said, give me the control of the *art* of a country, and you may have the management of its administrations. There can be no greater folly than that committed by our statesmen, when they treat art and literature as something quite aside from the great national interests. . . . Art is too often looked upon as an abstract thing, designed only for men of taste and leisure. . . . [But] there are more useful departments of art not to be overlooked. . . . *Pictures* are more powerful than *speeches*. . . . Patriotism, that noblest of sentiments, for it is a sentiment as well as a principle, and governs more in that capacity than in the other, is kept alive by art more than by all the political speeches of the land.[31]

This message was reiterated in its promotional materials, in which the AAU declared its *"patriotic purpose* [to be] the progress and elevation of American Art."[32]

The AAU managers wanted to bring the paintings to a larger group of Americans than just the subscribers by creating a "free gallery," hung with paintings submitted from April to December for the Christmas lottery.[33] During the earlier months of the year private collectors, often the managers themselves, loaned their own artworks to fill the galleries until more works had been purchased.

Artists also left works for sale, which the AAU agreed to hang, but for which it took no responsibility.[34] Visitors to the galleries reflected a cross-section of New York's population. In 1848 *The Literary World* (recall that its editor was AAU manager Evert Duyckinck) commented that during evening hours visitors came from "every section of the social system. There they all are, from the millionaire of 5th Avenue, to the B'hoy of 3d, from the disdainful beauty of Fourteenth Street . . . to the belle of the Bowery."[35] It has been estimated that some three million people visited the AAU galleries in those thirteen years, with the Christmas lottery a major social event of the season.[36]

THE AAU'S DOWNFALL

By 1850 the American Art-Union had begun to lose subscribers. The reasons for this decline were many and cumulative. By the late 1840s, the AAU had spawned a number of other similar organizations in the nation, notably in Cincinnati, Boston, Philadelphia, and Newark. Moreover, the for-profit "International Art-Union," set up in 1848 by the French print firm Goupil, Vibert and Company, had emerged in New York as a threatening competitor.[37] Another factor was the increasing defection of artists dissatisfied with the prices paid to them by the AAU. Stinging attacks from the genteel press, such as the *Home Journal*, edited by Nathaniel Parker Willis, did not help. Willis defended the more cosmopolitan International Art-Union and charged the AAU with mediocrity.[38]

The contentious political situation, however, was central to the AAU's decline and fall. When the powerful James Bennett of the *Herald* charged the AAU with being a partisan, abolitionist organization, its days were numbered. If the charges stuck, the AAU would have difficulty claiming an impartial nationalism attractive to both northern and southern subscribers. It began when the *Herald* rushed to the defense of Ohio artist Thomas W. Whitley, disgruntled over the AAU's treatment of him. Bennett's offensive—to attack the legality of the lottery—had not only political but also commercial motives.[39] A southern sympathizer and anti-abolitionist as well as an unscrupulous and highly successful newspaperman, Bennett knew he could sell papers by writing sensationalist articles about controversies he had helped to fan.

six engravings from the London Art-Union and other art unions. In addition there were 28 paintings, three engravings and one marble "left by their owners . . . for sale, and the institution has no connexion [sic] with or responsibility for them. They are placed upon the walls by permission while there is room, subject to be removed at the pleasure of the Committee." The AAU obviously wanted to distance itself from commercial galleries. It is most likely that many of the works for sale had been placed there by the artists themselves.

35 Quoted in Klein, "Art and Authority," 1548. A "B'Hoy" was a Bowery Boy, a member of one of the gangs of New York.

36 Baker, "The American Art-Union," 216.

37 The International Art-Union acquired 5600 subscribers in its first year, had its own gallery, and sold European as well as American art with the profits being skimmed by the directors; see Klein, "Art and Authority," 1549.

38 For a good discussion of Willis, see Klein, "Art and Authority," 1549-52.

39 See Bloch, "The American Art-Union's Downfall," 331-59.

40 Quoted in Bloch, "The American Art-Union's Downfall," 350. Bloch states that according to one Raymond biographer, Ernest Francis Brown, the AAU advertised in the *Times* in order to solicit new memberships; the AAU paid for the paper for the issues in which their circular appeared. That they also furnished the *Times* with a mailing list of potential subscribers would have galled the *Herald's* Bennett.

41 Quoted in Bloch, "The American Art-Union's Downfall," 352.

42 See Johns, *American Genre Painting*, 34. Johns does not cite the source of the quotation.

Mounting charges and countercharges volleyed between Bennett and the AAU. On January 1, 1851, Bennett sharpened his attack by targeting his competitor, Henry J. Raymond of the *New York Daily Times*:

> The Art-Union is in the hands of an *abolition clique* . . . in addition to paying for oyster and champagne suppers &c., &c., a *portion of the funds have been applied towards establishing a daily abolition journal* [the *Times*] *in this city, instead of being used for the legitimate purposes of the institution.* . . .[40]

By charging a new competing newspaper with having abolitionist sympathies, Bennett could discredit the *Times's* objectivity and thereby undercut its sales.

The AAU retaliated and sued the *Herald* for libel over the charge of the "oyster and champagne suppers." These hostilities escalated, and Bennett kept up the attack, writing on January 29:

> The Art-Union . . . tolerated, in their management, and aided with their money and means, the same anti-slavery agitator [Raymond] who introduced that subject in the Legislature of New York and almost ran the *Courier and Enquirer* into the ground. The same consequences will attend the destiny [of the *Times*], and such conduct and policy deserve, the result, which we now predict will befall them.[41]

Bennett was making explicit the politics of sectionalism (slavery versus antislavery), a politics that the AAU management had been striving to avoid. Raymond, having been elected to the New York Assembly by the Whigs in 1849, reelected in 1850, and named Speaker of the Assembly in January 1851, galled southern sympathizers such as Bennett. As Bennett charged, Raymond might have had major disagreements with his former boss, the AAU manager James Watson Webb, who considered abolitionists to be "foreign agitators."[42] We can certainly assume that Raymond's politics both alienated the southern subscribers of the AAU and was divisive within the ranks of the AAU managers themselves. The AAU managers had been a combination of Whigs and Democrats, and until the early 1850s they seem to have had cordial relationships as both groups strove to keep first and foremost the unity of the nation. The illusion of unity was shattered by the election of 1852, when both Whig and Democratic parties themselves split over the issue of slavery.

Aside from the attacks by Bennett and others, the AAU already found itself in financial troubles. The Committee of Management, which had projected continuous growth and was involved in expanding the art galleries, had brought the AAU close to bankruptcy. Many of its regular subscribers had not yet paid their dues. The AAU postponed its Christmas 1851 lottery until more subscribers had paid up; but because of Bennett's pending litigation the plan to hold the AAU lottery drawing in March 1852 was scrapped. In fact, the District Attorney, N. Bowditch Blunt, took the libel case to the New York Supreme Court, and in June 1852 the AAU's lottery was ruled illegal under New York law. With the growing polarization of New York citizens into anti-slavery versus pro-southern camps, there can be no doubt that politics, rather than the moral-

ity of lotteries, was the major, even if covert, consideration of the lawyers and judges involved in the decision. After a final auction of its holdings in December 1852, the AAU folded.[43]

THE BUSINESS INTERESTS
OF THE AAU MANAGERS

The managers who had guided the AAU were no different from other business leaders in the ways they were affected by political currents. Their decision to issue engravings appealing to both northern and southern interests paralleled efforts in the political sphere to compromise in order to ameliorate sectional strife and maintain a united nation. However, because of their business interests in railroads and shipping, they were also active participants in western expansionism, the second major theme favored as a subject for AAU engravings and reproductions.

The managers with business interests centered on railroad lines and shipping included a sizable and influential group. Francis W. Edmonds, the only artist among them, was a banker and director of the New York and Erie Railroad.[44] Merchant and

43 Nevertheless, the auction brought more staggering figures when the AAU sold 395 paintings for a total of $35,365, or about $90 per painting. To give an idea of the dollar's value at that time, 1852, a mason working on the Erie Canal made $10.50 for a six-day week. Hence, paintings costing an average of $90—and many cost $300 or higher—were certainly "luxury" items. But that was the point: the managers had all along sought to democratize the fine arts by making such luxury items available to a lower income but culturally ambitious audience and they deplored the fact that the works could not be distributed by lottery.

44 See N. Nichols B. Clark, *Francis W. Edmonds: American Master in the Dutch Tradition* (Washington, D. C.: Smithsonian Institution Press, 1988). Edmonds painted *Sparking*, engraved and distributed to AAU members in 1844, and *The New Scholar*, engraved and distributed in 1850. For brief biographies of all the AAU managers, see Nichols, "Merchants and Artists: The Apollo Association and the American Art-Union," 337-439.

45 For Sturges, see his obituary, *New York Times* (December 1, 1874), 2. His art collection was discussed in *The Crayon* 3 (February, 1846), 57-58.

46 For Leupp, see Allan Nevins, "The Century, 1847-1866," in *The Century, 1847-1946* (New York: The Century Association, 1947), 6. Leupp's collection was discussed in *The Crayon* 3 (June 1856), 186.

47 For Alsop, see Nichols, "Merchants and Artists: The Apollo Association and the American Art-Union," 38-39.

48 See Nichols, "Merchants and Artists," p. 432. See also the obituary of Wetmore in the *New York Times* (March 17, 1876), 5. Because of the clubby nature of the AAU, one can safely assume that other prominent managers had made investments in railroads as well, such as: Philip Hone, a former New York City mayor, prominent Whig and theater-goer (see Allen Nevins, ed., *The Diary of Philip Hone*, 2 vols. (New York, 1927); Abraham Cozzens, a merchant, amateur artist and prominent art collector, who served as president of the AAU from 1850 until the Art-Union folded in 1852 (see discussion of Cozzens's art collection in *The Crayon* 3 (April 1856), 123; and Harvard and Yale educated William J. Hoppin, who edited the Art-Union's *Bulletin* and brought it up to the standard of London's *Art Journal* (see *The National Cyclopaedia*, Vol. 5, 186). According to Nichols, "Merchants and Artists," 181-82, other AAU managers involved in the shipping industry were William Brown, Richard Demill, Moses Grinnell, Townsend Harris, Benjamin and Nathaniel Jarvis, Paul Spofford, and the marine lawyers Erastus Benedict and William Butler; other railroad men were William Kemble, Benjamin Nathan, and Charles Sandford.

49 See Nichols, "Merchants and Artists," 419-21; also the obituary in the *New York Times* (September 12, 1880), 5, and the *Dictionary of American Biography*, Vol. 15 (New York: Charles Scribner's Sons, 1946), 11-12. During the Civil War Roberts sold broken-down steamships at exorbitant prices to the government; see *Dictionary of American Biography*. Alsop was also at one time a director of the Ohio and Mississippi Railroad as well as the Illinois Central; see his obituary, *New York Times* (February 28, 1878), 4.

art collector Jonathan Sturges was a director of the Illinois Central railroad.[45] Merchant Charles M. Leupp was a director of the Tradesmen's Bank and of the Erie Railroad.[46] Joseph W. Alsop, Jr. co-founded the Pacific Mail Steamship Company in 1848.[47] Prosper Wetmore, described by art historian Arlene Katz Nichols as "the single most influential leader" of the AAU after James Herring, was a politically connected Democrat who joined the AAU managers in 1839 and took over the AAU presidency from 1847 through 1850.[48] He had interests also in the shipping business, along with his friend, the Whig Marshall O. Roberts, called in his *New York Times* obituary as "one of the wealthiest and best known" of the merchants of New York.

Although Roberts had interests in railroads, he obtained his considerable wealth through shipping and often partnered with Wetmore. Roberts's obituary in the *New York Times* stated that Prosper Wetmore helped Roberts secure a lucrative naval shipping contract through Wetmore's political ties with John Tyler, the U.S. president who annexed Texas. In 1850 when they were both associated with the AAU, Roberts and Wetmore along with others formed the United States Steamship Company. The company received a government contract to transport mail from New York to Panama. The Pacific Mail Steamship Company, which picked up the mail and carried it on to San Francisco, had Joseph W. Alsop, Jr. as one of its directors. Roberts expanded his shipping empire, with other lines plying the mails between New York and New Orleans.[49]

Roberts joined the managers in 1846, stayed on through 1851, and proffered a $10,000 mortgage to the AAU when it bought property to expand its quarters in 1849. In 1847 the AAU expanded its space by leasing property at 497 Broadway and an abutting lot on Mercer, after which it built a larger picture gallery. Two years later they bought another lot and built a new building. The last *Bulletin*, published in 1853, reveals that Roberts still held a $10,000 mortgage for the AAU. He was paid back when the building was sold.

Western expansion contributed greatly to the fortunes of these men, and they not surprisingly preferred pictures that celebrated western expansion. Indeed, to them expansion was the logical consequence to assertive nationalism.

THE ARTISTS AS PLAYERS IN THE NATIONAL DEBATE

One way to direct the course of art toward nationalistic themes was to patronize those artists whose art was "appealing to national feeling and rousing national sentiment" as called for by J. T. Headley. But the AAU managers did not attempt to exercise control of their artists with a heavy hand. They developed genuine friendships with the older artists through such social clubs as the Century Association; with the younger artists, they held out the promise of future purchases.[50]

It is thus no mere coincidence that a handful of talented younger artists developed themes of national unity and westward expansion so appealing to these managers. George Caleb Bingham, William Ranney, Charles Deas, Emanuel Leutze, and Richard Caton Woodville obliged the managers of the American Art-Union with pictures encoded with the expansionist ethos, many of which were selected for Art-Union engravings. These were illustrated and discussed at length in the *Bulletin* and ended up in the personal art collections of the managers.

50 See Hills, *West as America*, 105-6, for a brief discussion of the Century Club memberships of AAU managers and the older artists. As to the relationship of the AAU to younger artists, such as Eastman Johnson, see Patricia Hills, *Eastman Johnson* (New York: Clarkson N. Potter, 1972), 10, which describes how the corresponding secretary, Andrew Warner, persuaded Johnson to study in Düsseldorf rather than another art center in Europe.

51 See Nancy Rash, *The Painting and Politics of George Caleb Bingham* (New Haven and London: Yale University Press, 1991), 66-69. Quoted from the *Bulletin of the American Art-Union* 2 (October 1849), 12. In the same article the AAU also took credit for advancing the careers of portrait painter George Baker, and landscape painters Frederic Church and John Kensett.

52 See Hills, *The West as America*, 110-12 for more detailed analysis of Ranney's *Daniel Boone*.

53 Carol Clark, *Charles Deas and 1840s America*, Exh. Cat. (Norman: University of Oklahoma Press in cooperation with the Denver Art Museum, 2010), 194.

54 Clark, *Charles Deas*, 188-89.

The AAU, for example, issued Bingham's *The Jolly Flatboatmen* as a large engraving in 1847. The AAU managers would have considered the happy-go-lucky raftsmen carrying cargo along the Missouri river as a fairly accurate depiction of river life and commercial enterprise in the expanding west. Two years later the *Bulletin* boasted that "Bingham acknowledges his indebtedness to us as the first patron of his higher efforts, and his main-stay in all attempts beyond the line of portraiture."[51]

William Ranney became an Art-Union regular in 1845 when he submitted *The Wounded Trooper*. By 1847, the high point of the military campaigns against Mexico, his subjects were both nationalistic and clearly expansionist in their content. His *Washington's Mission to the Indians in 1753* and *First News of the Battle of Lexington* appealed to an audience eager to equate the Mexican War with a more acceptable, patriotic history. In 1848, the year the United States acquired vast amounts of land as the settlement from the Mexican War, Ranney showed two more historical scenes that would be read as metaphors for events of the late war, *Washington Rallying the Americans at the Battle of Princeton* and *Veterans of 1776 Returning from the War*. He also submitted western scenes, such as *Prairie Burial* and *Stampede*. Ranney's *Daniel Boone's First View of Kentucky* (page 123) was reproduced as the frontispiece to the May 1850 *Bulletin*, and *The Scouting Party* was illustrated in the September 1851 issue.[52]

Not insignificant was the fact that AAU managers were also enhancing their own collections by acquiring paintings that had hung at the AAU galleries. Charles Deas's *The Death Struggle*, shown at the AAU in 1846 was acquired by art collector George W. Austen, then treasurer of the AAU and on the Committee of Management.[53] Deas's *Long Jakes,"the Rocky Mountain Man"* (page 67), shown at the AAU in 1844 and distributed by lottery to Gilbert F. Everson, a New York importer, was acquired by Marshall O. Roberts.[54]

Without a doubt, the AAU darling was the German-American artist Emanuel Leutze, whose historical scenes in terms of quality and ambition were surpassed by no other American artist at that time and whose works were privately collected by AAU managers. Leutze showed in almost all of the Art-Union exhibitions.

FACING: T. Doney after George Caleb Bingham, *The Jolly Flatboatmen*, Powell & Co., engraving, 1847

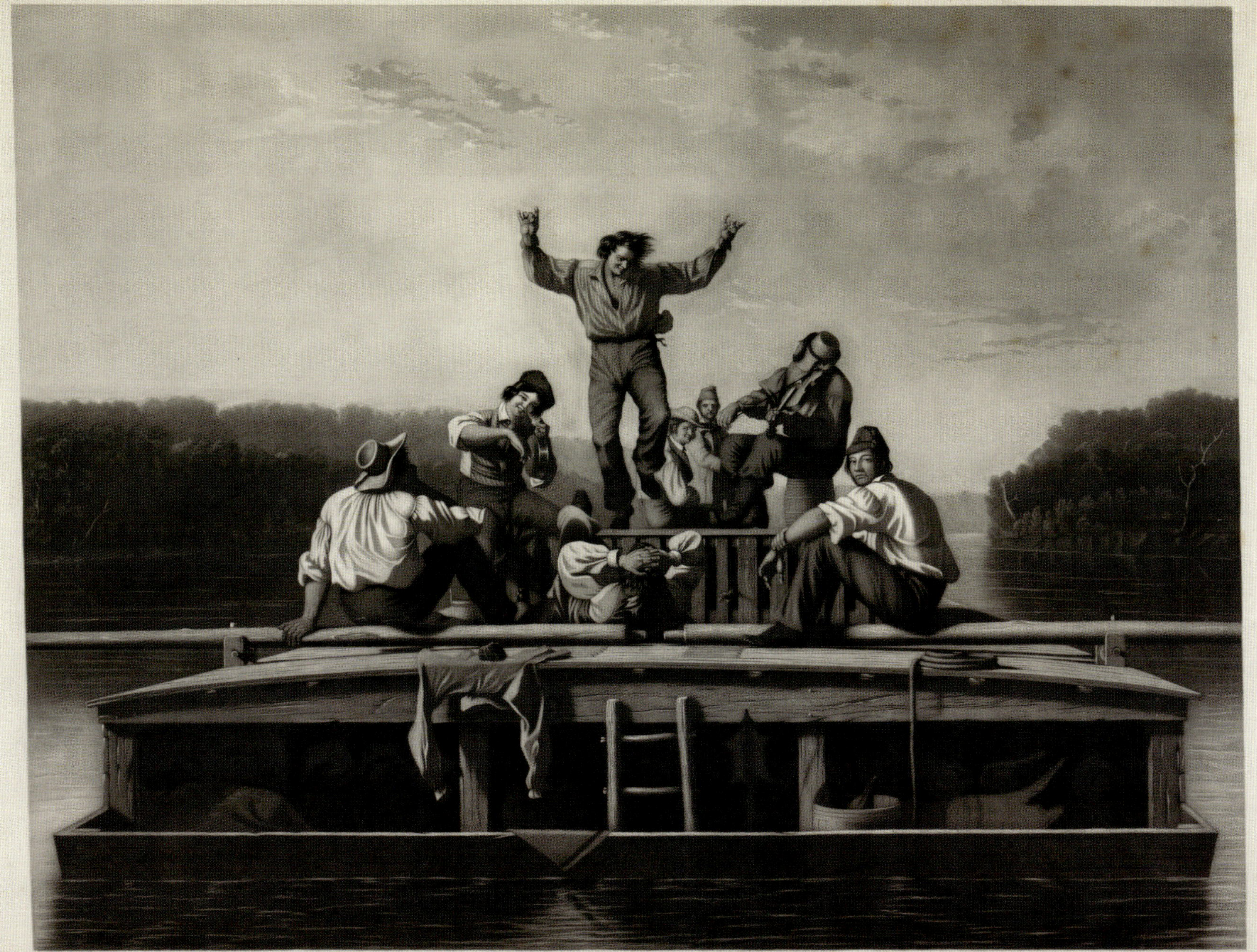

THE JOLLY FLAT BOAT MEN.

From the Original painting distributed   By the American Art Union in 1847.
Published exclusively for   the Members of that Year

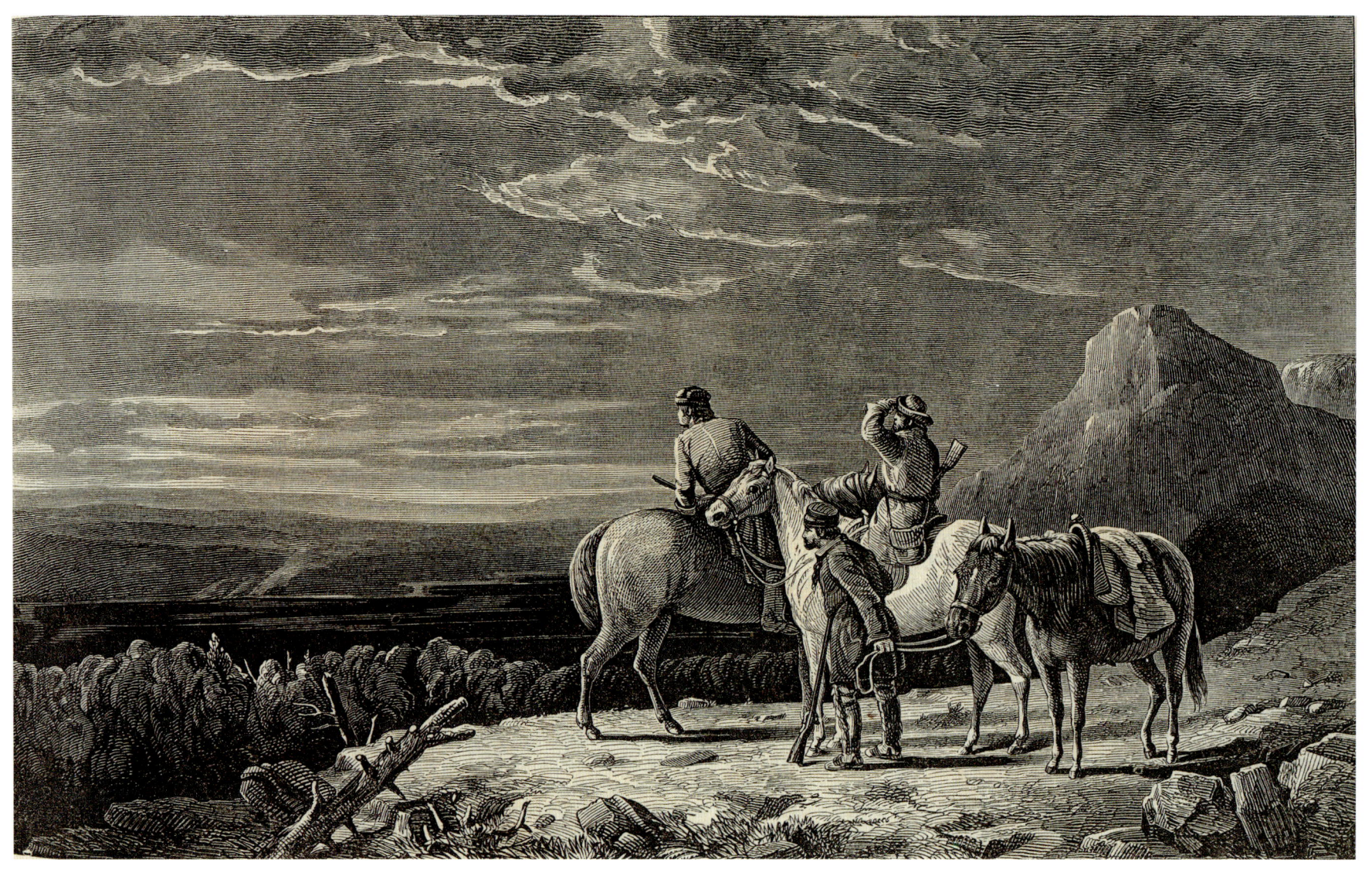

Richardson after William Tylee Ranney, *The Scouting Party*, American Art-Union, engraving, 1851, GM 5126.1061.89

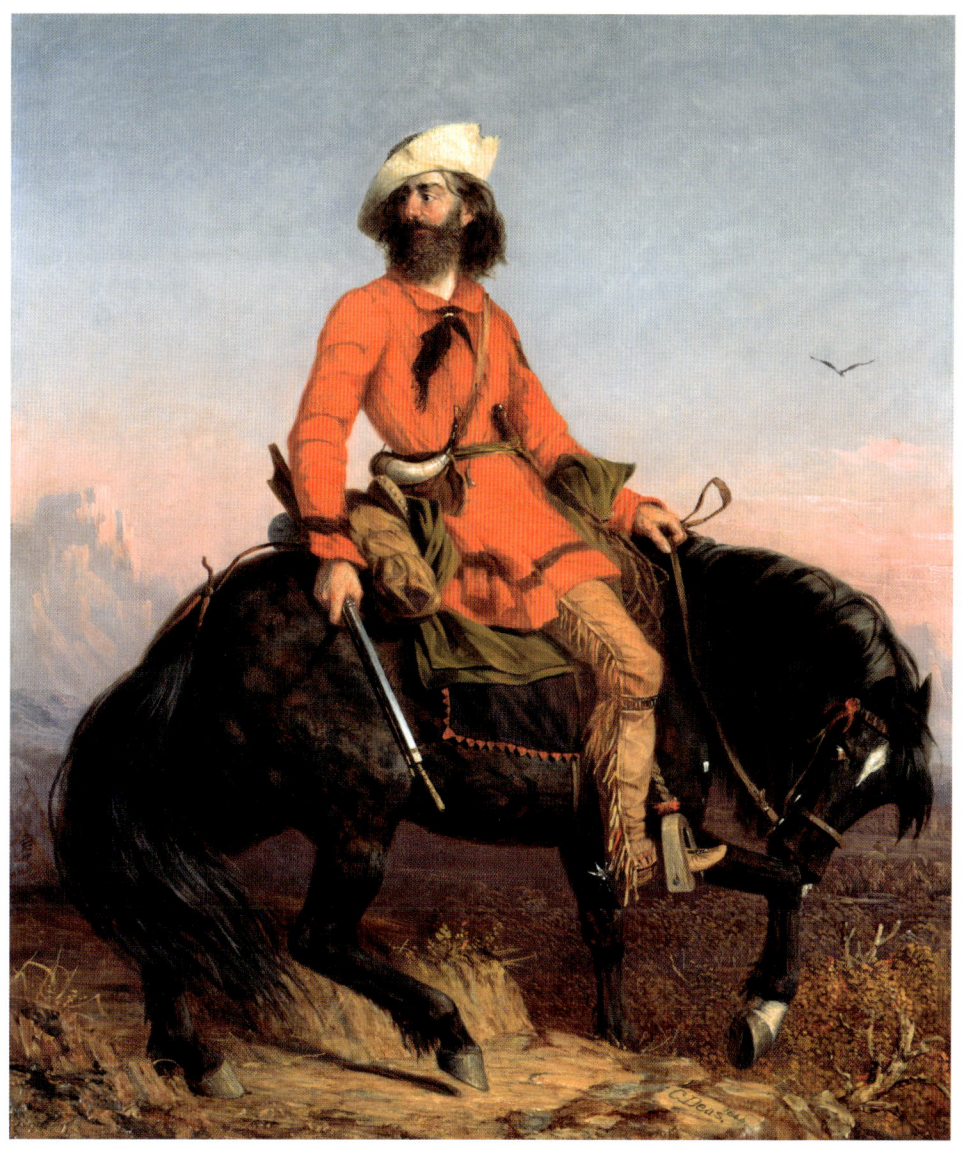

Charles Deas, *Long Jakes, "The Rocky Mountain Man,"* oil on canvas, 1844, Denver Art Museum Collection

55 See William H. Truettner, *The West as America*, 59-63. For a general discussion of Leutze, see Barbara S. Groseclose, *Emanuel Leutze, 1816-1868: Freedom Is the Only King* (Washington D. C.: National Collection of Fine Arts, 1975).

56 Roberts owned at least four other Leutze paintings. AAU director A. M. Cozzens was a major patron of Leutze and owned at least seven paintings including *Columbus before Ferdinand and Isabella*. Leutze even named one of his children "Abraham" after Cozzens. See Groseclose, *Emanuel Leutze*.

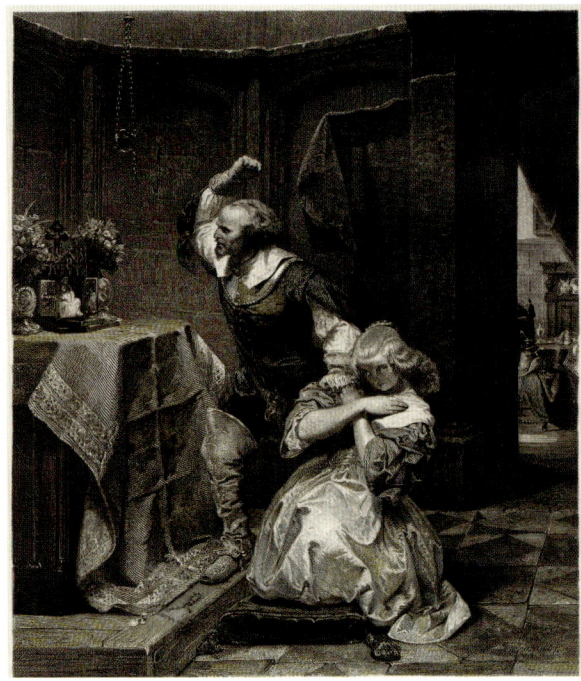

Alfred Jones after Emanuel Leutze, *The Image Breaker*, American Art-Union, engraving, 1850, GM 15.1147

Two of Leutze's works were engraved for distribution to all the members—*Sir Walter Raleigh Parting with His Wife* in 1846 and *The Image Breaker* in 1850. Although the former expressed manly virtue in pursuit of empire building, the latter is a curious work depicting a Puritan interrupting his daughter's devotion to a Roman Catholic image of the Madonna. The *Bulletin* consistently carried news about the Leutze atelier in Düsseldorf and followed the progress of his major works, such as *The Storming of the Teocalli by Cortez and His Troops*, 1848 (see page 44), which referred to the conquest of Mexico by the conquistadors, and by analogy, to the Mexican War and conquest of the west.[55] Leutze's *Washington Crossing the Delaware*, a revolutionary war scene, was purchased by Marshall O. Roberts from Goupil's New York gallery and went on exhibition in the AAU's galleries before traveling to Washington, D. C., in the early 1850s.

At the helm of a rowboat filled with ethnic and regional "American" types, including an African-American and a Scotsman, stands Washington, whose image and memory would rally the nation to the idea of a unified republic.[56]

FACING: Detail, Charles Burt after Emanuel Leutze, *Sir Walter Raleigh Parting with his Wife*, engraving

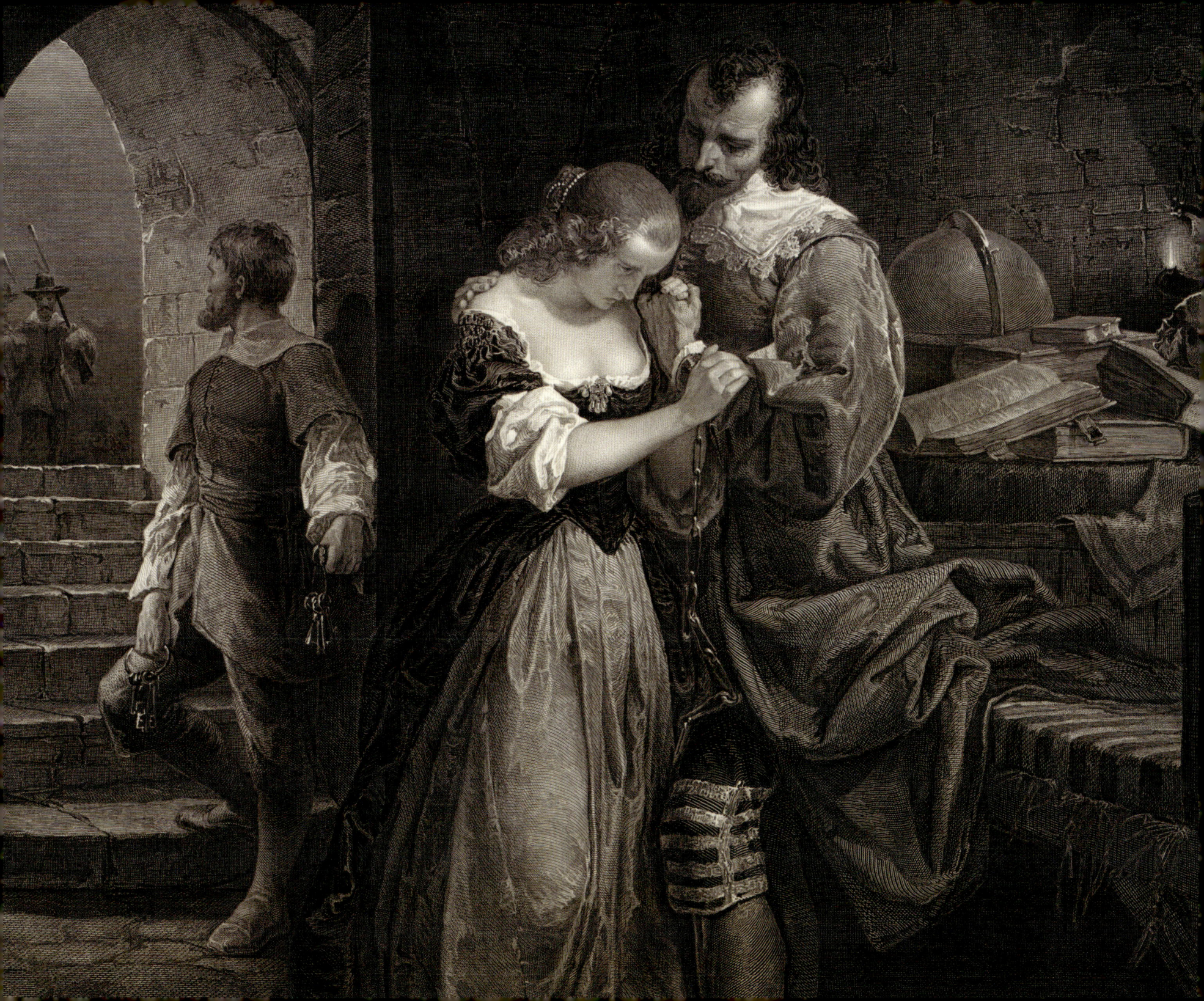

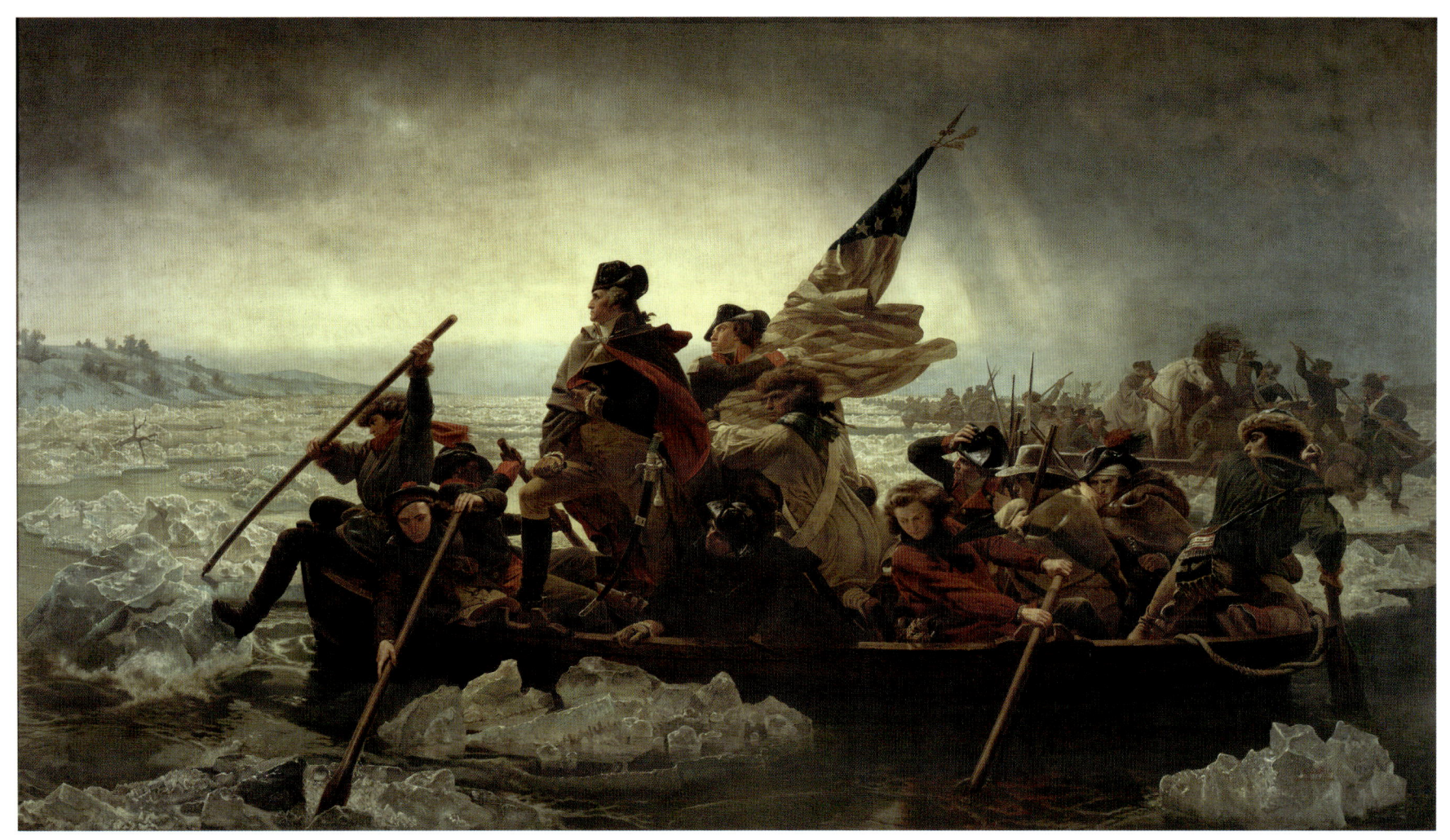

Emanuel Leutze, *Washington Crossing the Delaware,* oil on canvas, 1851, Metropolitan Museum of Art, Gift of John Stewart Kennedy, 1897, 97.34

The youngest AAU protégée was Richard Caton Woodville, a native of Baltimore then residing in Düsseldorf. Woodville's *War News from Mexico* (page 72), painted in 1848 and exhibited at the Art-Union in 1849, had a specific, topical subject, the first such to be promoted by the Art-Union. When it was reproduced in the April 1851 *Bulletin*, the editor wrote that it represented a group "gathered around the porch of a country inn and post-office, listening to the reading of a newspaper, which contains an account of one of the battles in the late war with Mexico. . . . The slouching barkeeper, the tavern-haunting scape-grace who finds something in the news to arouse him from his ordinary indifference, the deaf man, the exultant boy who is swinging his cap in the background, and the poor old negro upon the steps, all are treated with extraordinary fidelity to nature" and praised the subject of the print for being "perfectly AMERICAN in its character . . ."[57]

The large folio engraving went out to about 14,000 subscribers at the end of 1851. To celebrate the Mexican War three years after it had been concluded meant to celebrate the fact of westward expansion. And the inclusion of a heterogeneous mix of people on a porch labeled "American Hotel" delivered the message that successful empire building needed the unity of all regional groups. Woodville even included a woman and African Americans in the scene, but located them on the margins, as usual for the time.[58]

Woodville's next subject to be sent to the AAU, also focused on the Mexican War; *Old '76 and Young '48* (page 73) depicts a family interior in which a volunteer officer relates his adventures in Mexico to his old grandfather. In April 1849 the *Bulletin* had heralded it in a short notice about American artists living abroad. When shipped to the AAU galleries, the painting was not bought for the lottery but instead was held for the engraver. The AAU issued the engraving in 1851; in the final sale of the AAU in 1852, William Henry Webb, a shipping partner with AAU manager Joseph W. Alsop, Jr., bought the work.

The subjects of the majority of AAU prints and reproductions in the *Bulletin* were manly men. As Rachel Klein has pointed out, the engraving after White's *General Marion in His Swamp Encampment* and many other AAU engravings "betray [an] . . . attachment to republican images of

57 *Bulletin of the American Art-Union* (1851), 17.

58 Both *War News from Mexico* and *Old '76 and Young '48* are discussed at length in Hills, "Picturing Progress," 106-110.

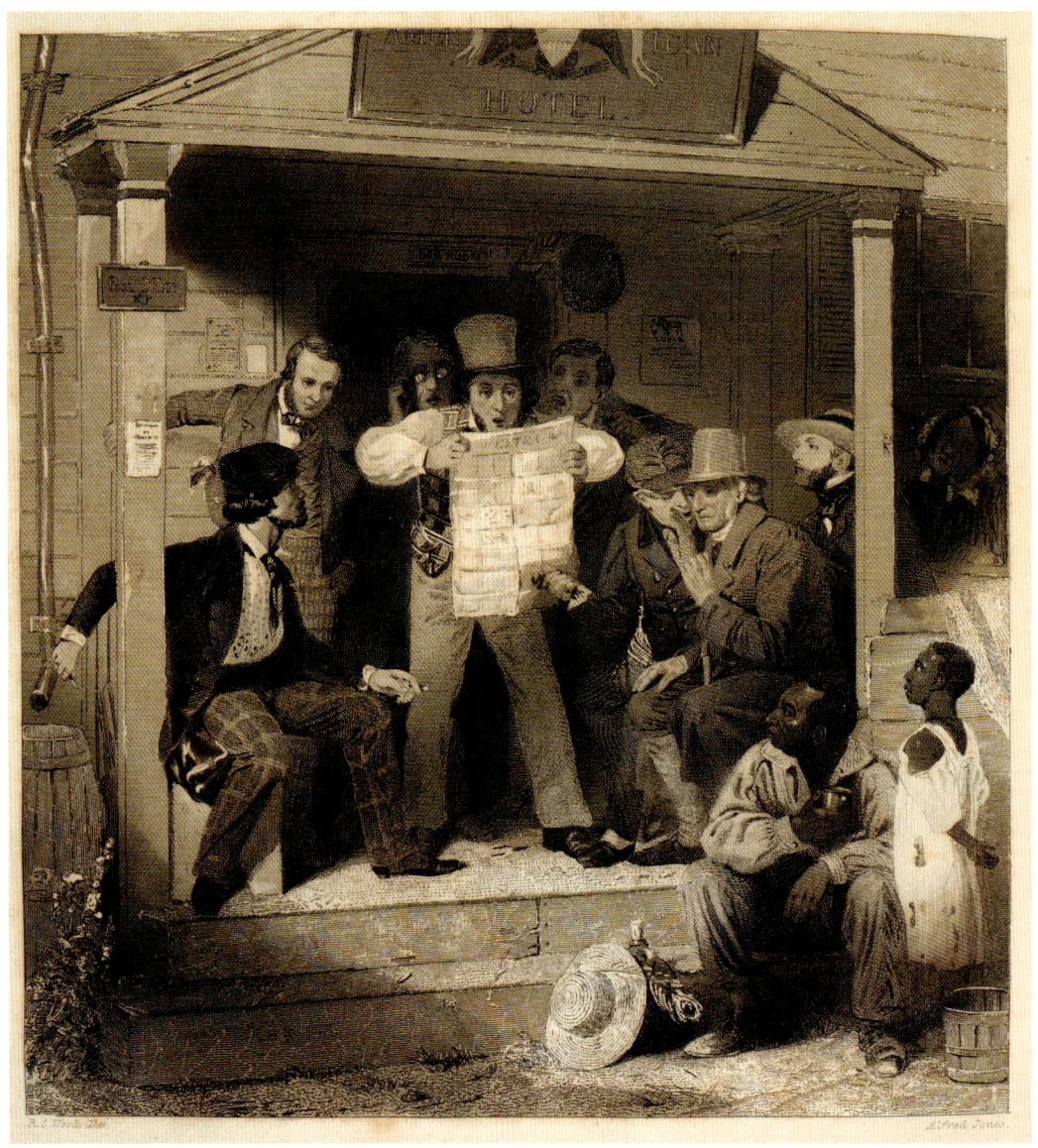

Alfred Jones after Richard Caton Woodville, *Mexican News or War News from Mexico,* American Art-Union, engraving, 1850

FACING: J. I. Pease after Richard Caton Woodville, *Old '76 and Young '48,* American Art-Union, engraving, 1851, GM 15.1148

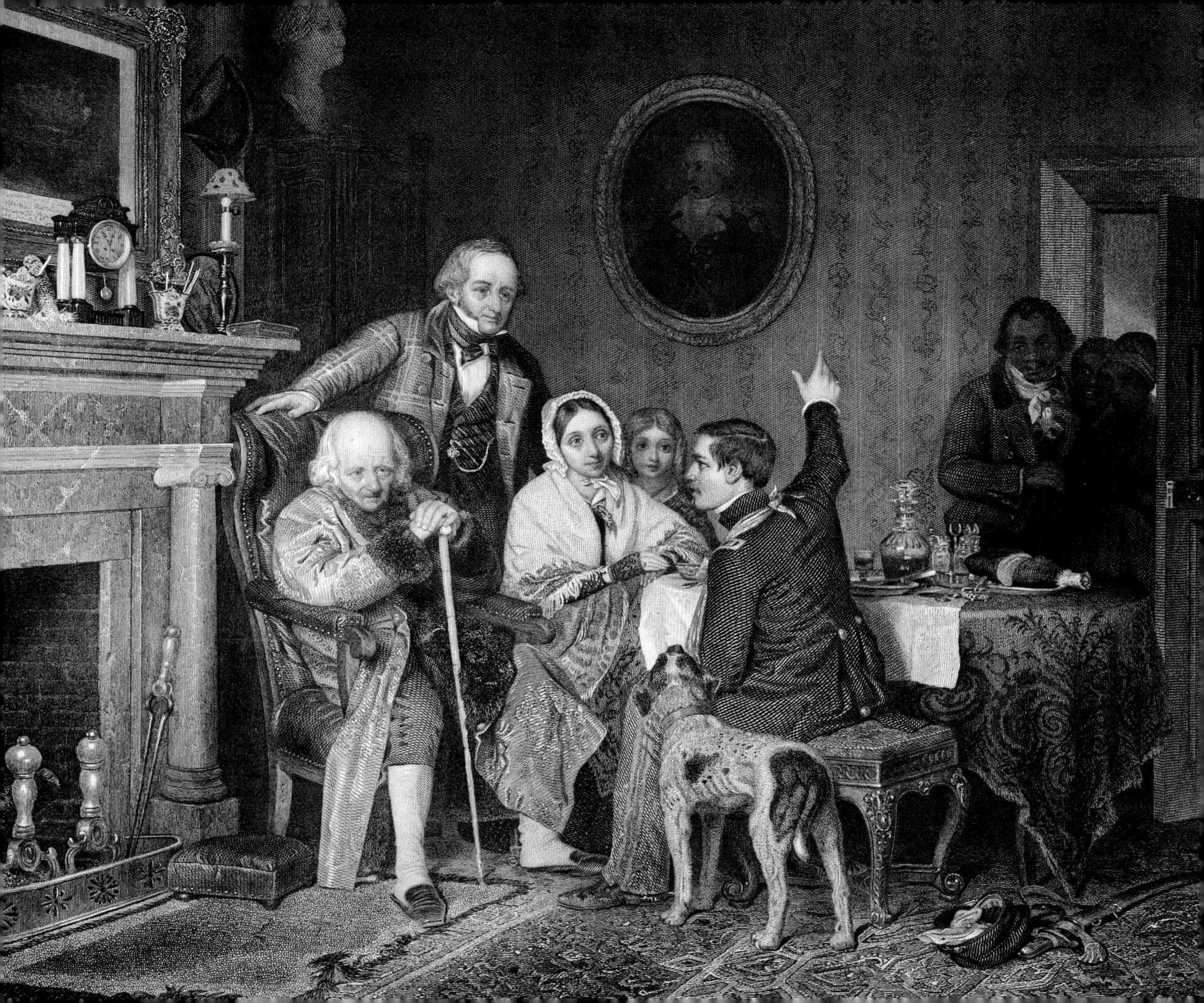

59 See Klein, "Art and Authority," 1543. Johns, *American Genre Painting*, 144-75, deals with issues of gender in genre painting.

60 For insight on this phenomenon, see Frederick Baekeland, "Psychological Aspects of Art Collecting," *Psychiatry* 44, No. 1 (1981), 45-59. To the successful businessmen of the nineteenth century, art collecting was a way to show refinement and taste beyond their material gains; in other words, it was their cultural capital that could be added to their actual economic capital. Pierre Bourdieu's writings are useful; see his *Distinction: A Social Critique of the Judgement of Taste*, trans. Richard Nice (Cambridge: Harvard University Press, 1984).

61 See Stephanie Mayer Heydt, "The Art of the Gift: William Sidney Mount, Daniel Huntington and the Antebellum Gift Book," (Ph.D. thesis, Boston University, 2008).

62 *Bulletin of the American Art-Union* (1851), 97.

manly virtue;" and, as she assesses the representation of women, the AAU "clung to imagery that emphasized more traditional notions of female malleability and submission," for example, the engraving after Daniel Huntington's *Mary Signing the Death Warrant of Lady Jane Grey*.[59] Although space constraints do not permit a full analysis of the ways AAU engravings represented issues of gender, I agree with Klein's observations. Men's activities—whether relating war experiences, inviting enemy officers to dinner, bringing cargo down western rivers, scouting western lands, fighting Indians, or reading newspapers—would have been considered paramount to both the uniting of the nation and the winning of the West. Also, in a period when American exceptionalism was everywhere trumpeted, it was the white male who served as the best gauge to mark the difference of the American from the European. However, two other observations are in order—both pertaining to the art market. The overwhelming number of AAU subscribers listed in AAU publications were men. Although custom dictated that 19th-century men pay the bills for household goods, patrons for art have been and continue to be men, since art

collecting confers a cultural status on men.[60] As for women: during the 1840s it was the gift books—those small, annual publications usually available in the Christmas season and often illustrated by engravings after leading artists—that contained the sentimental images felt appropriate for a female audience.[61]

Racial attitudes toward Native Americans were, of course, inherent in both the theory of Manifest Destiny and the practice of expansionism. To white Americans, expansion meant that the indigenous peoples must be subdued, if not eliminated. Horatio Greenough's over-lifesize sculpture *Rescue Group* could never have been included in an AAU lottery, nevertheless the September 1851 *Bulletin* wrote at length praising Greenough's image of an American hunter preventing a tomahawk-wielding Indian from attacking a mother and child: "The thought embodied in the action of the group and immediately communicated to every spectator is the natural and necessary superiority of the Anglo-Saxon to the Indian. It typifies the settlement of the American continent, and the respective destinies of the two races who here come into collision."[62] The persuasive imagery of expansionism depended

FACING: Charles Burt after Daniel Huntington, *Mary Signing the Death Warrant of Lady Jane Grey*, American Art-Union, engraving, 1848

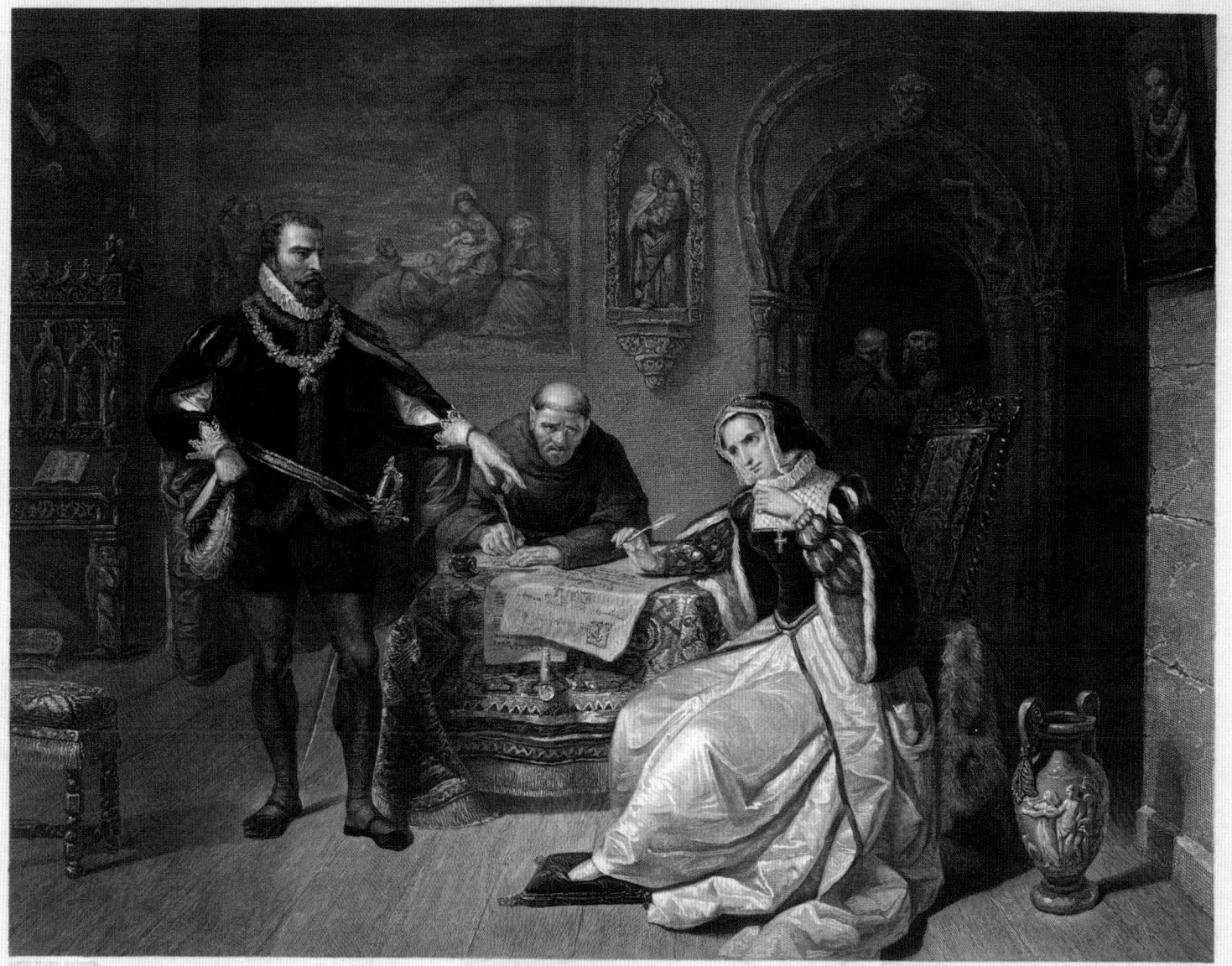

THE SIGNING OF THE DEATH WARRANT

OF LADY JANE GREY.

From the Original painting distributed   by the American Art Union in 1848.
Published exclusively for   the Members of that Year.

Entered according to Act of Congress in the year 1848 by the American Art Union in the Clerks Office of the District Court of the Southern District of New York.

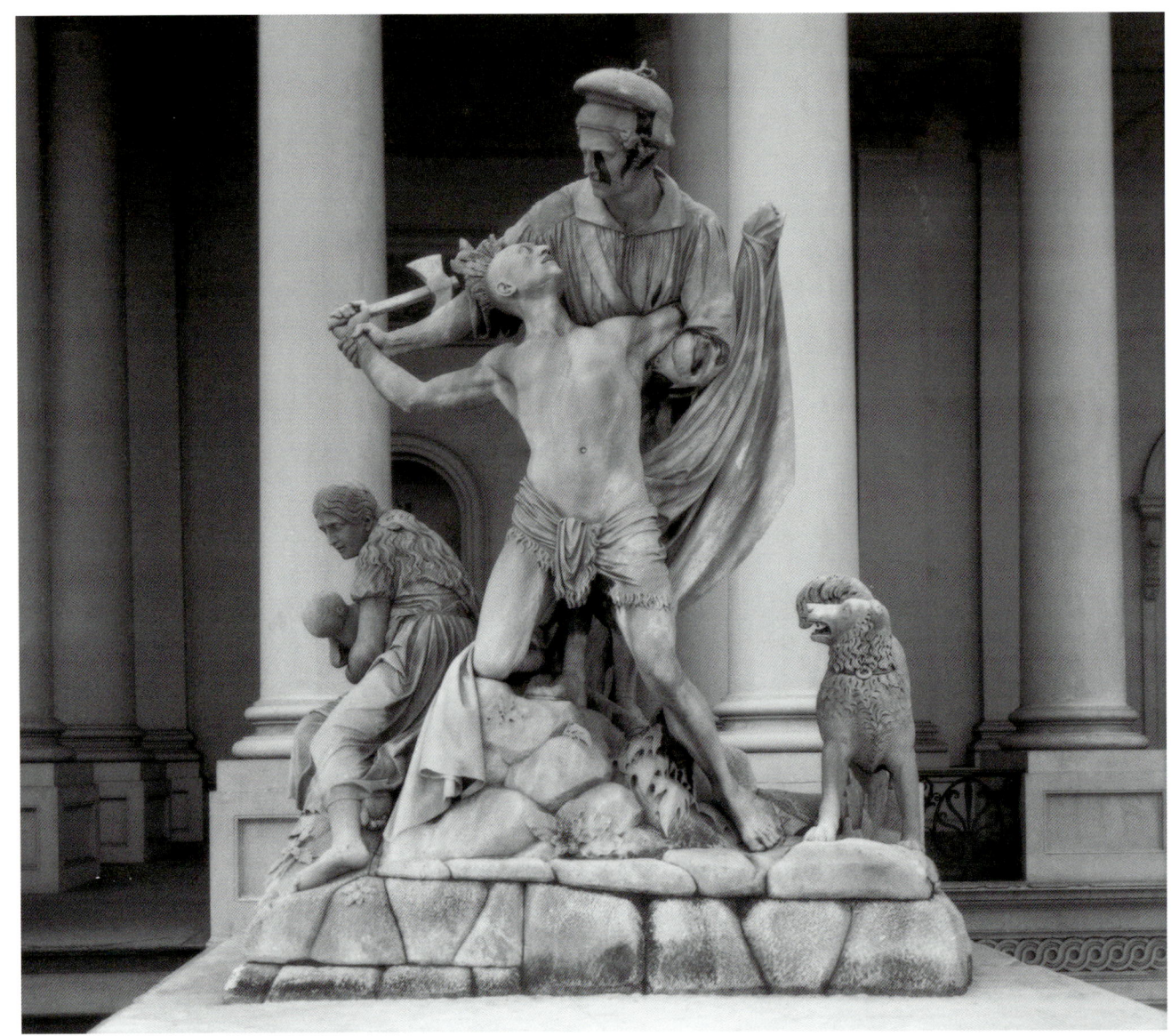

Horatio Greenough, *The Rescue*, marble, 1837-1850

PERFECTLY AMERICAN

on the rhetorical and pictorial heroicization of the scout and pioneer and, therefore, the necessary demonizing of American Indians whose tribes stood in the way of land conquest and development. The long article goes on to describe the differences between the American man and the European man; necessary for the credo of national unity was American pride in its own exceptionalism—often presented as Americans' manly differences from European men. Images of "last" or "dying" Indians were frequent representations in both paintings on exhibition in the AAU galleries and in the engravings included in women's gift books; such images, as we know, continued in the illustrated press and dime novels of the post-Civil War years.

Of course not all AAU fine arts engravings expressed the subject of nationalism or expansionism. Upon reflection, one notes how astute the managers of the Art-Union were in the selection of paintings for engravings—presenting history paintings (still considered at the apex of the painting hierarchy), landscape paintings (much admired), paintings based on American literature, genre paintings, including two by their friend and AAU manager Francis Edmonds, and paintings by leaders of National Academy of Design (Daniel Huntington), which they wanted to appease.

As to the subjects *not* chosen for engravings or reproductions in the *Bulletin*, I am reminded of what T. J. Jackson Lears said he had learned from Antonio Gramsci, that "the hegemonic culture depends not on the brainwashing of 'the masses' but on the tendency of public discourse to make some forms of experience readily available to consciousness while ignoring or suppressing others"[63]

IN SUMMARY

During the 1840s a group of New York merchants, lawyers, newspapermen, railroad directors and shipping tycoons, working through an ostensibly democratic institution—the American Art-Union—sought both to help artists and to develop a public that would admire and treasure the fine arts. At the same time the majority of AAU managers had an ideological stake in promoting a specific content for art and culture—the message of national unity. Not all of the AAU managers consciously thought of the subtext of expansion of empire when they selected AAU pictures, but it was an outlook to which they were won. Their

63 See T. J. Jackson Lears, "The Concept of Cultural Hegemony: Problems and Possibilities," *American Historical Review* 90 (June 1985), 577.

64 See Alan Wallach, "Long-term visions, short-term failures: art institutions in the United States, 1800-1860" in Hemingway and Vaughn, *Art in Bourgeois Society*. For attempts to bring about a unified culture for the North in the 1860s, see Charlotte Emans Moore, "Art as Text, War as Context: The Art Gallery of the Metropolitan Fair, New York City's Artistic Community, and the Civil War,"(Ph.D. thesis, Boston University, 2009).

goals for the encouragement of art did not contradict their business interests. Indeed, in their business lives they had experience in shaping the demands of middle-class consumers—cheap costs, expansion of markets, good distribution systems, and skills at making deals—while also molding opinion through the media (the newspapers) and through promotional devices that created consumer desires and, eventually, public consensus. That they did not succeed in extending the American Art-Union into the 1850s, because of the decade's irreconcilable ideologies and political economies, in no way diminishes their successes in nurturing the fine arts in America and supporting a number of major mid-century artists. The managers were themselves divided and caught up in the flux of U.S. history, even as they were making it. The country was not yet ready for a unified, national culture that they had envisioned—a culture that could not come until the years following a great and bloody Civil War.[64]

AUTHOR'S NOTE:

This essay extensively revises my chapter, "The American Art-Union as Patron for Expansionist Ideology in the 1840s," in Andrew Hemingway and Will Vaughn, eds. *Art in Bourgeois Society*, 1790-1850 (Cambridge: Cambridge University Press, 1998), 314-39, originally delivered as a paper in 1993 at the annual conference of the Association of Art Historians. I am grateful to the readers of the early drafts—Andrew Hemingway, Albert Boime, David D. Hall, Neil Larsen, and William Vance. For reading all the early drafts as well as the present version, I want to thank Kevin Whitfield. I also want to acknowledge Allen Kaufman, Stephanie Taylor, David Brody, Naomi Slipp, and Arlene Nichols for their help and suggestions. The first version published in 1998 meditates on the concept of "cultural hegemony," and draws on the writings of Raymond Williams, Antonio Gramsci, Edmund S. Morgan, Neil Larsen, and T. J. Jackson Lears; I emphasize there that the AAU represented a pre-hegemonic cultural situation. The extensive archive of publications, correspondence, and press clippings of the American Art-Union is held by the New-York Historical Society. Much information can be gleaned from the *Transactions of the Apollo Association*, issued annually for the years 1839 to 1843, and from the *Transactions of the American Art-Union*, issued for 1844-1849, herein after called *Transactions*. The *Transactions* for 1850 was published in the December 1850 *Bulletin*. The *Bulletin of the American Art-Union* was issued twice a month from April through December 1848; and monthly from April through December for 1849, 1850 and 1851. See also Charles E. Baker, "The American Art-Union," and Mary Bartlett Cowdrey, "Publications of the American Art-Union," in Mary Bartlett Cowdrey, ed., *American Academy of Fine Arts and American Art-Union*, Vol. 1, (New York: New-York Historical Society, 1953); E. Maurice Bloch, "The American Art-Union's downfall," *New-York Historical Society Quarterly* 37 (October 1953), pp. 331-59; Maybelle Mann, *The American Art-Union* (Otisville, NY: ALM Associates, Inc., 1977; revised 1987); and Lillian B. Miller, *Patrons and Patriotism: The Encouragement of the Fine Arts in the United States,* 1790-1860 (Chicago: University of Chicago Press, 1966), 160-72.

Unless otherwise noted, my history of the AAU is based primarily on my close readings of both the *Transactions,* the *Bulletins,* and the correspondence on microfilm at the New-York Historical Society.

A valuable analysis, which emphasizes different issues from my own, is Rachel N. Klein, "Art and Authority in Antebellum New York City: The Rise and Fall of the American Art-Union," *The Journal of American History* 81 (March 1995), pp. 1534-1561. Arlene Katz Nichols, "Merchants and Artists: The Apollo Association and the American Art-Union," (Ph.D dissertation,

The City University of New York, 2003), is valuable for its new look at the AAU, its synthesis of the 1953 scholarship, and its extensive biographical discussion of the AAU managers and Officers.

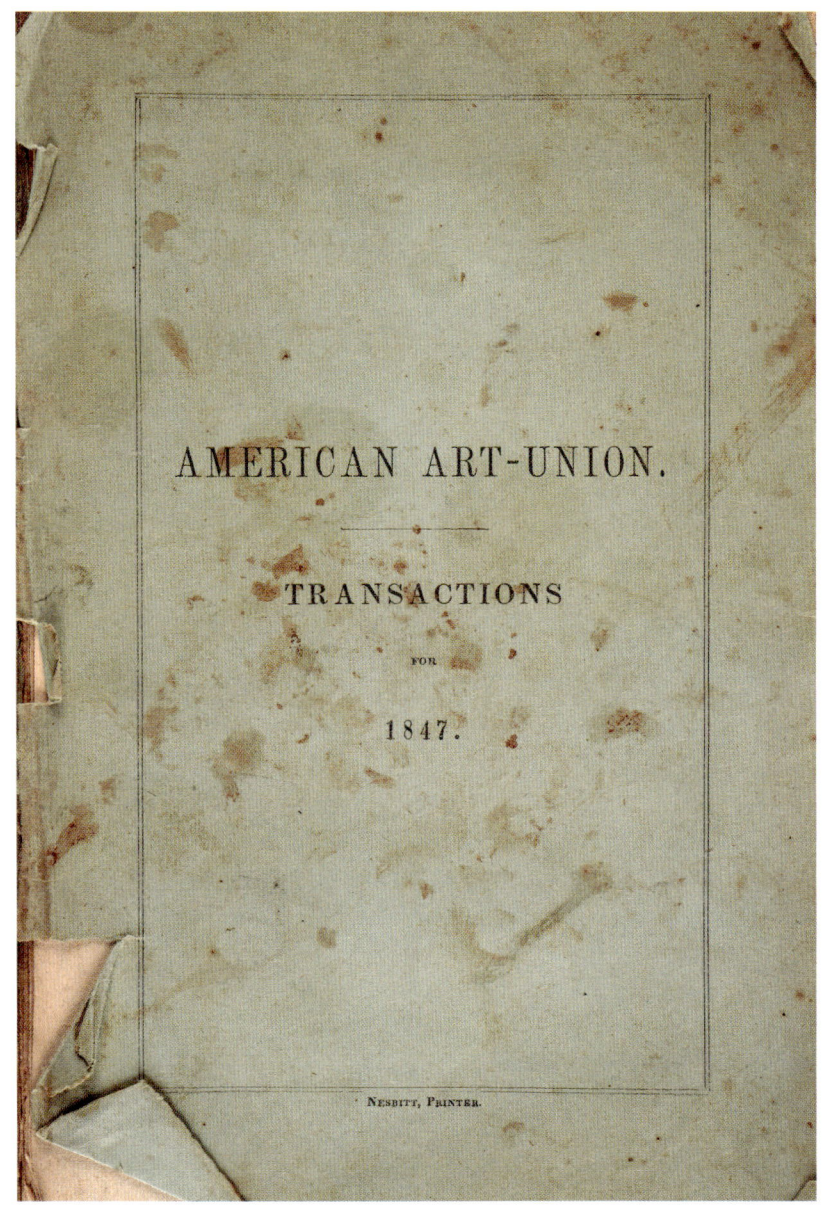

AMERICAN ART-UNION.

———

TRANSACTIONS

FOR

1847.

NESBITT, PRINTER.

THE AMERICAN ART-UNION,

In the City of New-York, was incorporated by the Legislature of New-York for the promotion of

THE FINE ARTS IN THE UNITED STATES.

THE Committee of Management have already in progress for the members of the year 1848, the large engraving of "QUEEN MARY SIGNING THE DEATH WARRANT OF LADY JANE GREY," in line, by BURT, after the original picture by HUNTINGTON, of which engraving, each member will receive a copy. They have the pleasure to announce that a large painting by *Leutze*, representing THE MISSION OF THE JEWS TO FERDINAND AND ISABELLA, a MOONLIGHT SCENE, by DURAND, besides several other works of great merit, have already been purchased for distribution among the members for 1848.

The annual meeting and distribution will take place this year or the 22d day of December.

It is very desirable that the dues of the members should be paid early in the year, that the Committee may make their purchases at the best advantage.

Subscriptions and payments may be made to either of the Honorary Secretaries, whose names are given within, or to John W. Moore, Superintendent, at the Art-Union Rooms, by letter or otherwise, or to Mr. John Erhardt, the Collector for the City of New-York.

Remittances and all letters should be addressed to Andrew Warner, the Corresponding Secretary, New-York. Drafts, *payable in New-York* to the order of G. W. Austen, Treasurer, should be sent when practicable.

NESBITT, PRINTER.

Blank or Prize?

The fledgling Apollo Association for the Promotion of the Fine Arts and its more vibrant offspring, the American Art-Union, emerged in the wake of the Panic of 1837, a financial crisis brought on by an expansion and sudden contraction in the circulation of paper bank notes that enabled the rampant speculation in public lands characteristic of the decade. Throughout the 1830s, debates over the primacy of specie, typically gold or silver, over paper currency and the proper role of national and local banks in utilizing and distributing it spilled out in popular literature and political cartoons. As this discourse drifted into the cultural field during the 1840s, it equated banking and other forms of speculative commerce with gambling and games of chance. It is amid this atmosphere of economic uncertainty and widespread mistrust of banks

1 On antebellum banking, see Bray Hammond, *Banks and Politics in America: From the Revolution to the Civil War* (Princeton, NJ: Princeton University Press, 1957); Henry Wysham Lanier, *A Century of Banking in New York, 1822-1922* (New York: The Gilliss Press, 1922); Margaret G. Myers, *The New York Money Market, Volume I, Origins and Development* (New York: Columbia University Press, 1931); Howard Bodenhorn, *A History of Banking in Antebellum America: Financial Markets and Economic Development in an Era of Nation-Building* (New York: Cambridge University Press, 2000).

2 Ann Fabian, "Speculation on Distress: The Popular Discourse of the Panics of 1837 and 1857." *Yale Journal of Criticism* 3, 1 (1989), 127. On literary expressions of financial panic, see also David Anthony, "Banking on Emotion: Financial Panic and the Logic of Male Submission in the Jacksonian Gothic." *American Literature* 76, 4 (December 2004): 719-747.

and other financial institutions that the American Art-Union evolved from a local to a national network of art patronage, appreciation, and distribution. The Art-Union's membership and the extent of its geographic reach peaked in 1849, with 18,960 members in 30 states and the District of Columbia, but soon after met its demise in the early 1850s, charting yet another cycle of "boom" and "bust."[1]

Cultural historian Ann Fabian advances the argument that financial panics such as this provided occasions for particular kinds of creative expression and cultural critique. I want to extend Fabian's discussion by suggesting that these forms of expression did not stop at sermons, poetry or jokes, but came to define certain cultural practices and the formation of cultural institutions like the American Art-Union that utilized economic structures of profit, loss, and even speculation, as bases for their operation. The Art-Union's plan modeled its annual distribution of membership premiums on the circulation of paper notes, a bedrock of antebellum banking practice, while its annual distribution of paintings, the organization's metaphoric "specie," took the form of an annual lottery. For a time the business plan worked, making the Art-

Union the most successful of its kind. But by the late 1840s, a chorus of detractors lambasted the organization's management, its selection and distribution of works, and particularly its central lottery mechanism as speculative enterprises that undermined trust and distorted true value. Emphasis was placed on the moral perils they posed and their stress upon and detriment to the social fabric. Though criticisms came from a variety of constituencies, including but not limited to institutional rivals such as the National Academy of Design, evangelical revivalists, and disgruntled artists, a general consensus began to emerge by around 1850 that the organization had, in numerous ways, overextended itself. In economic terms, the inflation brought on by the Art-Union's increasingly prodigious output of prints, medallions, and publications during the 1840s, was followed by a precipitous deflation as the number, and particularly the quality, of paintings purchased for the annual distribution and exhibited in the Art-Union's Perpetual Free Gallery failed to keep pace. Like a paper bank note in circulation without an adequate amount of specie to back it, the Art-Union failed faster than a wildcat bank, a period term reserved for the most unsound and risky banks chartered under state law who issued money without proper gold in stock to back up the supply. Banknotes, lottery tickets, Art-Union prints—all were sheets of paper of questionable value. In the fluctuating cultural economy of antebellum America, did each represent a "blank" or "prize"?[2]

In his State of the Nation speech delivered December 5, 1836, President Andrew Jackson stressed that "variableness must ever be the characteristic of a currency of which the precious metals are not the chief ingredient," a point he expanded upon in his Farewell Address the following March. "The paper system being founded in public confidence, and having itself no intrinsic value, is liable to great and sudden fluctuations, thereby rendering property insecure, and the wages of labor unsteady and uncertain."[3] The "illusory wealth" of what he and other critics often called "rag money" benefited speculators and victimized farmers and small producers who traded their labor for continually fluctuating values represented by bank notes whose "true character," as hard money economist William Gouge asserted in 1833, were merely "simple *evidences of debt* due by banks."[4] "One of the most serious objections to paper money," wrote Universalist minister and reformer Theophilus Fisk in 1837, "is that it deranges the measure of value; making that which should be permanent and fixed as the everlasting hills, liable to the most ruinous fluctuations and distressing revulsions." Like banks and other commercially inspired ventures, including the American Art-Union, "the value of their currency is perpetually changing as they expand or contract the quantity, and yet it is made the measure of prices, as if it remained fixed."[5]

Such critiques of paper money and speculation as cultural practice increased dramatically in the 1840s as the mechanisms of the speculative economy infused the broader culture with what Fisk called "a spirit of cold calculation, which is carried into all the relations of society, making barter and merchandise of the best feelings of the heart."[6] For some, the Art-Union enacted a commercialized art world that functioned like a lending bank, selectively purchasing and amassing stores of paintings as its metaphorical "specie" and issuing paper "notes" in the form of small and large folio engravings for dissemination among its patrons.

3 Quoted in Robert Sobel, *Panic on Wall Street: A History of America's Financial Disasters* (New York: Beard Books, 1999), 52.

4 William M. Gouge, *A Short History of Paper Money and Banking in the United States, To Which is Prefixed an Inquiry into the Principles of the System* (1968, Philadelphia: Printed by T. W. Ulstick, 1833), 54.

5 Theophilus Fisk, *Labor the Only True Source of Wealth; or, the Rottenness of the Paper Money Banking System Exposed, Its Sandy Foundations Shaken, Its Crumbling Pillars Overthrown. An Oration Delivered at the Queen-Street Theatre, in the City of Charleston, S. C. July 4, 1837* (n.p. 1837), 20.

6 Theophilus Fisk, *Labor the Only True Source of Wealth*, 7-8.

7 John H. Gourlie, Letter to Francis W. Edmonds, (February 9, 1841). Francis W. Edmonds Papers, William L. Clements Library, University of Michigan.

8 Charles E. Baker, "The American Art-Union," in Mary Bartlett Cowdrey et al., *American Academy of Fine Arts and American Art-Union* (New York: The New-York Historical Society, 1953), I: 243-255.

9 Miner K. Kellogg, "Art-Unions: Their True Character Considered." *The International Monthly Magazine of Literature, Science, and Arts* 2, 2 (January 1, 1851), 193.

10 The quote continues "who, in its celebrity and in the distribution of its patronage, found a much coveted distinction and personal influence, and of course they better understood the management of the business part of the rivalship. The Art-Union has enriched—the National Academy has impoverished— accordingly. The *merchant* Institution has brought the *Artist* Institution to its last gasp. While the *merchant amateurs* confess that they do not know what to do with their superfluous money, the *whole body of our great Artists* are

Contrasting the fledgling Apollo Association with the already established though not thriving National Academy of Design, founded more than a decade earlier in 1826, New York businessman and committee member John H. Gourlie hit upon his upstart organization's central premise: "the people who visit academy exhibitions have no *permanent* interest beyond their *two shillings worth*. In the Apollo," on the other hand, "the subscriber *feels* a personal interest and when at the end of the year he gets a picture or an engraving he thinks he is encouraging the arts—and so he is."[7] Just as one invested in a corporation or other financial venture by purchasing its stock, the patron of the arts as Art-Union subscriber sought a return on his investment. As the 1840s unfolded, and as the Art-Union evolved from the Apollo Association, the benefits of membership expanded considerably.

For a five-dollar membership fee, subscribers received the annually published *Transactions*, which meticulously recorded the proceedings of annual meetings and provided an exhaustive list of managers, honorary secretaries, members, and recipients of prizes at the annual drawings. Between 1848 and 1852, members also received the *Bulletin of the American Art-Union*, which appeared as a semi-monthly from April through December 1848, and as a monthly through the same months of 1849, 1850, and 1851.[8] These publications included summaries of annual activities, news of upcoming events, notices of paintings purchased for the gallery and the annual distribution, news of artists' activities, works selected for engraving, and engraved illustrations of selected works along with set pieces of art criticism and reviews of gallery exhibitions. For every five dollars paid, subscription also entitled members to receive each year one or more large folio engravings after works purchased by the Art-Union, and it entered them in the lottery to distribute that year's selection of paintings. With the subscription funds, the Committee of Managers solicited paintings from artists and made selections from works submitted, operating, some charged, "as mere speculators upon the labors of artists."[9]

By 1849, it was widely felt that the Art-Union's management had "fallen into the hands of 'businessmen.'"[10] Indeed, merchants, auctioneers, and bankers rotated through the ranks of the Art-Union's Committee of Management throughout the organization's lifespan.[11] Their professional sensibilities certainly helped to rescue the struggling Apollo Association, recasting it as a nationally scaled clearinghouse for the visual arts modeled on the mechanisms of the lending bank. Shrewdly guiding the organization beyond financial equilibrium toward fiscal solvency, committee members found more ways than one to stretch its capital. The Art-Union routinely paid the majority of its artists far below their asking price for paintings, as evidenced in its treasurer's ledgers for its peak years.[12] To help populate, and thus accentuate, the walls of its Perpetual Free Gallery, the Art-Union also yearly showed several paintings belonging not to the Art-Union, which would include them in the annual lottery, but to individuals including members of the Committee of Management and others involved in administering the organization. Short-changing its artists and exhibiting borrowed paintings—some of the most select ever shown at the Gallery, in fact—inflated the value of its yearly yield of artworks assembled for lottery distribution to members. What it did distribute, in great quantity following the example of banks wildcat or otherwise, were lower costs works on paper, essen-

tially notes intended to secure one's membership to and investment in the organization. Indeed, as the ranks of membership swelled and the quantity of paintings purchased peaked in the late 1840s, the number of prints made available to members via distribution or Art-Union publications also increased dramatically between 1840 and 1851.

In 1840, members received a single print— *General Marion in His Swamp Encampment Inviting a British Officer to Dinner*, engraved by John Sartain after a painting by John Blake White. By 1844, the first year prints were published by the newly christened American Art-Union, membership entitled subscribers to two engravings: the large folio line engraving of Francis W. Edmonds's *Sparking* engraved by Alfred Jones and a medium folio outline engraving after T. F. Hoppin's *Escape of Captain Wharton*, a scene from James Fenimore Cooper's *The Spy*, etched by F. F. E. Prudhomme. A smaller version of the print after Edmonds provided the front plate illustration for the *Transactions* for 1843. Also that year, ten bound sets of four plates each of *Harvey's American Landscape Scenery* were purchased by the Art-Union and distributed by lot that December.[13] But in 1847, the offer-

in perplexity to know how to meet their current Academy expense." Nathaniel Parker Willis, "Crushing of the National Academy of Design and True Art by the Amateur Merchants of the Art-Union." *Home Journal* 44, 194 (October 27, 1849), 2.

11 Bankers who served on the Art-Union's Committee of Management between 1838 and 1852 include George Curtis, E. B. Corwin, Francis W. Edmonds, Ebenezer Platt, Paul Spofford, Samuel Ward, and Benjamin R. Winthrop. For the professions of these and other members, see Rachel N. Klein's helpful appendix, "Managers of the American Art-Union," that concludes her article "Art and Authority in Antebellum New York City: The Rise and Fall of the American Art-Union," *The Journal of American History* (March 1995), 1561.

12 See Treasurer's Accounts, 1849-1860. American Art-Union Papers, The New-York Historical Society.

13 Cowdrey, 286-287.

14 For more on Art-Union prints, see Jay Cantor, "Prints and the American Art-Union," in *Prints in and of America to 1850.* Ed. John D. Morse (Charlottesville, VA: Published for The Henry Francis du Pont Winterthur Museum, 1970): 297-326.

15 "An unknown number of bronze medals were distributed in later years. The exact number of the bronze "edition" is unknown." Cowdrey et al., *American Academy of Fine Arts and American Art-Union,* 288.

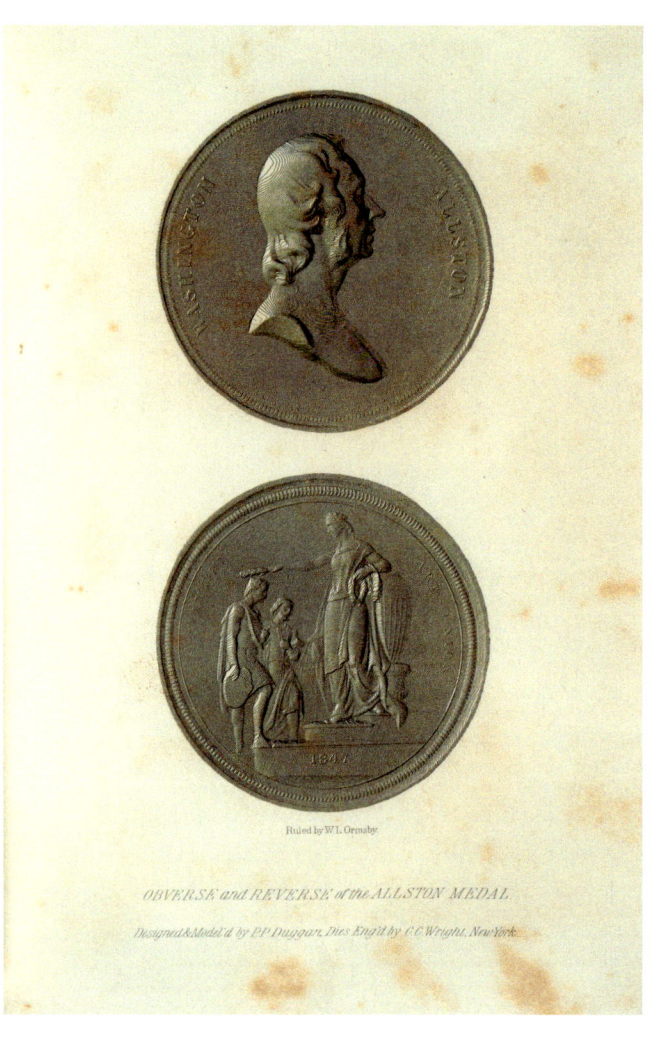

OBVERSE and REVERSE of the ALLSTON MEDAL.

Designed & Model'd by P.P.Duggan, Dies Eng'd by C.C.Wright, New York.

P. P. Duggan and C. C. Wright, *Washington Allston Medal,* American Art-Union, engraving, 1847, GM 5126.1062.2

ings on paper swelled yet again. That year, George Caleb Bingham's *The Jolly Flatboatmen* was engraved by T. Doney in a large folio mezzotint from the original painting distributed by the American Art-Union in 1847. Another version of this image illustrated the front plate for the 1846 edition of *Transactions.* A small folio line engraving was made after Daniel Huntington's *A Sibyl,* then in the possession of the American Art-Union, which also illustrated the *Transactions* for that year.[14] As the size of prints alternated between large and small folio, iterations of these reproductions began to multiply.

Perhaps to substantiate its offerings on paper, to back it with a material form of "specie," the Art-Union issued its first medal commemorating the artist Washington Allston. Designed and modeled by P. P. Duggan and engraved by C. C. Wright, the medal featured Allston's profile on the obverse and the seal of the Art-Union on the reverse. Fifty copies in silver and 250 in bronze were distributed by lottery in 1847.[15] A reproduction of the medal's dies provided the front plate of the *Transactions* for 1847. Two additional medals followed, in 1848 of Gilbert Stuart backed by the Art-Union

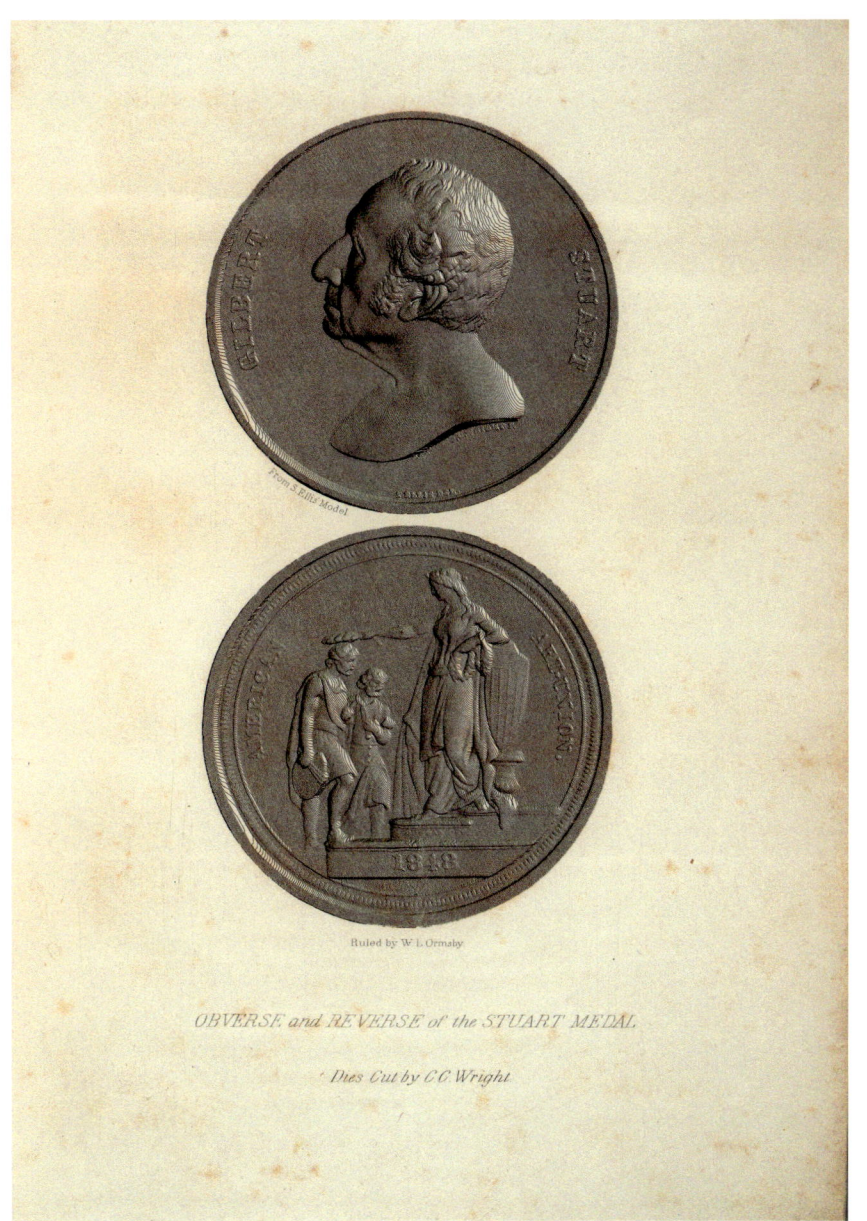

OBVERSE and REVERSE of the STUART MEDAL.

Dies Cut by C.C. Wright

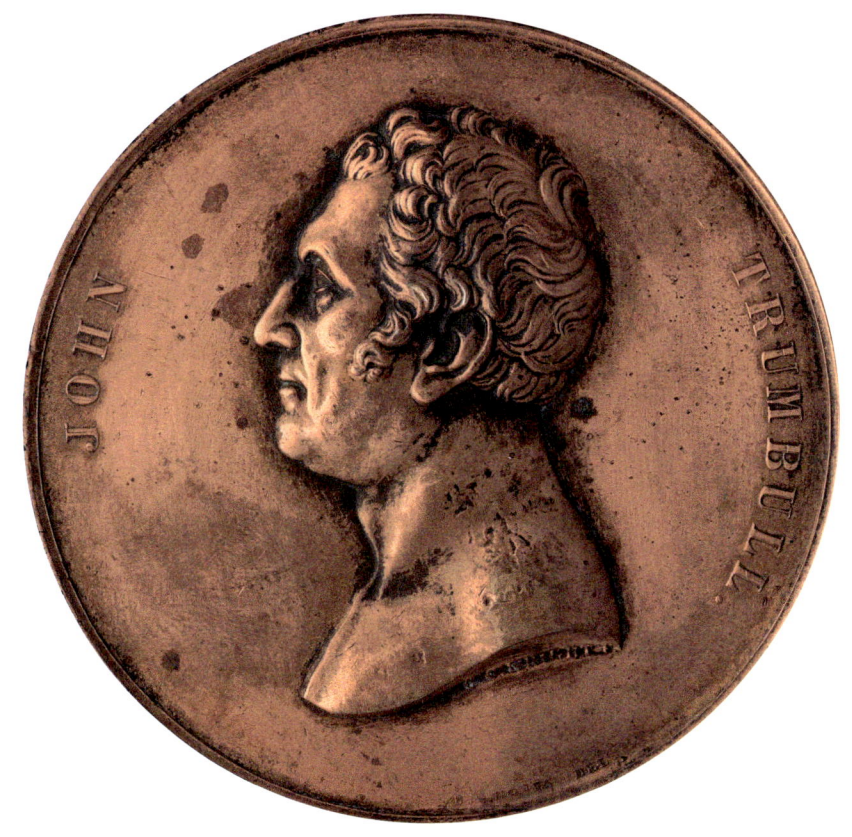

P. P. Duggan and C. C. Wright, *John Trumbull Medal,*
American Art-Union, bronze, 1849, GM 08.219

P. P. Duggan and C. C. Wright, *Gilbert Stuart Medal,*
American Art-Union, engraving, 1849, GM 5126.1063.3

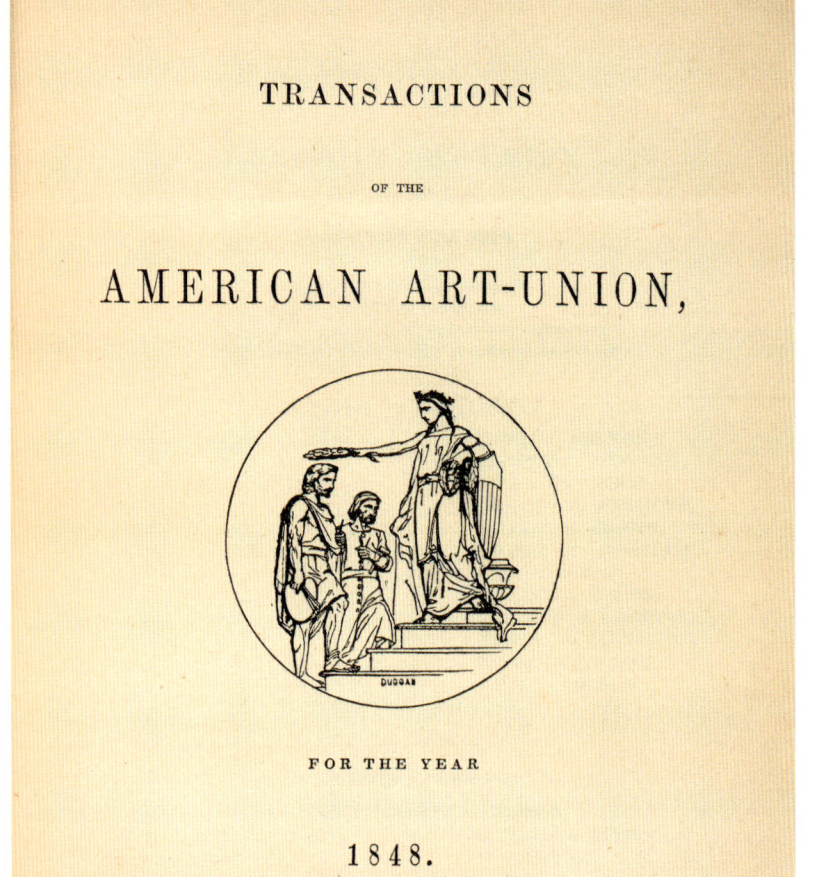

TRANSACTIONS

OF THE

AMERICAN ART-UNION,

FOR THE YEAR

1848.

———

NEW-YORK.
GEORGE F. NESBITT, PRINTER.
1849.

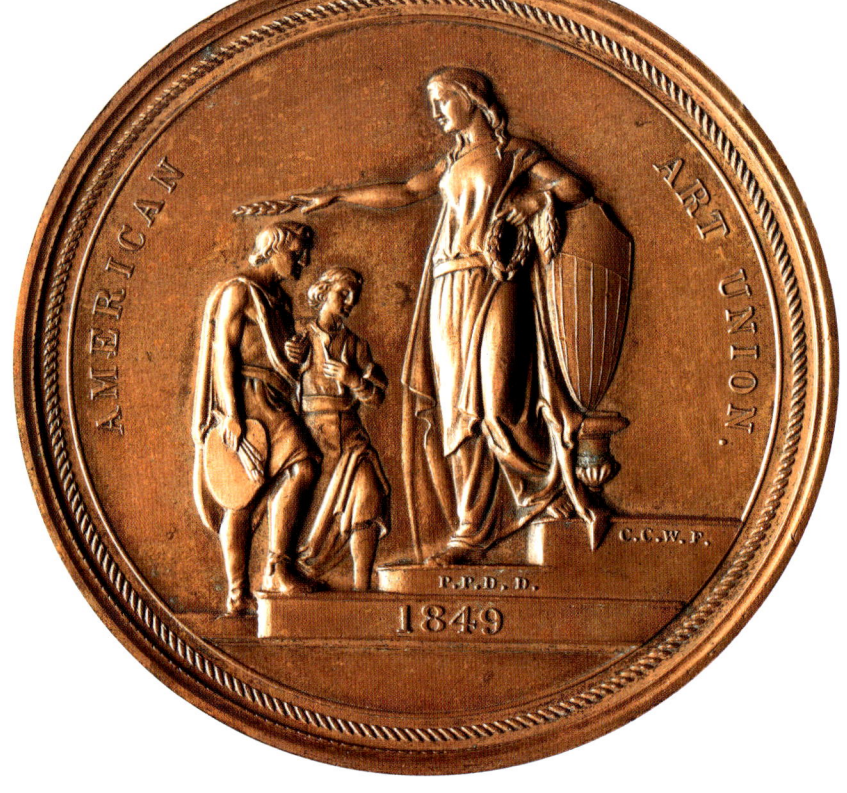

P. P. Duggan and C. C. Wright, reverse side, *John Trumbull Medal*, American Art-Union, bronze, 1849, GM 08.219

seal issued only in bronze, and in 1849 of John Trumbull backed in the same fashion and issued, again, solely in bronze. The distribution of precious metal medallions bearing engravings of American Art's true "gold" augmented the increasingly brisk circulation of paper prints, which some suggested merely served to distract members from what some saw as the declining quality of the oil paintings it raffled. The Art-Union credited their production to a surplus of revenues.[16]

Featuring the figure of "Fame" (or a benevolent muse) placing a laurel on a painter's head while a second awaits his turn, the Art-Union's seal vivifies its rhetoric of stimulating "to exertion" the nation's "native and resident men of genius" who will "reap their full share of fortune and fame."[17] The imagery also echoes the engraved vignettes of allegorical figures of justice, bounty, and laborious production gracing the borders and corners of antebellum bank notes. In a note, for instance, issued by the Broadway Bank in 1849, the figure of Commerce is seated resting against a pile of containers and a horn of plenty while in the distance, ships sail in and out of a harbor. Athena is seated at the bottom left; above her the Comptroller's die

ensures justice and balance. These vignettes imbued banknotes with the compositional balance and allegorical meaning needed to fortify their value as they circulated far and wide in great quantity. Over time, though, their value, like the ink and rag paper used to print them, simply wore out.

By 1850 the distribution of prints grew to five small folio line engravings of works after a select group of the most prominent artists affiliated with the Art-Union, including Richard Caton Woodville, Asher B. Durand, Francis W. Edmonds, and Emmanuel Leutze, along with *Dream of Arcadia*, another image after Thomas Cole. The following year's distribution of five small folio line engravings featured images after Jasper Cropsey, William Sydney Mount, William Ranney, John Kensett and another by Woodville.

The sheer multiplicity of these images begins to suggest a troubling pattern of inflation and balances overdrawn, as paintings by these particular artists had, by the late 40s, become increasingly rare in the annual distributions. Perhaps to counter this tendency, or at least the perception of this tendency, the Art-Union raffled in its annual distribution of 1848 Thomas Cole's four-part series,

16 Prosper M. Wetmore, "Proceedings at the Annual Meeting, 1847," *Transactions of the American Art-Union* (1847), 18.

17 Prosper M. Wetmore, "Proceedings at the Annual Meeting, 1847," 15.

18 "Proceedings at the Annual Meeting, 1849," *Transactions of the American Art-Union* (1849), 32.

19 Prosper M. Wetmore, "Proceedings at the Annual Meeting, 1849." *Transactions of the American Art-Union* (1849), 26.

Voyage of Life, in a single lot to J. T. Brodt of Binghamton, New York. Thought to have single-handedly increased subscriptions for that year, Cole's ambitious and moralizing series accrued a value for the Art-Union inversely represented in its comparatively paltry offering the following year of a large folio engraving of *Youth*, the second image in the four-part series (see pages 117-119).

Though its calculated bait and switch methods for attracting subscribers often lacked poise in the eyes of critics, Art-Union activities were reported with the utmost eloquence. Robert Kelly, on behalf of the Committee of Management, presented the Annual Report of the operations of the year 1849 in the following terms:

> The American Art-Union has accomplished results which the local patronage of wealthy centres of population could not accomplish at all. It has scattered its engravings and distributed its prizes over the whole length and breadth of the land. The taste of the people has been cultivated, and the latent germ of Art unfolded in the mind of many a youth. The mode of distribution we have adopted for disposing of our accumulated treasures, by the awards of Fortune's wheel, is a convenient method of scattering them with impartial hand. The works we send out are messengers and missionaries of Art.[18]

In order to "scatter" its premiums, the Art-Union relied primarily on the growing ranks of its "Honorary Secretaries." These roving field agents, some 600 in number by 1849, were based in places like Mobile, Alabama, Lexington, Kentucky, and Galena, Illinois. Earning a percentage on every subscription, Secretaries were responsible for soliciting memberships and for the local delivery of prints and other premiums. They were, as Art-Union President Prosper M. Wetmore, a dry goods merchant and amateur poet boasted: "some of the most intelligent, refined, and active spirits in our country."[19] The labors of these individuals can be read in the growing membership rolls assiduously listed in every issue of the *Transactions*, but their faults, typically involving late delivery of prints and other premiums, drew the ire of members and critics alike.

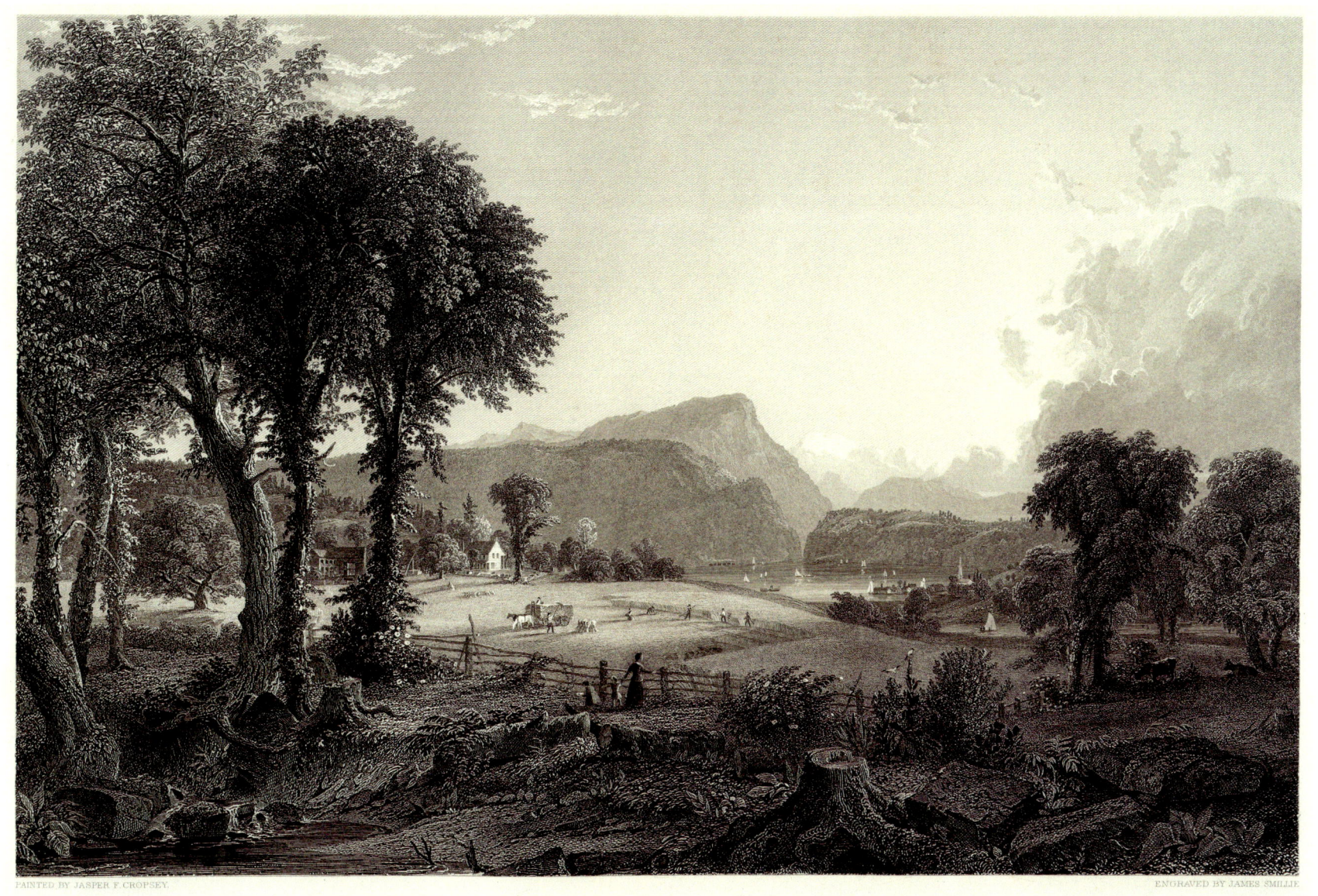

PAINTED BY JASPER F. CROPSEY.

ENGRAVED BY JAMES SMILLIE.

James Smillie, after Jasper Cropsey, *American Harvesting*, J. Dalton, engraving, 1851, GM 15.1144

TRANSACTIONS

OF THE

AMERICAN ART-UNION,

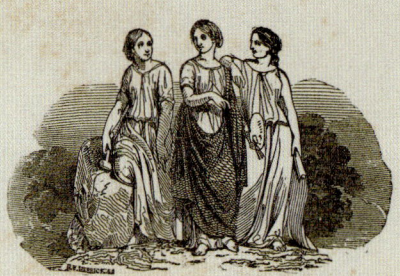

FOR THE YEAR

1847.

~~~~~~~~~~~~~~~~~~~~

NEW-YORK:

G. F. NESBITT, STATIONER AND PRINTER, TONTINE BUILDING,

CORNER WALL AND WATER STREETS.

1848.

PLAN

OF THE AMERICAN ART·UNION.

~~~~~~~~~~

The AMERICAN ART-UNION in the city of New-York, was incorporated by the Legislature of New-York, for the PROMOTION OF THE FINE ARTS in the United States.

It is managed by gentlemen who are chosen annually, by the members, and receive no compensation. To accomplish A TRULY NATIONAL OBJECT, uniting great public good with private gratification at small individual expense, in a manner best suited to the situation and institutions of our country, and the wants, habits and tastes of our people, the Committee have adopted the following PLAN:

Every subscriber of five dollars is a member of the Art-Union for the year, and is entitled to all its privileges.

The money thus obtained (after paying necessary expenses) is applied:

FIRST:—*To the production of a large and costly Original Engraving* from an American Painting, of which the plate and copyright belong to the Institution, and are used solely for its benefit.

Of this Engraving every member receives a copy for every five dollars paid by him.

Members entitled to duplicates are at liberty to select from the Engravings of previous years.

Whenever the funds justify it, an extra Engraving, or Work of Art, is also furnished to every member.

Every member also receives a full Annual Report of the Proceedings, &c., of the Institution.

SECOND:—*To the purchase of Paintings and Sculpture* by native or resident artists.

These Paintings and Sculptures are publicly exhibited at the Gallery of the Art-Union till the annual meeting in December, when they are *publicly distributed by lot* among the members, each member having one share for every five dollars paid by him.

Each member is thus certain of receiving in return the value of

---

Methodist minister Thomas H. Pearne, for example, viewed the prints circulated by the Art-Union not as "missionaries of art" that cultivated taste and encouraged an appreciation for art, but as chances in the lottery worth far less than five dollars apiece. "It is, to my mind," Pearne wrote, "an inquiry of no little interest, what the actual cost of the engraving which each member really receives is; and what proportion of the amount contributed is expended in the purchase of those works of art which are distributed by lot."[20] Simultaneously minimizing its expenditures and inflating its value during the late 40s, the Art-Union paid less and less for greater numbers of paintings while producing larger quantities of prints intended to both swell and appease the rank and file membership. As if to corroborate this view, and to placate critics of the lottery, *The Literary World* sought to assure readers who might also be Art-Union members: "It will be seen that the Art-Union is thus diminishing the lottery feature, by expending large amounts upon engravings and other works of Art, and *securing* to each member the full value of his subscription."[21] But the following month, a writer for the *Buffalo Courier* proposed "A New Art-Union," prefacing his list of improvements with the following critique, revealing just how far the Art-Union had overextended itself:

People are beginning to get tired of the huge humbug known as the 'American Art-Union.' Undue predominance, in number, of blanks over prizes; the miserable character of many of the pictures distributed; the evident clannishness and favoritism which govern the management of the institution, all combine to cast odium upon it and disgust the public.[22]

It was the Art-Union's "system of prizes," wrote Boston's Reverend Robert C. Waterson for the *Christian Examiner and Religious Miscellany* in March 1850, that constituted the "moving wheel" of the organization's plan to "promote the knowledge and love of the fine arts, to encourage talent," and "to raise the standard of taste."[23] The annual raffle drawing, which offered "the prospect of obtaining, for a small sum, that which is of great value," constituted the single feature that made the Art-Union so successful and popular among its

20 Thomas H. Pearne, "Art-Unions." *Christian Advocate and Journal* 23, 45 (November 8, 1848), 177.

21 "The Fine Arts." *The Literary World* 6, 166 (April 6, 1850), 352.

22 "A New Art-Union," *Home Journal* 20, 222 (May 11, 1850), 4.

23 Robert C. Waterson, "American Art and Art-Unions," *Christian Examiner and Religious Miscellany* 48, 2 (March 1850), 216.

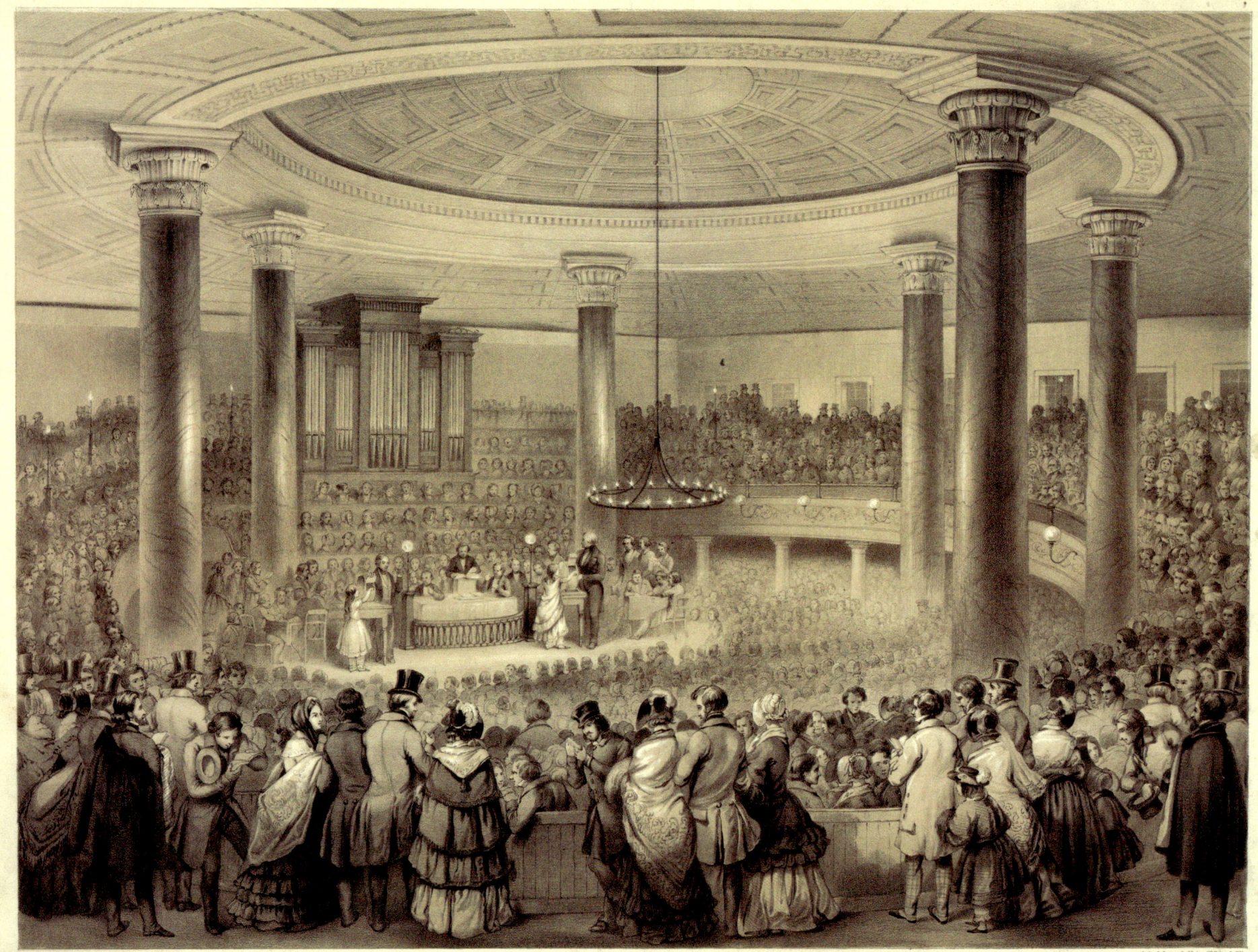

DISTRIBUTION OF THE AMERICAN ART UNION PRIZES,

at the Tabernacle, Broadway, New York, 24th Dec. 1847.

Published by John P. Ridner, 497 Broadway Art Union Building New York.

members. But many questioned the practice, leading several commentators, including Nathaniel Parker Wills, then editor of the *Home Journal*, and a spate of others to openly question whether the distribution was "more likely to refine the popular taste, or to excite a spirit for gambling."[24] In artist Miner K. Kellogg's anonymously penned invective, "Art-Unions: Their True Character Considered," published in January of 1851, the author asserts that "numbers rather than quality seem to govern the Art-Unions in their purchases of works, that they may give subscribers a greater number of *chances* to draw something for their money and thus encourage them to future *patronage*." Art-Unions, for this writer, were "nothing else but lotteries, under another and more popular name" and, like lotteries, tended to "attract men from legitimate pursuits, into the speculative, uncertain, and, morally, illegitimate pursuit of fortune."[25] Pearne, writing for the *Christian Advocate and Journal* in 1848 explains, "The process is this. The numbers of the paintings, or of the given sums of money to be drawn for, are put into one wheel, and the numbers of the subscribers' names severally are put into another, and then by *lot* it is determined what each subscriber draws, whether a blank or a prize, as the one may be, and, if a prize, what amount."[26]

In 1848, the Art-Union commissioned this lithograph after Tompkins Matteson's *Distribution of the American Art-Union Prizes at the Tabernacle, Broadway, New York*. Depicting the annual drawing held on Christmas Eve, the lithograph was distributed primarily to Honorary Secretaries for use in soliciting subscriptions. Several of the figures in the foreground, especially the man turned to scan his ticket at center, fasten our gaze. Like children eagerly awaiting Santa Claus, ticket holders eagerly scan their cards to determine their value as the names of paintings, prints, or medallions are pulled from a box and read aloud. With each number called, with each turn of the wheel, worthless pieces of paper accrued enormous value in an instant, a value that dissolved as winners collected their prizes and losers cast aside their unlucky "blanks." But in this engraving, produced for the purpose of enticing would-be subscribers, transparency and order reign in this spectacular and highly respectable middle class event. The scene has none of the raucousness and moral debauchery that critics considered characteristic of lotteries.

24 Nathaniel Parker Willis "The Two Art-Unions," *Home Journal* 42 (October 13, 1849), 192.

25 Miner K. Kellogg, "Art-Unions: Their True Character Considered," *The International Monthly Magazine of Literature, Science and Art* (1 January 1851), 191-95.

26 Pearne, "Art-Unions," 177.

FACING: Francis D'Avignon after Tompkins Matteson, *A Lottery Distribution of American Art-Union Prizes at the Tabernacle, Broadway, New York, December 24, 1847*, Sarony and Major, engraving, 1847, GM 5027.4405.218

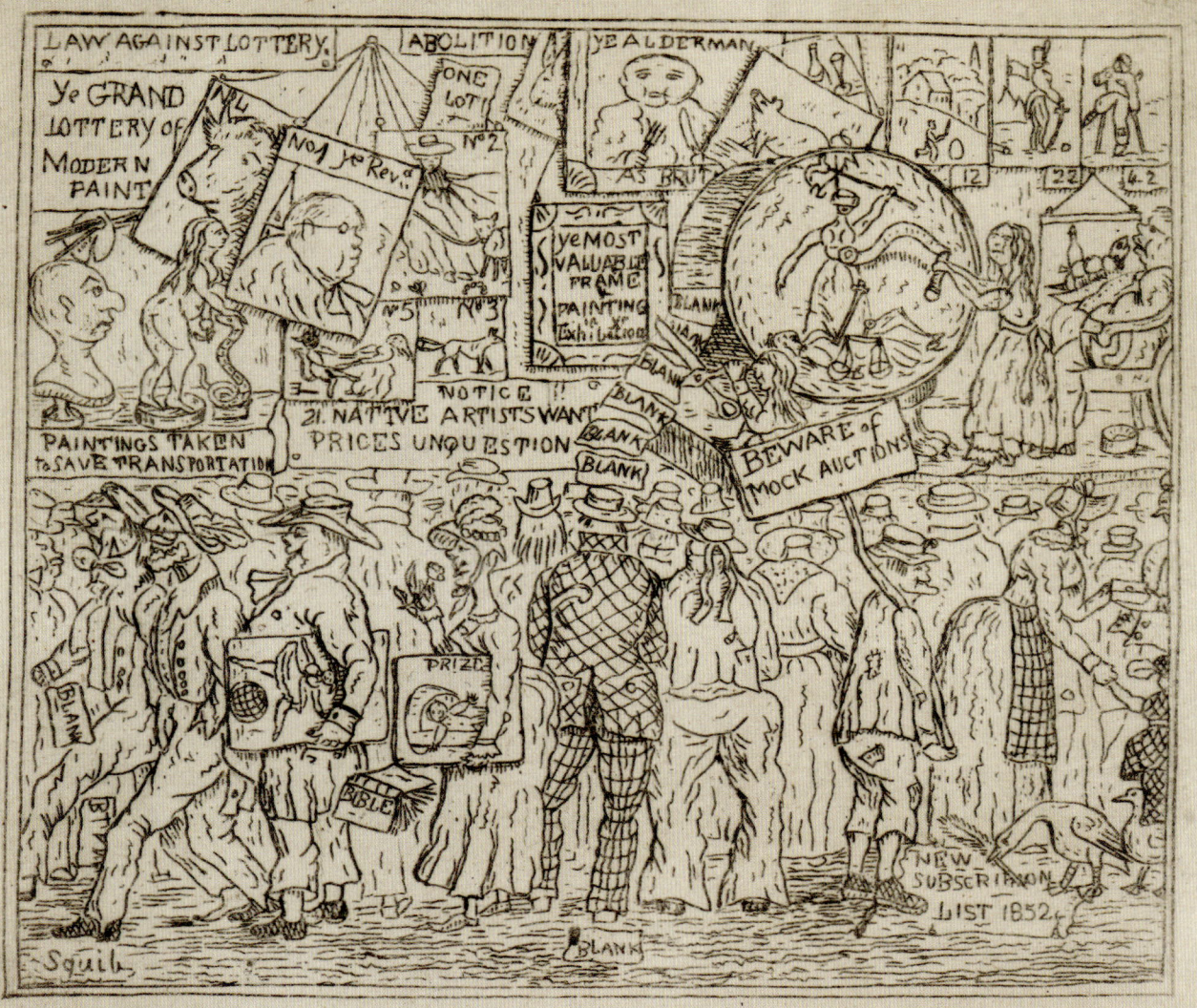

But contrast the Art-Union's image of refined and orderly distribution—in which the "wheel of fortune" works without assistance, in which the crowds remain mostly seated, where decorum throttles speculative fever—with another made just a few years later. In this dense graphic "ye Drawing of ye Grand Lotterie," a clear reference to the 1852 acution sale, "fortune showers her favours on ye multitude!!!" Lampooning the rhetoric employed by the Art-Union's Committee of Management, this enigmatic little engraving, measuring roughly three by six inches, approximates the size of an average bank note of the antebellum period. Like the allegorical import of banknotes, this engraving condenses much information into its compact space. But unlike those notes, in which abundance frames the activities of graceful allegorical figures of plenty and the assiduous labors of carpenters and coopers, chaos, and confusion animate the scene.

The engraving is attributed to Townend Glover (1813-1883), a lifelong student of fruits and insects and amateur artist. In 1834, he traveled to Munich where he studied fruit and flower painting with painter and drawing instructor Carl Mattenheimer (1791-1852), which quickly became a specialty. Glover's artistic skills would serve him well during expeditions far from his Fishkill, New York, home to document and collect specimens of fruits and insects—especially those injurious to cotton—in South Carolina, Florida, Mississippi, and elsewhere. Throughout his life, Glover made satirical caricatures, often engraved in copper. Of these images, Glover's biographer noted "the drawing is frequently grotesque and the action superb, while the satire is most pointed."[27]

Through meeting Andrew Jackson Downing in the late 1840s, Glover took up an interest in pomology, the study and practice of cultivating fruit, and embarked on a series of illustrations of various fruits depicting changes produced by differences of soils and climates. He exhibited these at state fairs and elsewhere in Albany, New York, at the exhibition of the New York State Agricultural Society in 1851 and at a meeting of the American Institute in New York. Glover's correspondence reveals that in 1852, the year of the Art-Union engraving, he arranged for an exhibition in Horticultural Hall, Boston. This eventually led him to Washington, D.C., where he was commissioned by the newly

27 Charles Richards Dodge, *The Life and Entomological Work of the Late Townend Glover, First Entomologist of the U. S. Department of Agriculture* (Washington D. C.: Government Printing Office, 1888), 13-20.

FACING: Attributed to Townend Glover, *Manners and Customs of Ye Yengesse*, etching on paper, 1852, Smithsonian American Art Museum, 1971.203

28 Dodge, *The Life and Entomological Work of the Late Townend Glover*, 20.

29 "Beware of Mock Auctions," *The Subterranean* 3, 15 (September 6, 1845), 2.

30 Rachel N. Klein, "Art and Authority in Antebellum New York City: The Rise and Fall of the American Art-Union," *The Journal of American History* (March 1995), 1557.

31 For more on the Art-Union and the changing practices of American artists, see Peter John Brownlee, "Francis Edmonds and the Speculative Economy of Painting." *American Art* 21, 3 (Fall 2007): 30-53.

formed Bureau of Agriculture to collect statistics and other information on seeds, fruits, and insects in the United States. Roughly ten years later, he would be appointed the first United States Entomologist by the new Department of Agriculture.[28]

Signed "Squib" in the lower left hand corner, Glover's engraving is a far cry from the precise illustrations populating the book for which he is best known, *Illustrations of North American Entomology*, first published in 1872. Regardless, it is clearly of its moment in taking the American Art-Union, or some institution very similar to it, as the target of its critique. In a direct twist on the seal of the Art-Union, the figure of justice with her scales lies slain by sword at the feet of a beleaguered figure of blind luck, holding a weathervane above her head in apparent triumph. With eyes covered, she hand cranks a wheel that spits out a steady supply of "blanks." Nevertheless, a few individuals at left walk away with paintings tucked under their arms. Below this emblem of abundance, a ragged man toting a sign that reads "Beware of Mock Auctions" ineffectually parades to the right. In an 1845 article of the same name, the author suggested the idea of "sending chaps with sign boards

or muslin banners to parade in front of swindling establishments, with cautionary instructions . . . painted on them."[29] The word "Abolition," which appears just below the border at top left, may refer to a charge made against the alleged use of Art-Union funds to aid manager Henry J. Raymond in the founding of his *New York Daily Times*, which the *New York Herald* labeled an "abolition journal."[30] But this charge, one of several leveled at the Art-Union, is nearly lost amid the fray. Intoxicated with the frenzy, someone has cast aside a Bible as if it were a worthless "blank" to accept the often-warned-against prize. The culprit is unclear, being either the man in the broad-brimmed hat walking to the left, or the woman to his right who has taken to tippling.

Like the ideological divide separating the Art-Union's proponents from its opponents, the contrast between these two views of the annual lottery could not be more pronounced. Promoted as an event of middling gentility by Art-Union managers and ridiculed by critics as a chaotic carnival, a mock auction churning out paper blanks along with the occasional prize, it was the central feature that made the organization so appealing, and yet so divisive. Because of this mechanism a gulf had opened during the 1840s between those who favored and promoted the distribution of prints and paintings by lottery, and those who felt it encouraged only excitement for gambling. That the rifts between the two camps were articulated in the language of speculative business practices and gambling underscores the economically reckless and rapidly developing cultural milieu in which the American Art-Union rose and fell. The organization's plan, of course, had ramifications for the creative impulses and business practices of its artists, but its design and operations shaped a particularly speculative framework for the appreciation of American art at a pivotal moment in its development. The Art-Union functioned as a node in the market economy that so thoroughly transformed the cultural landscape of antebellum America. Indeed, the ebb and flow of its success and failure mirrored the economic fluctuations of its time, for as the Art-Union closed its doors, another financial calamity, the Panic of 1857, lay just over the horizon.[31]

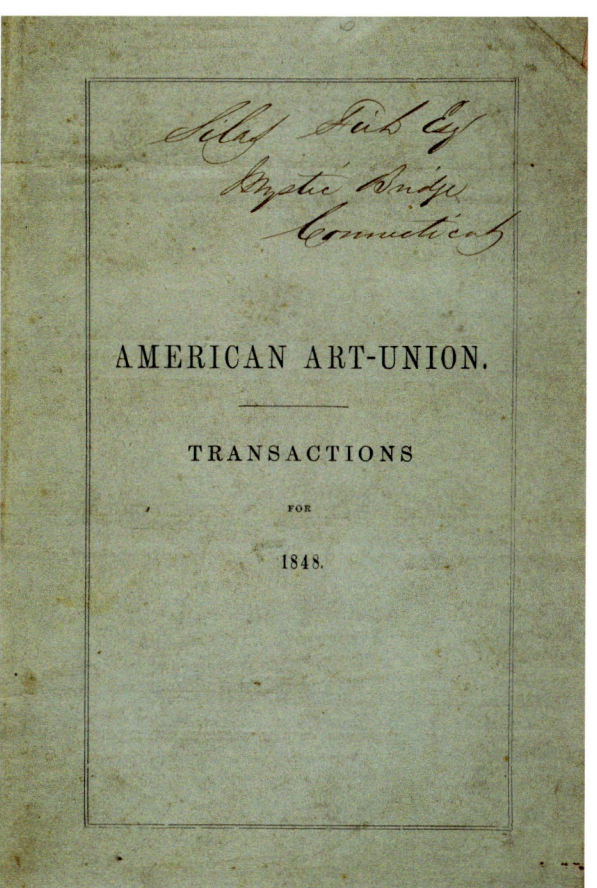

AUTHOR'S NOTE

I wish to thank Kimberly Orcutt at the New-York Historical Society for facilitating my access to the storehouse of American Art-Union materials housed there. Thanks also to Denise Wamaling, Smithsonian American Art Museum, for help with obtaining images, and to Helena Wright, Division of Graphic Arts, National Museum of American History, Smithsonian Institution for generously sharing information on Townend Glover. Additional assistance with images was provided by Annelise K. Madsen, Curatorial Assistant, Terra Foundation for American Art. Additional assistance with images was provided by Annelise K. Madsen, Curatorial Assistant, and Carley Moseley, Grants Intern, Terra Foundation for American Art.

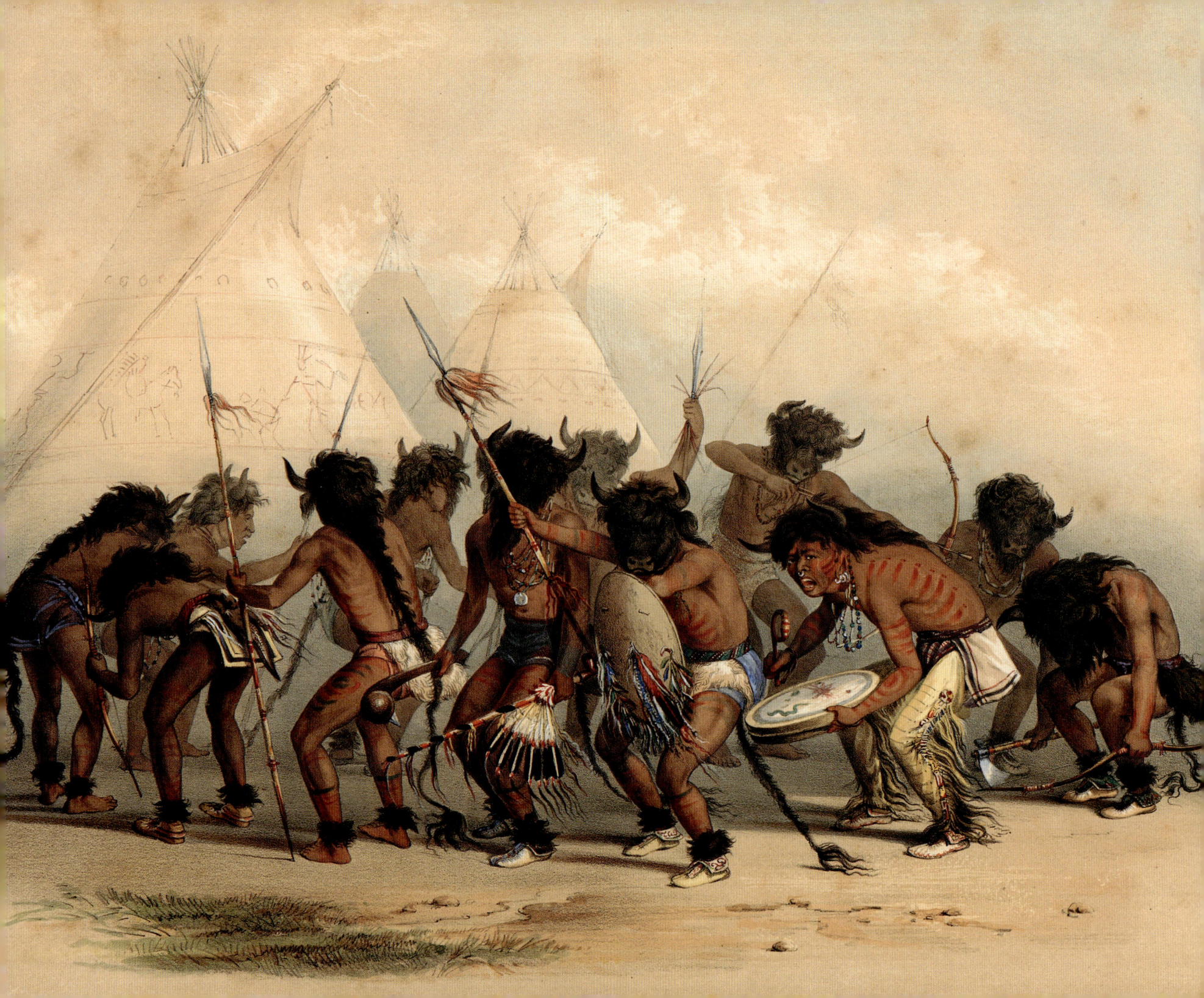

Free to the World THE ART=UNION GALLERY

The institution, if not the creator of a taste for art in the community, disseminated

a knowledge of it and largely stimulated its growth. Through it the people awoke to

the fact that art was one of the forces of society. — Asher B. Durand

On Christmas Eve, 1847, the ninth annual meeting of the American Art-Union convened at the Broadway Tabernacle in New York City. Hundreds gathered for the event, which would culminate in distribution of the year's acquisitions of art. AAU president Prosper M. Wetmore called the meeting to order and delivered remarks on the institution's recent undertakings. It had been the Art-Union's most successful year to date. Subscribers had virtually doubled over the previous year, from 4,450 to 9,666 at the close of business that day. Significantly, the Art-Union had opened a new exhibition space at 497 Broadway—the "Perpetual Free Gallery" had at last found a permanent home. Wetmore's opening remarks reminded the members of the Art-Union's enduring perspective:

FACING: George Catlin, *Buffalo Dance*, in Catlin's Indian Portfolio, engraving, 1847, GM 4576.93.8b

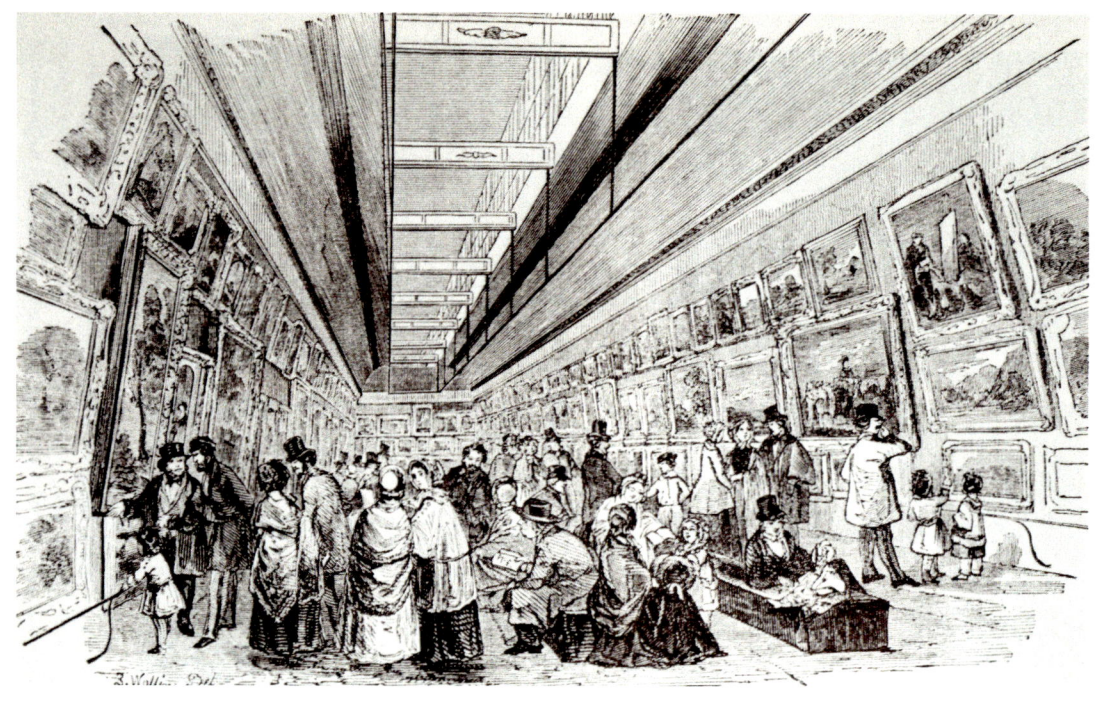

Who that has visited the spacious gallery of this Institution, erected under your auspices, and sustained by your liberality, has failed to remark the effect of this popular exhibition upon the public mind? Thousands of visitors are daily met within its walls, of every degree and condition, from the humble artisan fresh from his daily toil, the poor child of genius who comes perhaps to gather inspiration from the breathing canvas, to the educated and critical observer, who drinks in streams of pleasure from this fountain of the beautiful in Art… And that stately gallery, with its fine collection of pictures and statuary, is free to all, free not merely to subscribers, but through your generosity, free to the world…[1]

The opening of the new gallery at 497 Broadway in October 1847 had proved successful beyond the Art-Union's managers' wildest imaginings. The display was "thronged with visitors" eager to get a glimpse of the gallery's latest additions, including engravings from George Catlin's Indian Portfolio.

1 *Transactions of the American Art-Union for the Year 1847* (1848), 14-16.

2 *Transactions of the American Art-Union for the Year 1847* (1848), 14-16.

3 Mary Bartlett Cowdrey, *American Academy of Fine Arts and American Art-Union, 1816-1852* (New York: New York Historical Society, 1953), 202.

Samuel Wallin, *Gallery of the Art-Union, 497 Broadway, New York City*, American Art-Union, engraving, 1849, GM 5027.4405.200

The Art-Union's exhibitions had reached a milestone. The event marked the culmination of nearly a decade of Art-Union activities. Earlier exhibitions were organized in a series of rented galleries, ever-evolving and with sporadic success. Indeed, the Art-Union's "rooms" had seen a number of iterations since the group's organization under the auspices of the Apollo Association and James Herring's Apollo Gallery in 1839. The early exhibitions relied heavily on artworks borrowed from collectors and often loaned by the artists themselves. The modest displays of the early years were poorly attended, and those who did attend were charged an admission fee to help defray exhibition expenses. In 1842, however, the Art-Union opened the free gallery in rented space not far from its eventual "stately" home on Broadway. The move to make the gallery "free not merely to subscribers" but more significantly, "free to the world" began a new era in the life of the institution.[2] Before the end of the decade, the free exhibitions of the American Art-Union would meet the challenges of lofty rhetoric to become "the best attended the country had ever known."[3]

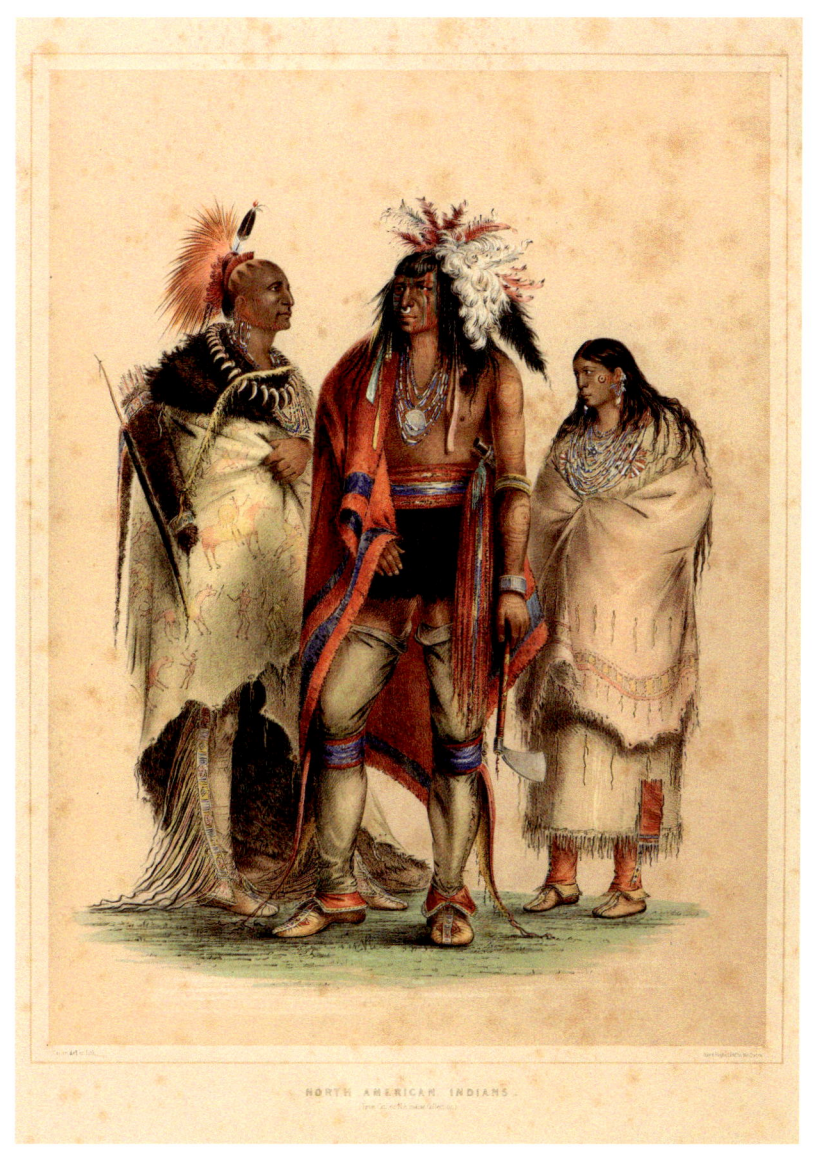

George Catlin, *North American Indians,* in Catlin's Indian Portfolio, engraving,1847, GM 4576.93.1b

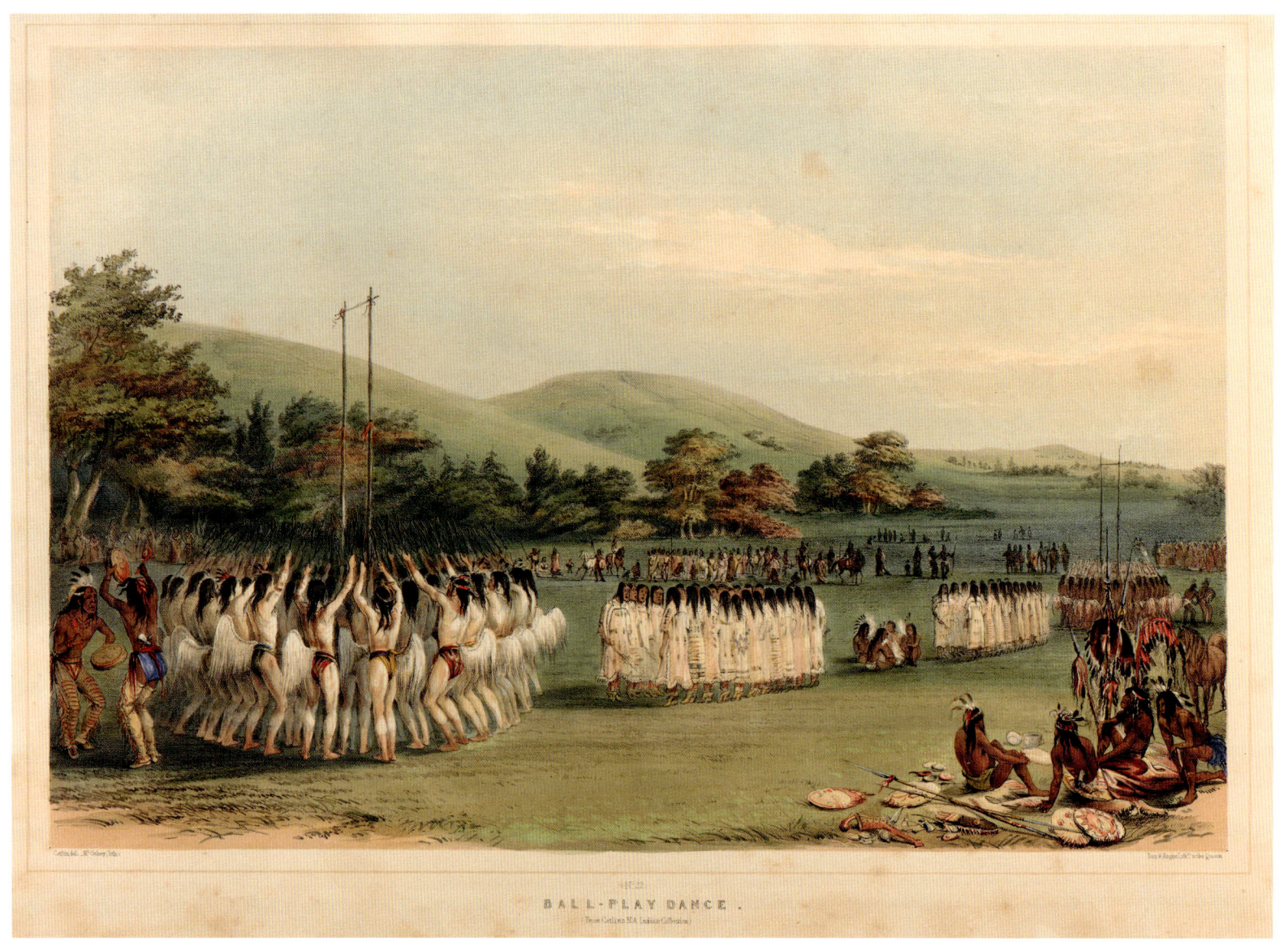

BALL-PLAY DANCE.

George Catlin, *Ball Play Dance*, in Catlin's Indian Portfolio, engraving, 1847, GM 4576.93.22b

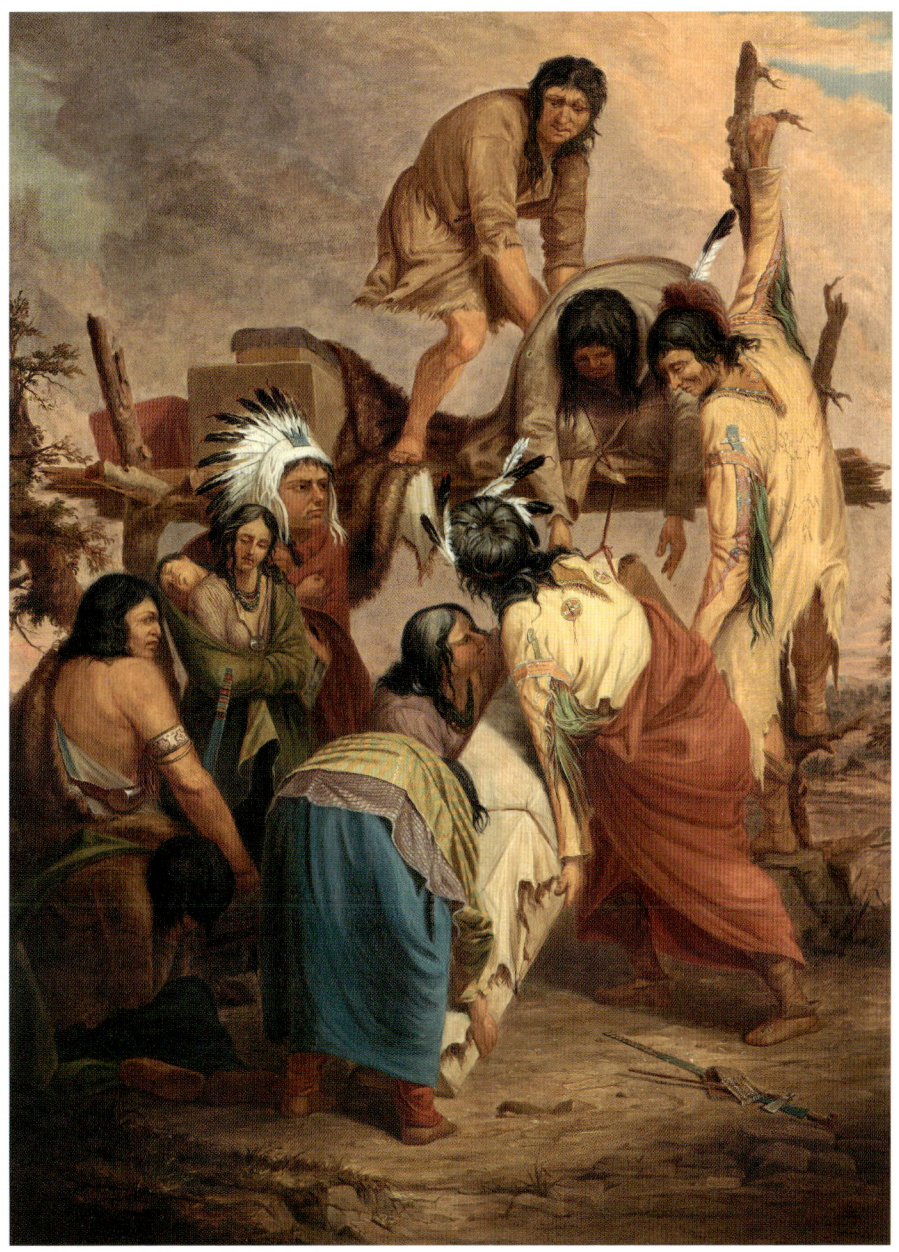

Seth Eastman, *Indian Burial,* oil on canvas, 1848, GM 0126.1122

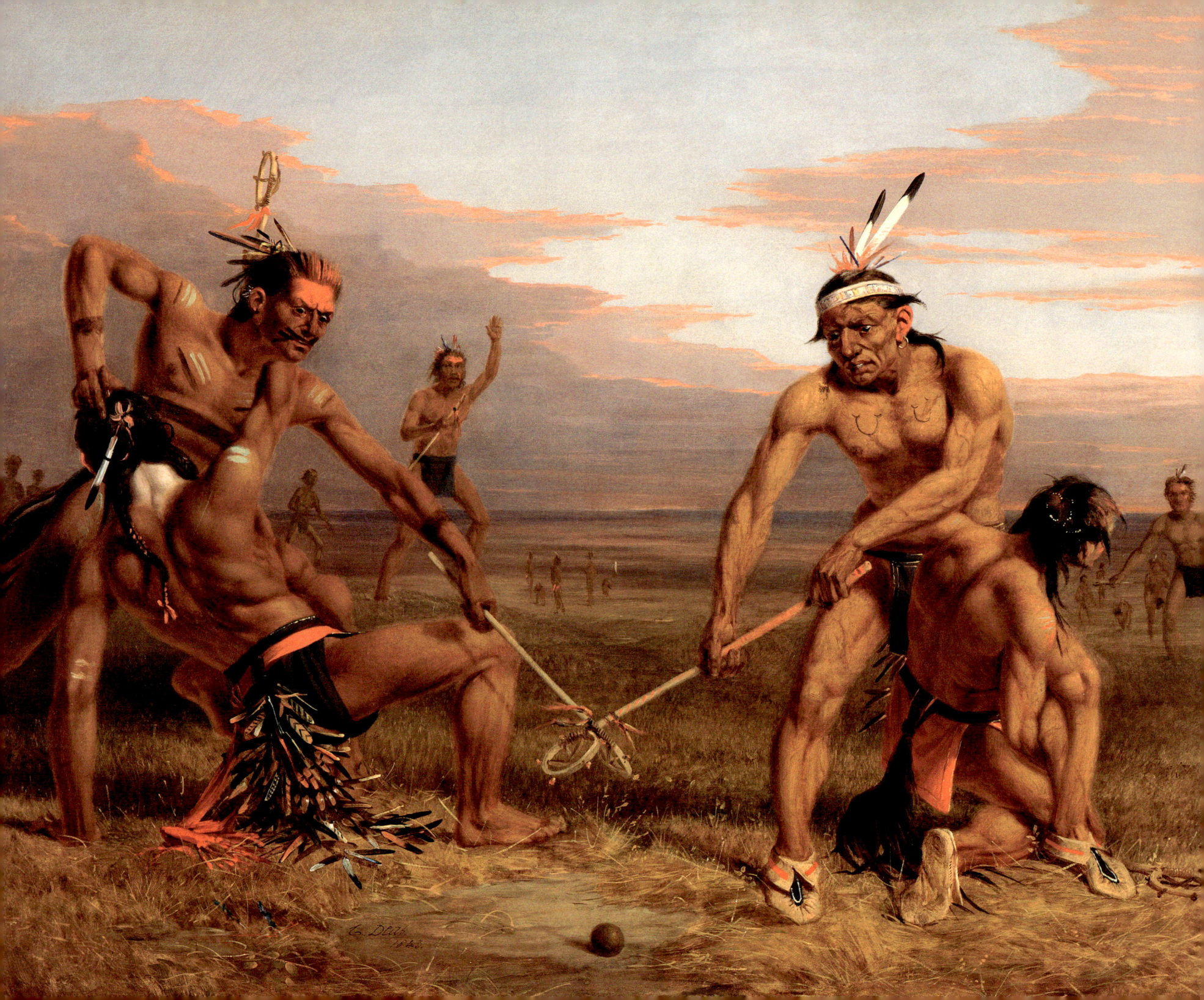

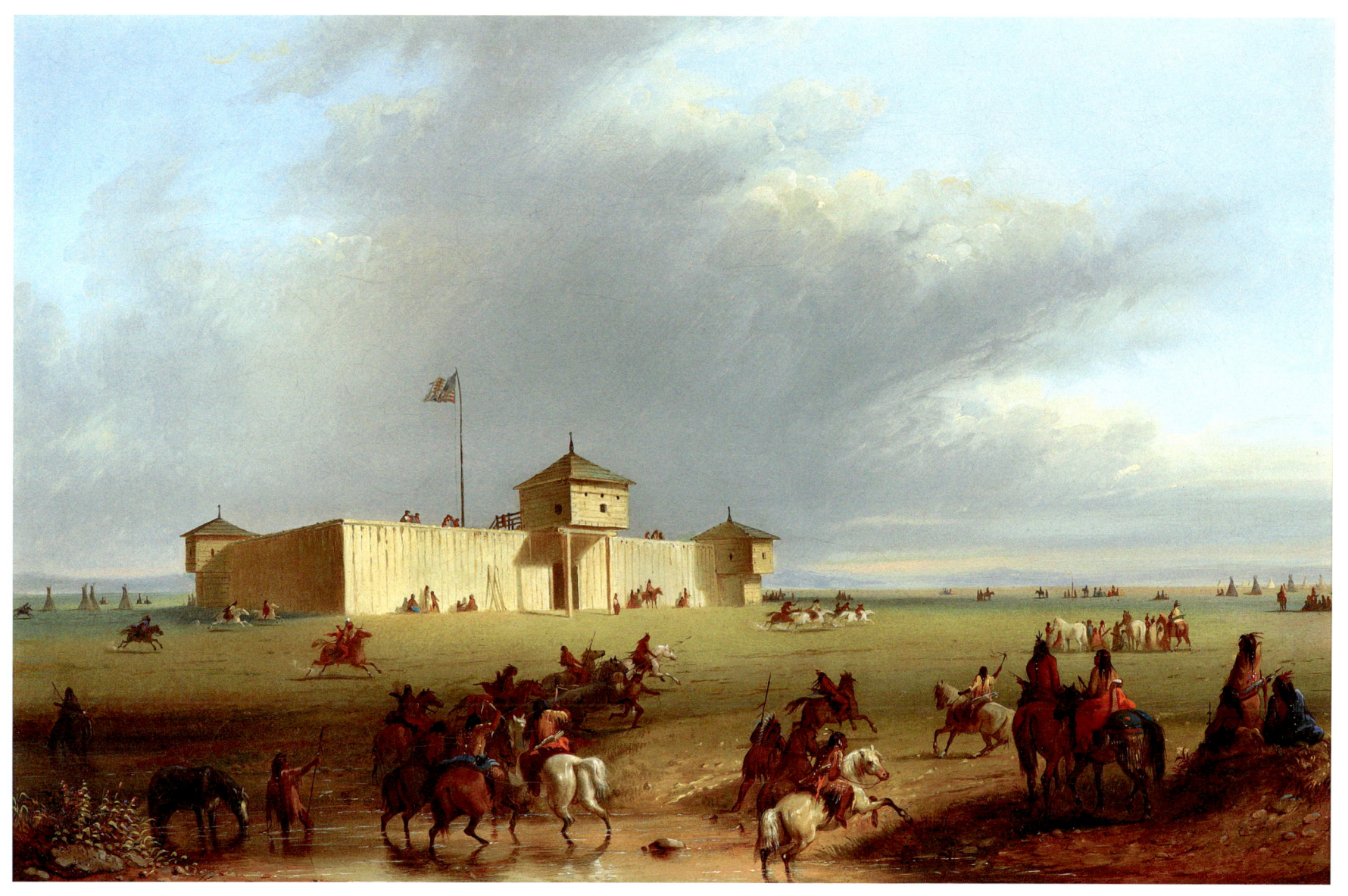

Alfred Jacob Miller, *Fort Laramie*, oil on canvas, 1852, GM 0126.727

FACING: Charles Deas, *Sioux Playing Ball*, oil on canvas, 1848, GM 0126.1152

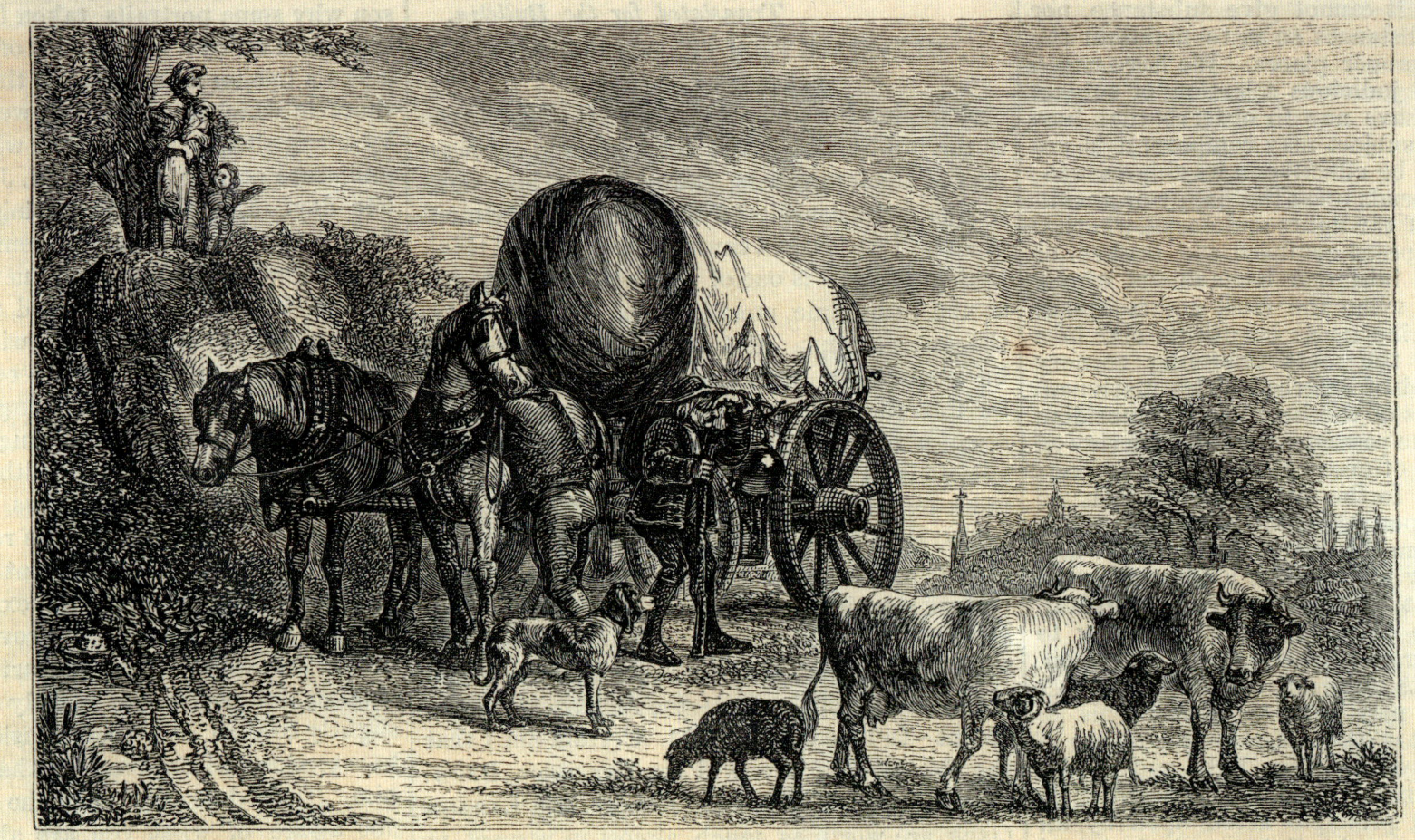

THE EMIGRANTS' LAST LOOK UPON HOME.

Designed and drawn upon wood by THOMAS F. HOPPIN.   Engraved by BOBBETT & EDMONDS.

Bobbett and Edmonds after Thomas H. Hoppin, *The Emigrants' Last Look Upon Home*, American Art-Union, engraving, 1851, GM 5126.1061.88

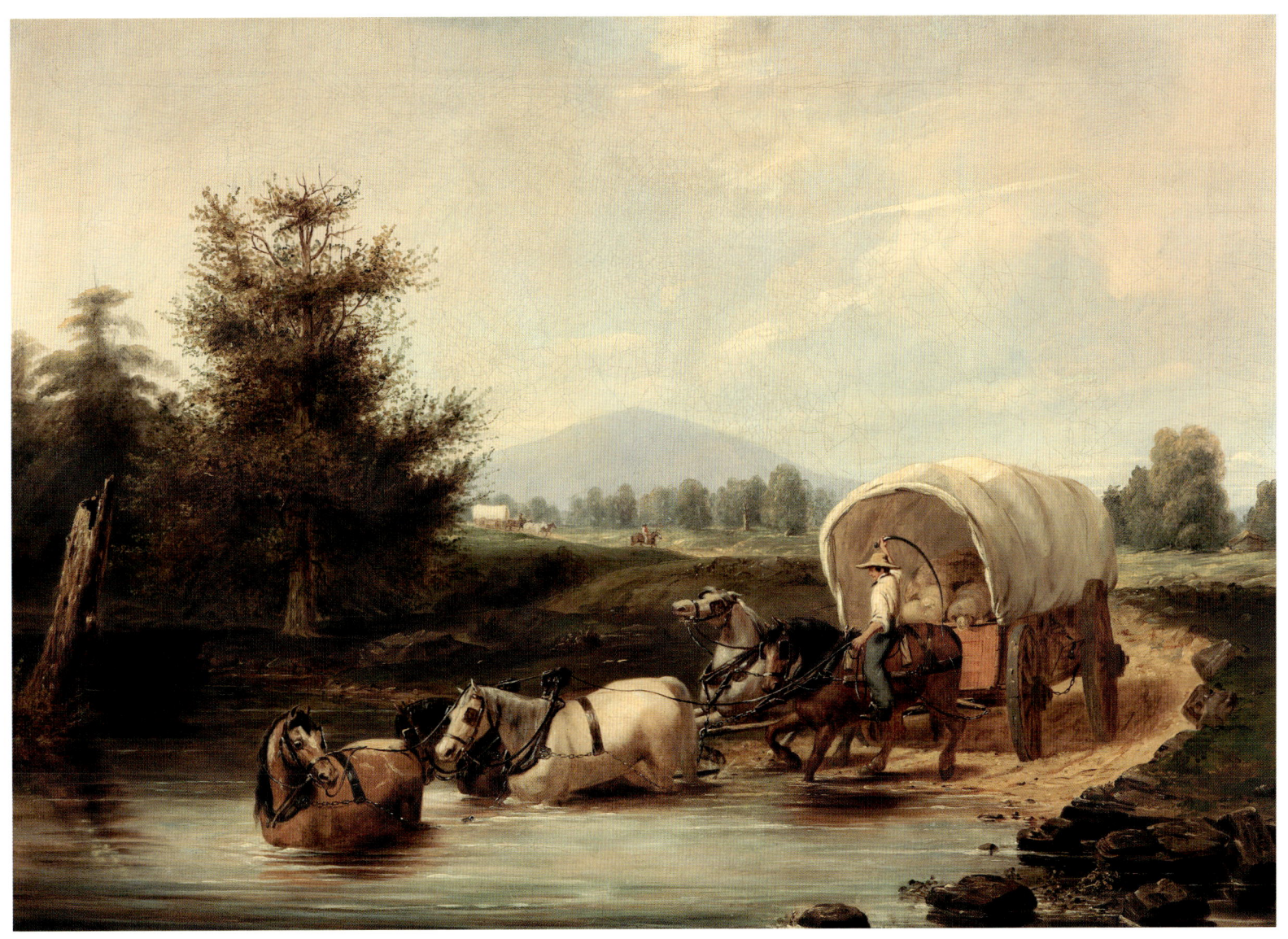

William Tylee Ranney, *Crossing the Ferry,* oil on canvas, 1846, GM 0126.1234

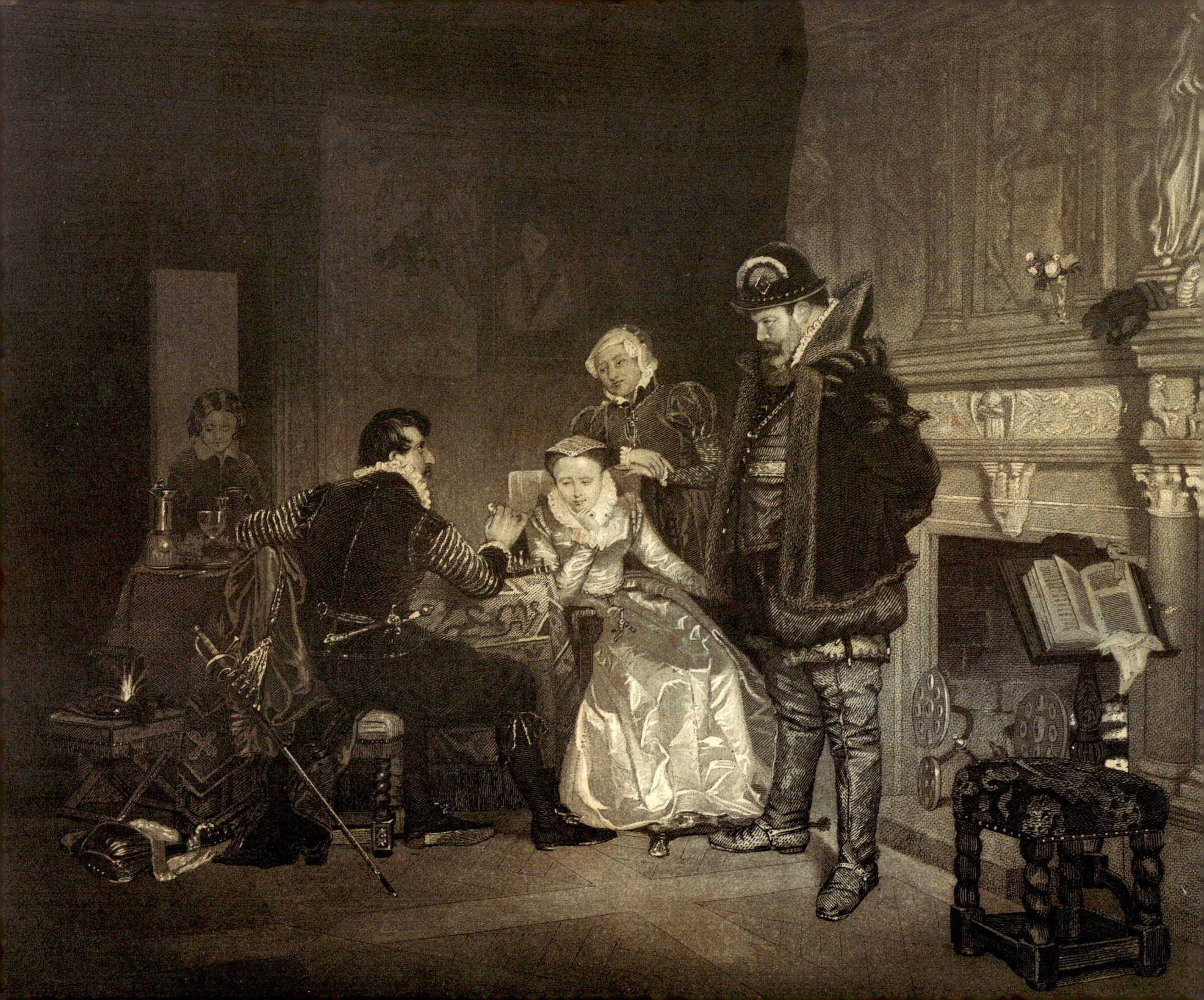

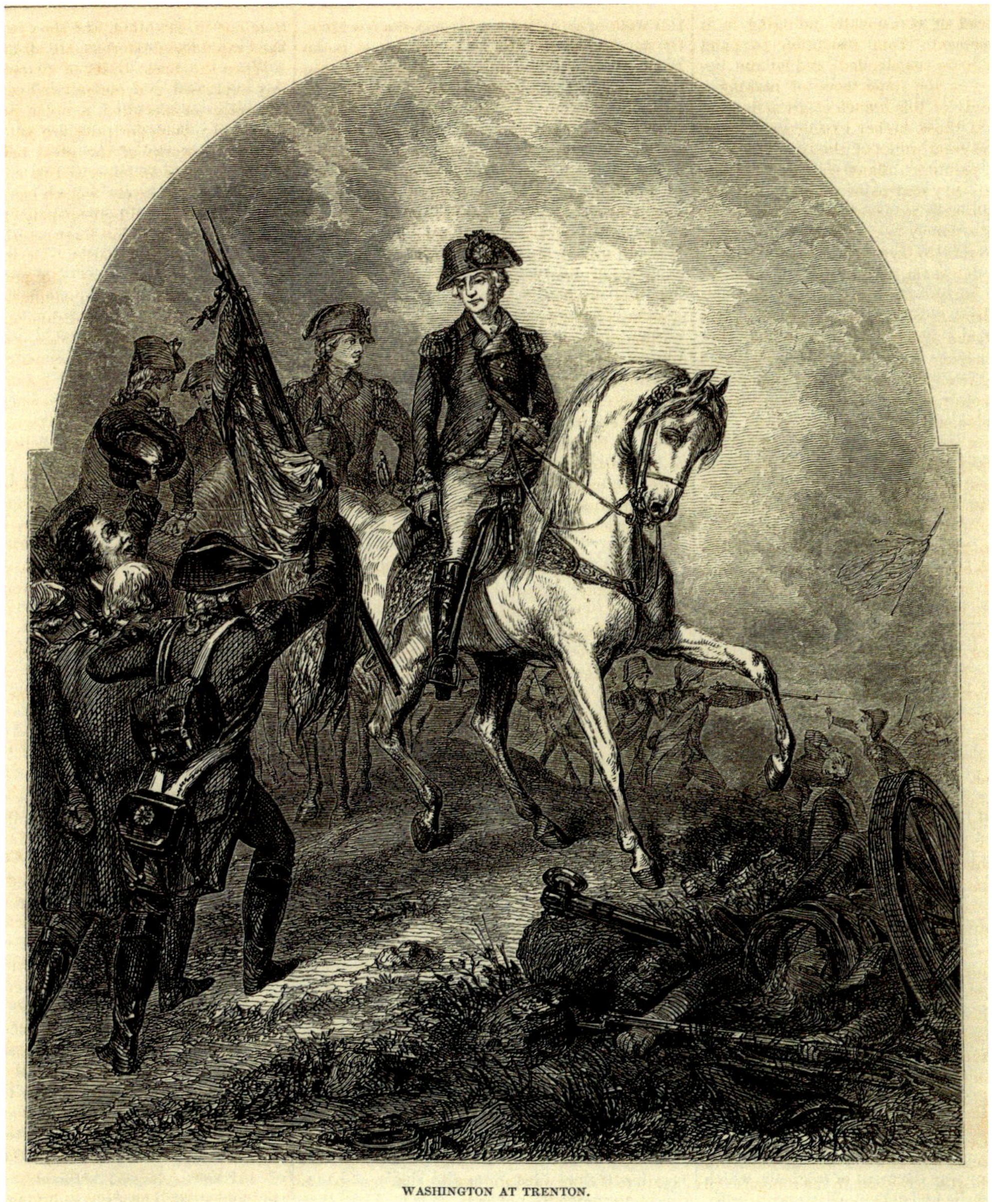

WASHINGTON AT TRENTON.

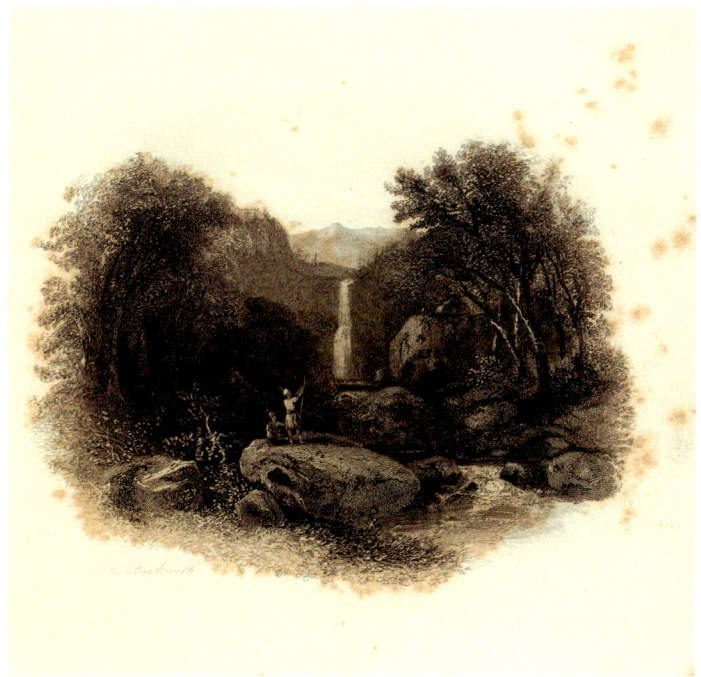

H. Beckwith after John Frederick Kensett, *Catskill Mountain Scenery*, American Art-Union, engraving, 1851, GM 5126.1061.101

LEFT: Bobbett and Edmonds after Wenderoth, *Washington at Trenton*, American Art-Union, engraving, 1851, GM 5126.1061.73

FACING: Charles Burt after Richard Caton Woodville, *The Game of Chess*, American Art-Union, engraving, 1851, GM 5126.1061.53

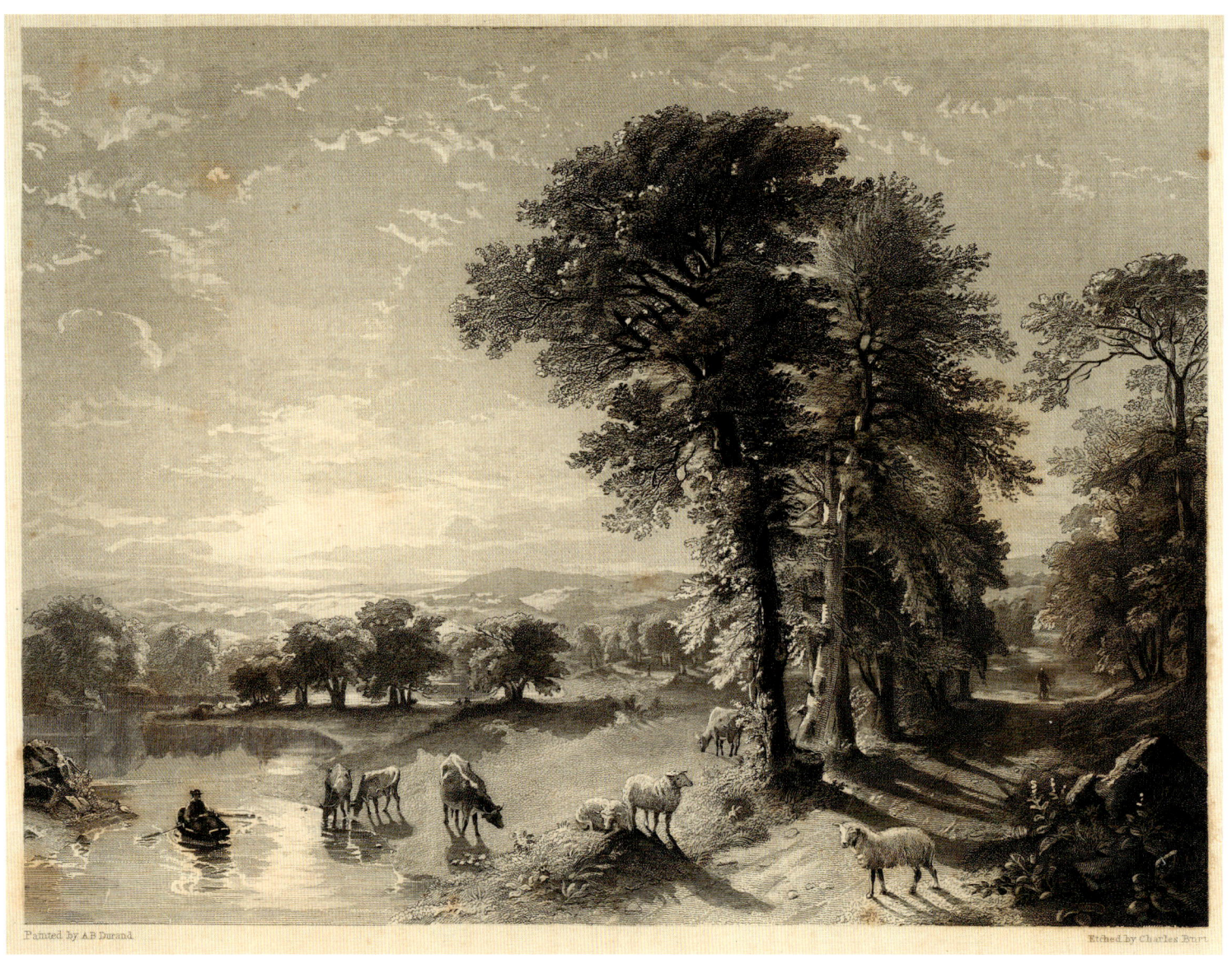

Charles Burt after Asher B. Durand, *Landscape,* American Art-Union, engraving, 1851, GM 5126.1061.119

Prosper Wetmore continued his enthusiastic account of the Art-Union's efforts and the worthiness of its mission on that Christmas Eve of 1847:

It has been asserted that republican institutions are unfavorable to the cultivation of the Arts of design; that the influences of a free public opinion must of necessity be indicated in something 'savage and wild,' rather than in graceful forms and gentle outlines. The daily exhibitions of this Institution, the events of this night, are a complete refutation of such a charge. Let us look for a moment at facts within our knowledge. We need not go beyond the limits of our own city to find the evidence that the freest institutions ever formed, have had a tendency to expand the mind to its greatest limits and most natural action. It would indeed be strange if this were not so, for Art must flourish most when its wings are widest spread, and its ascent is unchecked by the shackles of any master.[4]

The Art-Union's president's remarks captured the intensity with which members of the group viewed the role of art and its potential impact on society. Their sociopolitical ideals conflicted dramatically with those who asserted that "art was incompatible with the new American democratic form of government."[5] The construction of the new free gallery was a demonstration of the Art-Union's ongoing commitment to bring art to every class of people. For the AAU managers and their supporters, the fine arts had too long been the sole domain of the wealthy and privileged. The annual art distribution would offer a chance at owning an artwork for a small fee, the gallery provided access to those "citizens of the laboring classes, to whom the expenditure required to visit other exhibitions, is an indulgence which they cannot conveniently afford."[6]

The Art-Union's Perpetual Free Gallery was a unique social experiment for 19th-century antebellum America. It was believed that the exhibitions offered a means to enrich the lives of all visitors but particularly for the less advantaged. In his formal comments on the evening of the 1847 distribution, manager William J. Hoppin summed

4 *Transactions of the American Art-Union for the Year 1847* (1848), 14.

5 Anne Farmer Meservey, "The Role of Art in American Life: Critics' Views on Native Art and Literature, 1830-1865," *American Art Journal*, Vol. 10, No. 1 (May 1978), 74.

6 *Transactions of the American Art-Union for the Year 1847* (1848), 21.

7 *Transactions of the American Art-Union for the Year 1847* (1848), 21.

8 *Transactions of the American Art-Union for the Year 1847* (1844), 6.

9 *The New York Herald,* December 21, 1844.

up the Art-Union's advocacy on the benefits of art for the common man:

> To men pent up in the dark streets of cities, and deprived of the free air and bright sunshine of rural life, the painted canvas affords a substitute not wisely to be neglected, of the living landscape—a reflection, not always faint and without comfort, of the smile of God in nature. And it is not with the visit to the gallery that its benefits terminate. It begets taste, simple and cheap in their gratification, which strengthen the domestic ties. It suggests employments which add new charms to home, however poor and scanty be the accommodation to which that sacred name is applied.[7]

However lofty their goals, the Art-Union managers understood that providing access to all classes would still be hindered by the prevailing attitude that "paintings and statues are regarded as luxuries to be indulged in only by the rich and effeminate." In his address at the annual distribution in 1844, Charles F. Briggs lamented that "this misconception is found one of the greatest obstacles to success in an undertaking like this of the Art-Union. And when it is remembered that works of art are rarely found but in the houses of the rich, or else shut up carefully in galleries, where the inquiring glances of the vulgar poor rarely penetrate, it cannot be wondered at that such a feeling should exist. But, it is the aim of the Art-Union to dispel such errors as these, and to convey to the abodes of common life works of intrinsic merit, which wealth does not always possess the discrimination to appropriate to its own use."[8]

Throughout the mid 1840s, the Art-Union's free exhibitions in New York garnered attention and support. Even the *New York Herald*, which contributed to the eventual demise of the AAU, wrote enthusiastically of the Art-Union gallery's impact on city life in 1844. "Never before has there been so much excitement manifested in the city on the subject of the fine arts—by which we especially mean painting and sculpture—and it is quite evident that a new feeling in regard to them is taking root and rapidly spreading among our citizens."[9] As the successes of the Art-Union's exhibition program continued to build, so too did its support in the press. "A spare hour cannot be more pleasantly spent than in a visit to the rooms of the American Art-Union…The productions are all by American artists and afford a gratifying proof of the progress of art in our country."[10]

Some saw the Art-Union exhibitions as evidence of a growing international artistic prowess. "We visited this institution in company with an amateur friend and were exceedingly gratified at the number of gems deposited… Here are works worthy of that clime that gave birth to art and matured it till it became divine. These noble productions impress us with the idea that art must ultimately be restored to its lost grandeur and exert upon the American mind a reverence for the beautiful and true parallel to that which lifted Italy above her barbaric contemporaries… Italy is the Mecca of art and the American has drawn inspiration from her treasures… Nature has lavished her beauty with such variety in this land that those who rely on her for truth have found where the secret of true art lies."[11]

The Art-Union's experiment in democracy extended not only to the subscribers and visitors to the gallery but to the careers of the participating artists. The Art-Union encouraged the work of new artists and through its purchases offered a means by which the production of art was not reliant on the whim and commissions of wealthy patrons. The free gallery also offered an opportunity for selected artists to bring additional works not purchased by the AAU before the general public. In 1844, Charles F. Briggs reported to the committee that "the rooms of the Art-Union have been made a depository for many fine works of art, in addition to the pictures owned by the Association, and have been much visited both by our own citizens and by strangers, and an opportunity has been afforded many of our young artists to make themselves known, which has been the means of bringing them, in many instances, patrons as well as admirers."[12]

Thousands were drawn to the gallery's exhibitions each week. In 1848, *The Literary World* noted that the Art-Union had contributed "by its free gallery of paintings, one of the most elevating and attractive public exhibitions of this city; diffusing everywhere, by means of its agents and publications, the most authentic information respecting the progress of American art; and above all, directly

10 *The Rondout Freeman*, November 21, 1846.

11 *The Constitution*, December 8, 1847.

12 *Transactions of the American Art-Union for the Year 1844* (1845), 9.

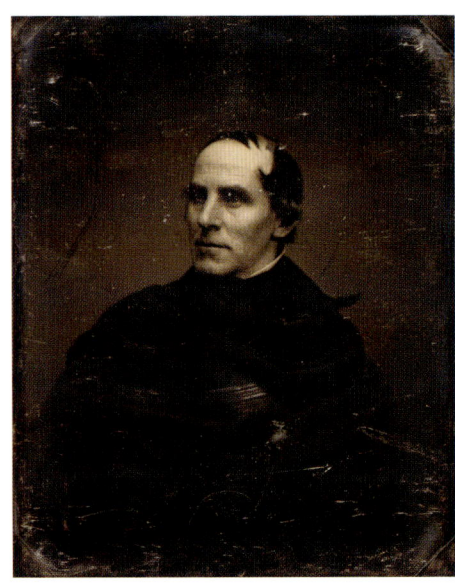

Mathew Brady, *Thomas Cole,*
daguerreotype, ca. 1844

13 *The Literary World,* October 13, 1849.

14 *The Portsmouth Journal,* October 7, 1848

15 *Bulletin of the American Art-Union,*
October 1849.

16 *Transactions of the American Art-Union for
the Year 1848* (1849), 46-47.

assisting in the support and education of hundreds of American artists."[13] That same year, the *New York Evening Express* reported that "the American Art-Union in this city is getting to be one of our greatest lions. It keeps its gallery of paintings open free to all every day but Sunday and when the day is cool enough to moderate the heat of near 200 gas lights, the room is brilliantly lighted through the evening and thousands of all classes keep it continually thronged…Last year it was estimated that an average of thirty thousand persons visited weekly, toward the end of the season. The four pictures, the *Voyage of Life*—Cole's masterpiece—are worthy of a hundred visits."[14] As the crowds continued to grow, even the new gallery became "insufficient for the purposes of the institution" and a second exhibition space was planned for construction on a lot adjoining the Broadway gallery—the adjoining galleries to be "thrown open for gratuitous public exhibition" the following year.[15]

It was a grand social experiment. As the exhibitions continued to be "thronged with admiring visitants from country and city," proof of the free gallery's success in shaping the social behavior of the city was believed to be demonstrated in the overall good manners of the masses of visitors to the exhibition. "Cheerful testimony is here borne to the uniform decorum there observed, and to the peculiar fact, that notwithstanding this immense concourse of visitors, no part of the property there so openly exposed, has been in the least mutilated or abstracted—undeniable evidence of the humanizing effect of this exhibition upon the general character of the community. Our Free Gallery has thus become one of the most attractive places of resort in this metropolis of the New World—inviting all, in the true spirit of republican liberality…"[16]

In November 1848, *The Knickerbocker* published its enthusiastic support of the Art-Union gallery and its impact on the social life of the city:

The Gallery is no longer a superfluity,
it has become a necessity. It is part of the
public property as much as the fountains,
the parks, or the City-Hall. The retired
merchant from Fifth Avenue, the scholar
from the University, the poor workman, the
news-boy, the beau and the belle, the clerk
with his bundle—all frequent the Art-Union.
Its hall shows the progress of the hours as

Johann Micheal Enzing-Müller after Thomas Cole, *The Voyage of Life—Youth,* J. Dalton, engraving, 1851

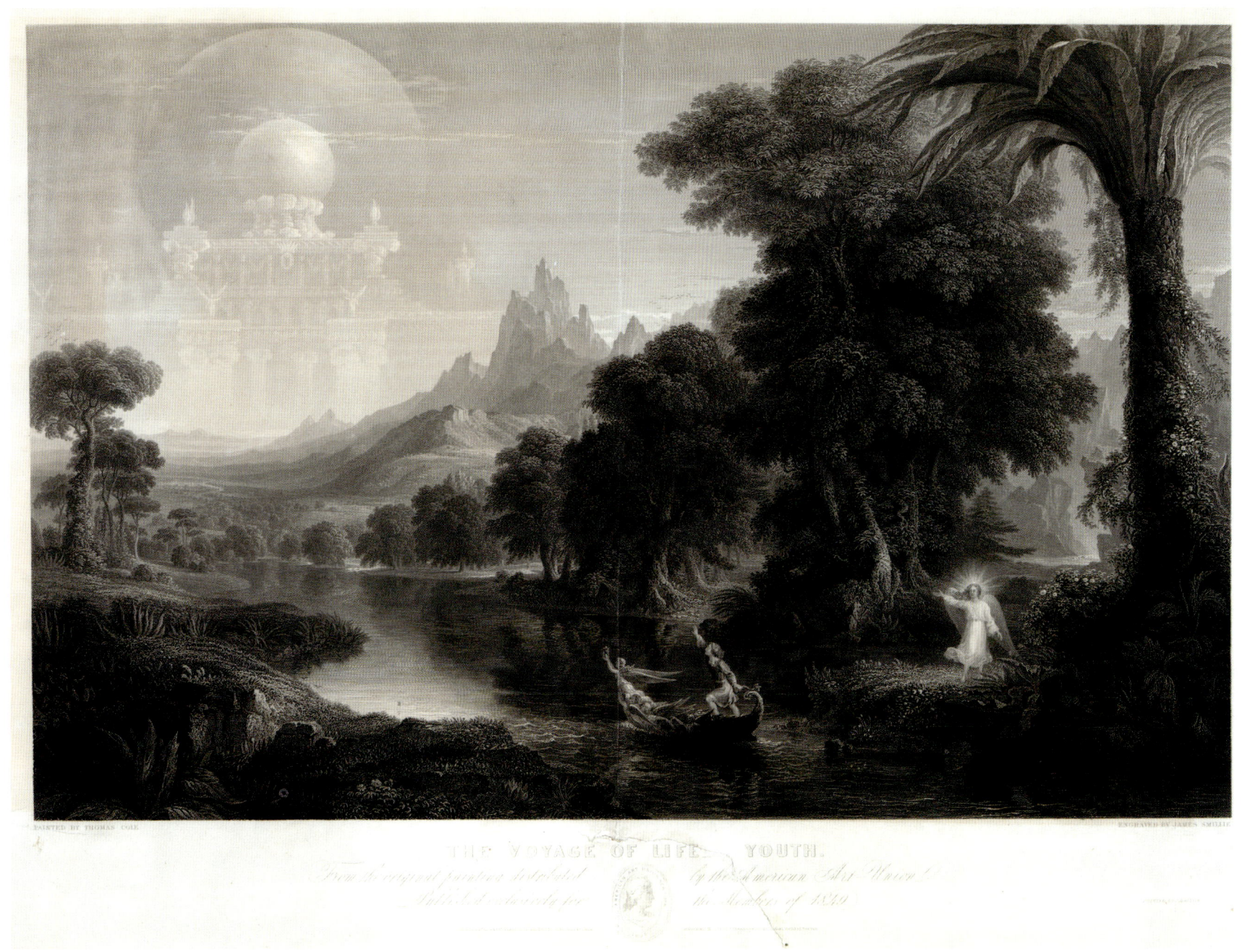

PAINTED BY THOMAS COLE   ENGRAVED BY JAMES SMILLIE

THE VOYAGE OF LIFE   YOUTH.

From the original picture completed   by the American Art Union.
Published exclusively for   its Members of 1849.

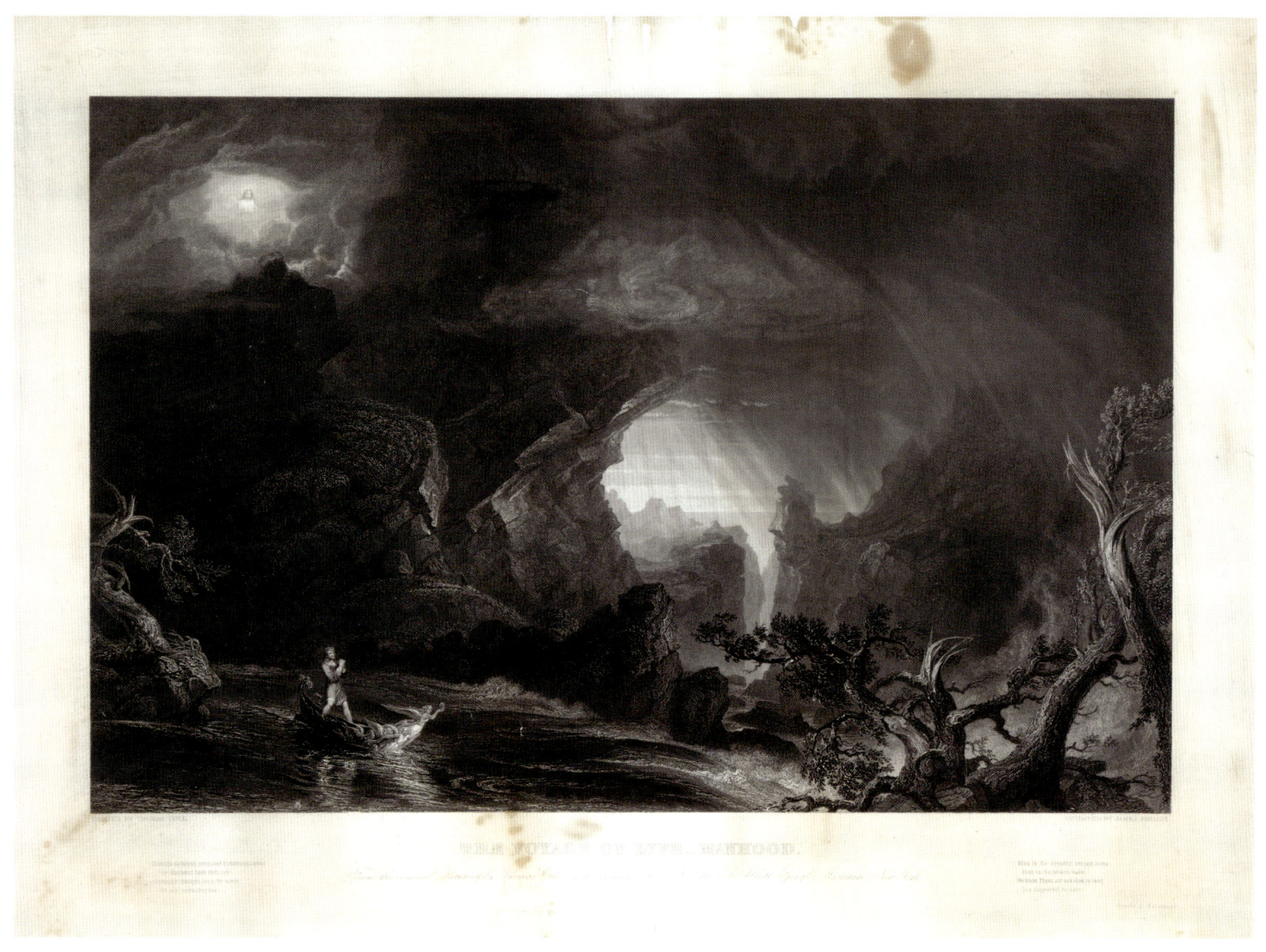

James Smillie after Thomas Cole, *The Voyage of Life—Manhood*, R. Holdgate, engraving, 1850

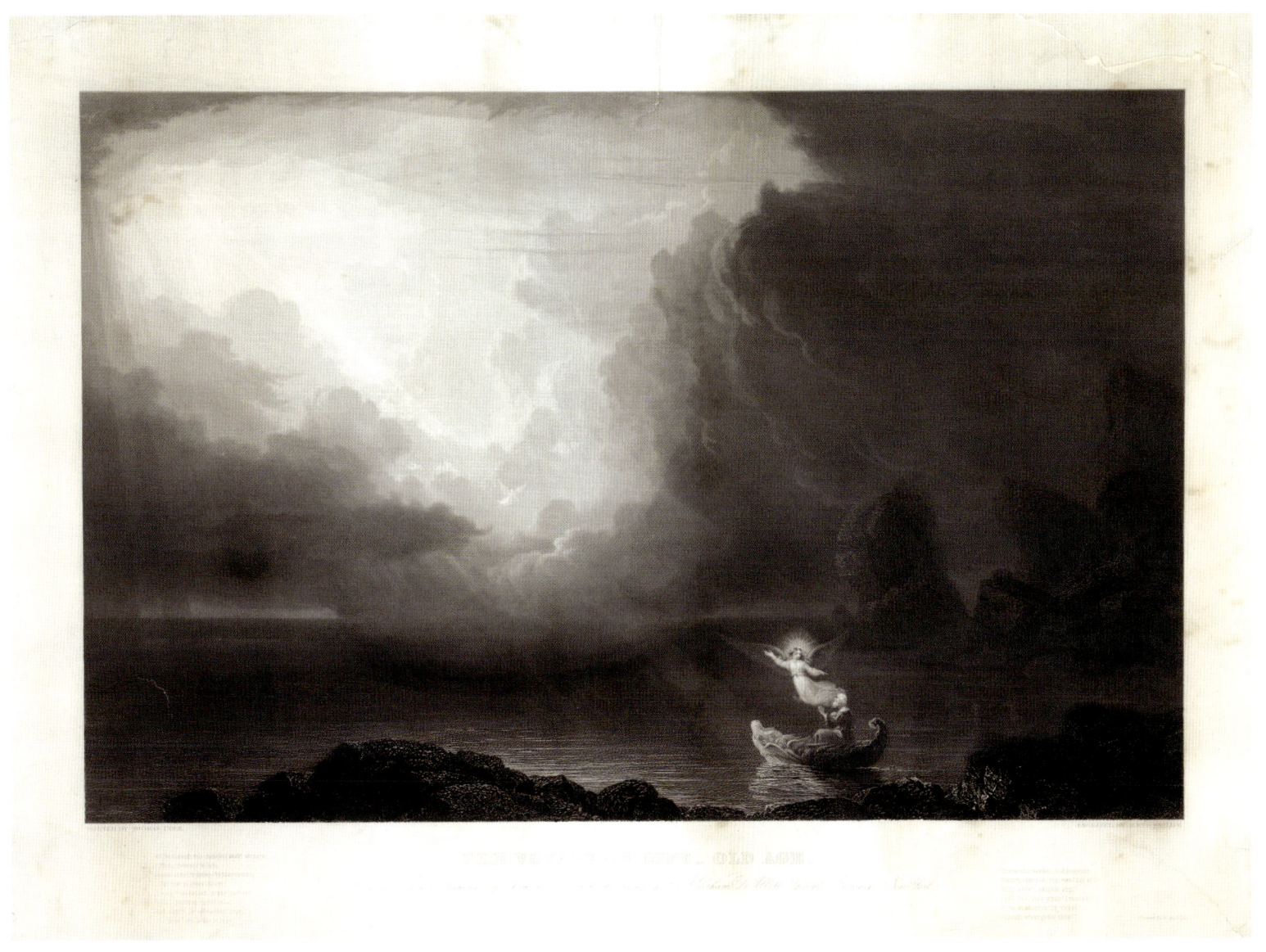

James Smillie after Thomas Cole, *The Voyage of Life—Old Age*, American Art-Union, 1850

17 *The Knickerbocker,* or *New York Monthly Magazine,* July, 1848, Vol. XXXII. No.1.

18 Duyckinck Collection, Mss. Division, New York Public Library.

19 *The North American,* March 10, 1849.

well as Trinity clock. First come the noisy boys and girls, on their way to school; then the staid merchants drop in as they go down to their counting-houses; then appear the strangers from the country, who set off early after breakfast to see the lions; about noon the gentlemen in moustaches and yellow kids lounge about the seats, yawning in the faces of the fashionable ladies who alight from their carriages here on their road to Stewart's; in the afternoon comes the returning throng from the offices and counting-houses, while in the evening the working men, whose shoulders through the day have been free from the restraints of broad-cloth and buckram, don their uneasy Sunday-coats and come hither by hundreds, escorting their wives and children, and all their female relations. Now of all these motley crowds, is it not certain beyond a doubt that many go forth from this gallery with minds elevated by what they have seen, with manners and feelings refined, with new checks fastened upon coarse and unruly passions. Is it not certain that tastes are begotten here which afterward shed the charm of quiet and content over many a household. Nay, is it not certain that sparks of genius have been kindled here in poor neglected bosoms which shall dazzle us with their glorious light at some future day."[17]

The *Knickerbocker's* remarks captured the essence of nearly a decade of public interaction within the continually-evolving galleries of the American Art-Union in New York City. In 1849, New York lawyer and poet William Allen Butler captured it in verse with the following lines:

The Free Gallery of the American Art-Union

> *Here at last the arts of beauty*
> *In their fittest home abide,*
> *Not beneath the gilded ceilings*
> *Of the palaces of pride;*
> *Not in lordly shrines sequestered.*
> *For the favored few alone,*
> *But in simple halls whose portals*
> *Open to the world are thrown!*

Close beside the whirl incessant
Of the city's ceaseless din,
Free to all who choose to enter,
Is the wealth of art within;
And the rich man and the poor man,
Turning from the crowded street,
In the fellowship of feeling,
Here as equals still may meet![18]

While the Art-Union exhibitions continued to draw praise from many quarters, the gallery was not without its detractors. A scathing critique from *The North American* in 1849 questioned not only the overall quality of the Art-Union's purchases but also its buying practices: "I have not been very seriously impressed with the excellence of these pictures and think that an institution with an income of over eighty thousand dollars per annum ought to do something a little better than this. There are some half dozen good pictures but, with these exceptions, the whole collection appears to me very much like the refuse of the artist's studios. And such, too, I fear is the fact. The difficulty—and it is a serious one–seems to be this. Instead of giving our acknowledged first artists positive orders for good pictures, and leaving them to their own price, they go about the studios haggling with the artists for cheaper prices like a lady buying a new dress. If a thousand dollars, for instance, is asked for a picture, the committee offer three hundred dollars, afterwards, perhaps, proposing a compromise by paying five hundred. Under these circumstances, the artist either refuses the negotiation or, if he happens to be poor, (which is somewhat frequently the case with artists) paints a picture *down to the price* he is to receive for it. Now, how can we expect any real and permanent benefit to art or public taste to arise from such a course as this, on the part of the wealthiest and most ostentatious institution in this country?"[19]

The most damaging criticism of the Art-Union's practices was not of the gallery and its exhibitions but of the annual distribution, viewed by some as constituting an illegal lottery. In 1849, the *New York Journal of Commerce* reluctantly observed that while "it is not a part of our present design to speak of this institution, whose objects none can more heartily approve than we. But we cannot forebear a passing remark on the Lottery, by which it distributes its prizes. Is this lottery in any

20 *New York Journal of Commerce*, January 1849.

21 *The New York Times*, December 18, 1852.

22 *The New York Times*, December 16, 1852.

23 Mary Bartlett Cowdrey, *American Academy of Fine Arts and American Art-Union*, 1816-1852 (New York: NewYork Historical Society, 1953), 216.

sense different from others which are forbidden by State Law? And is there not danger of encouraging gambling by this plan? Already we see many plans of money making advertised 'on the plan of the American Art-Union.' It is very certain that the object of an immense majority of the subscribers is not the encouragement of art but the winning of a picture, often to be sold as soon as drawn."[20]

The New York Supreme Court's ruling that the American Art-Union's distribution methods did indeed constitute an illegal lottery brought to an end one of the most ambitious and popular efforts toward the promotion of the arts in the history of the United States. The Perpetual Free Gallery closed in December of 1852, and the Art-Union's remaining holdings were sold at auction that month "dispersed among the true lovers of art."[21] The *New York Times* reported that "there was a large attendance but a glance at the names of the purchasers, confined comparatively to a few, would show that by far the greater numbers present attended to take a 'last fond look' at works of beauty and masterpieces of art which had for years been a source of elevating and refined enjoyment to our citizens."[22]

In her 1953 study, Mary Bartlett Cowdrey confirms the success of the Art-Union galleries thus: "During the whole thirteen years of Art-Union activity, its exhibitions were viewed by an estimated total of no less than three million visitors— an enormous attendance for those days… Indeed, when one considers that the average population of New York City during the period 1839-1851 was not more than 400,000 and that the average yearly attendance at the Art-Union galleries, including the lean initial years, amounted to 230,000, the phenomenon becomes astounding…The fact stands striking and unshaken that the Art-Union galleries elicited a keener interest among a greater proportion of the population than has any other museum or gallery of art over an equal period at any time before or since, anywhere in America."[23]

The promotion of the arts and the support of artists both established and new was an essential feature of the Art-Union's overall success. In *Young America: The Flowering of Democracy in New York City*, historian Edward L. Widmer asserts that "despite its abridged history, the Art-Union irrevocably enlarged the nation's art consciousness and facilitated the emergence of a professional class

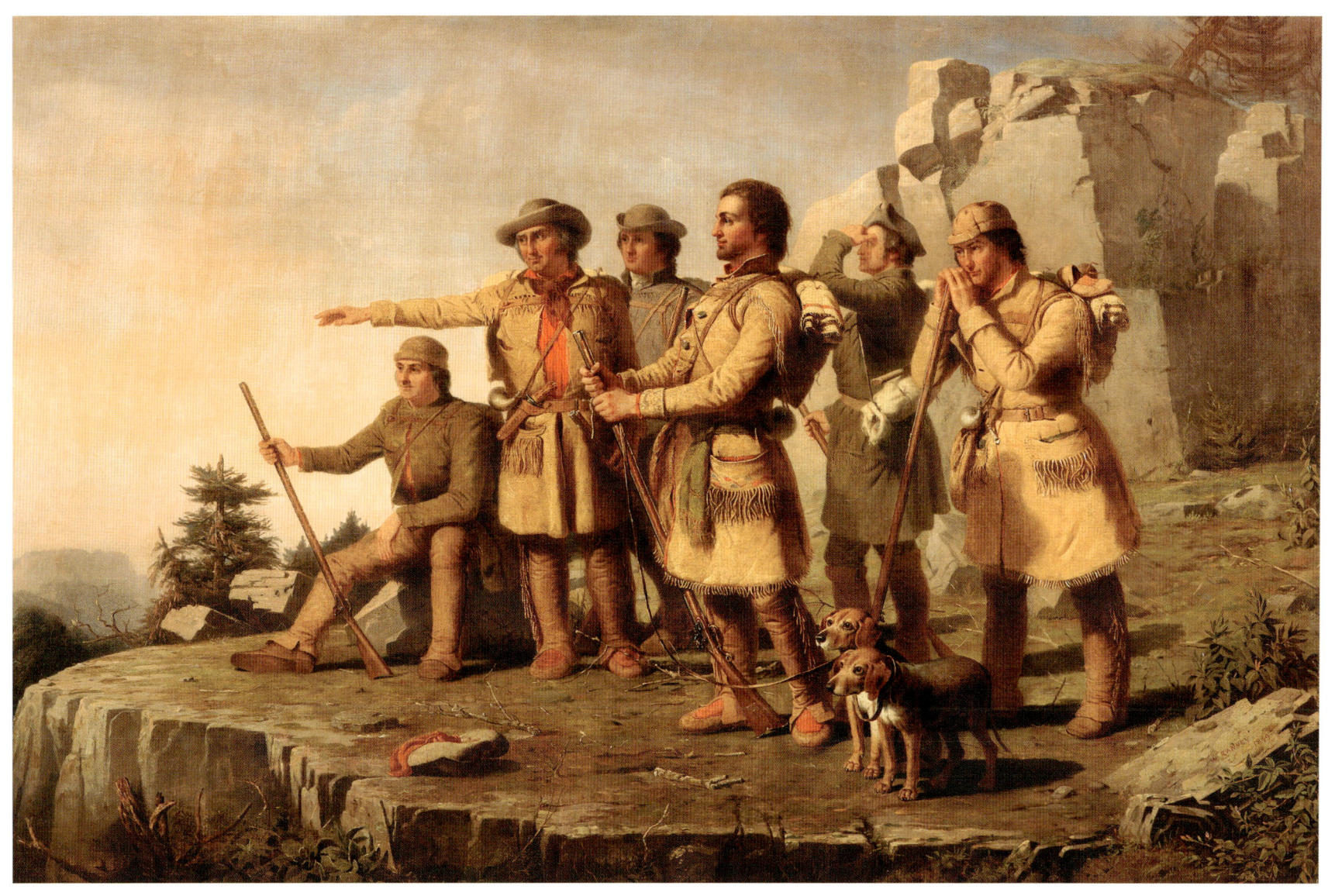

William Tylee Ranney, *Boone's First View of Kentucky,* oil on canvas, 1850, GM 0126.1233

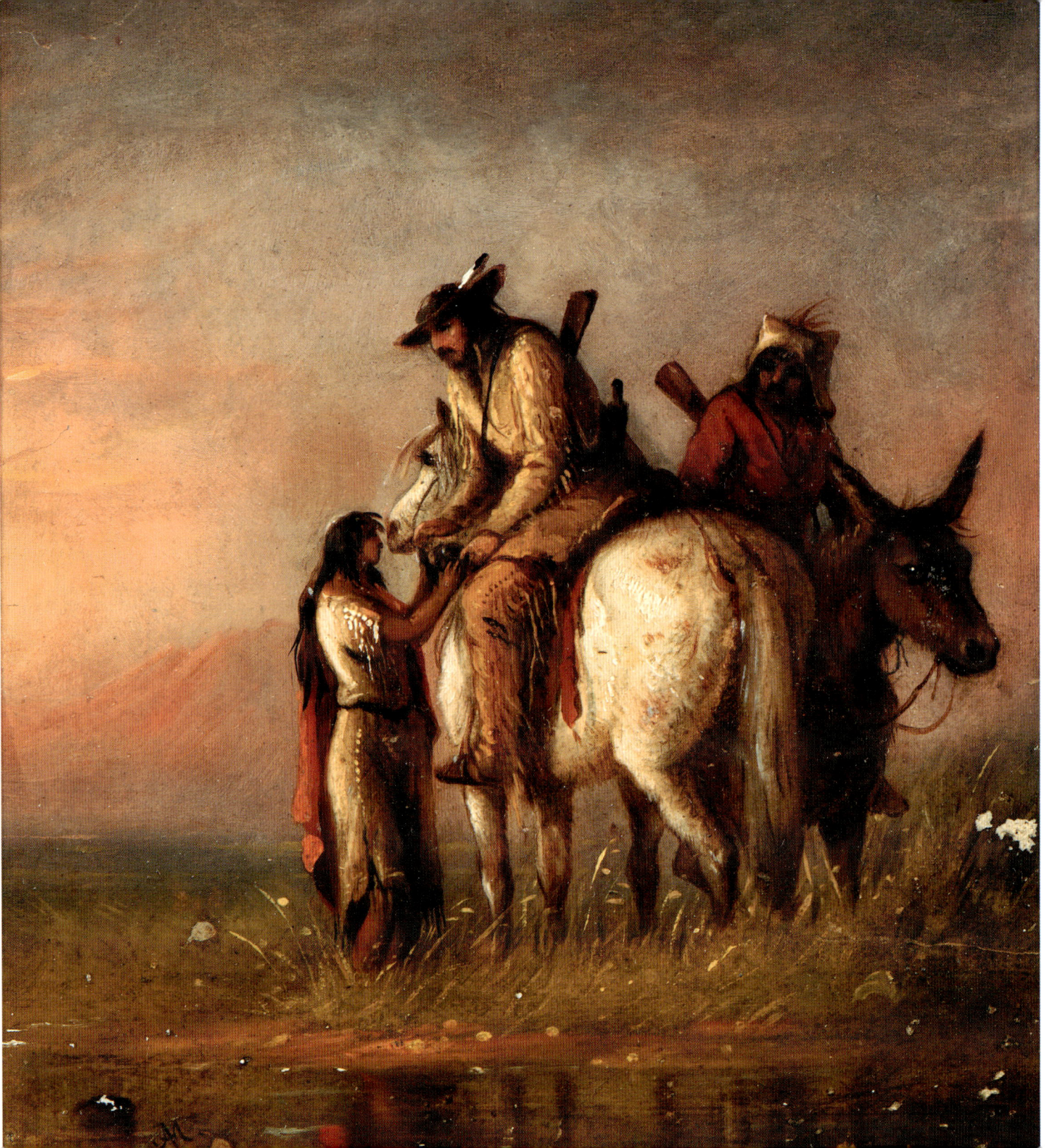

of artists and art mongers. Besides the encouragement it provided genre painters like Edmonds, it gave younger artists a place to learn their craft. If it did nothing else, it brought art appreciation out of the few private salons it had inhabited and forced it out into the open. No matter how the resulting art itself was evaluated, this was a path breaking achievement."

Free access to art by the general public was perhaps novel at first but was a critical breakthrough in the early years of the Republic. The lofty rhetoric of the Art-Union managers was followed with deeds. The enactment of the Art-Union's democratic principles in the rooms of its ever-evolving galleries remains a fundamental accomplishment of its distribution and exhibition program. "If the widespread representation of ordinary, unposed Americans did not in itself constitute an extraordinary artistic achievement, then the increased participation of those same people in the larger art-distribution process did. Together, the human realism of the genre artists and the widely felt influence of the American Art-Union enhanced the lives of countless numbers of "unaccredited" citizens whose lives had never been touched by art previously. Despite the brevity of this participatory moment, it introduced the democratic principle into what had been an ill-defined and aristocratic enclave of American culture."[24]

The last years of the old Art-Union gallery on Broadway were marked by neglect and inner city decay. The once thriving art center had given way to more random commercial pursuits. Only a few years after its closing, the grand salon of the Art-Union was converted to a "lager-bier saloon" where "theatrical performances, comic singing and dancing" took place "for the delectation of the beer drinkers."[25] The old gallery was converted to the stores of Harris & Russak furriers in the late 1870s.[26] The final days of "that stately gallery" were belatedly announced on August 16, 1896 when the *Brooklyn Eagle* published the following article on the Art-Union gallery's demolition—perhaps a fitting obituary to the passing of an era in American life:

There is now in process of destruction a building on Broadway, New York that would have had columns written about it had the demolition been undertaken a few years

24 Edward L. Widmer, *Young America: The Flowering of Democracy in New York City* (New York: Oxford University Press, 1999), 152-154.

25 *The New York Times*, November 8, 1858.

26 *The New York Times*, June 14, 1879.

FACING: Alfred Jacob Miller, *The Thirsty Trapper*, Oil on Canvas, 1852, GM 0136.743

earlier. It is the old home of the American Art-Union. This was one of the earlier and perhaps more spasmodic attempts of native art to get itself recognized and the methods then adopted would hardly be endorsed at present. It put up this marble building… where exhibitions might be seen and sales effected, for in those days a new work of Church or Bierstadt was hippodromed about the land…and shown in the principle towns at a quarter of a dollar a head and drawing good audiences, too. That kind of thing is growing difficult to do now…and pictures that the people were once eager [to see] would attract but slight attention. They were works of the Hudson River School, careful, truthful, full of interesting detail but lacking in force and breadth. But the Art-Union existed for more than this; there was a social side to it and the social side of the artist life in New York was also more considerable than it is now. In the first place, there were so many fewer painters then that society not only tolerated them but ran after them. Society before the war was based on gentleness and refinement and courtesy and intelligence, not on pomp and money and pride in families about thirty years old…The vulgarity of an overdressed multitude screaming its remarks across each others' heads in an over-decorated drawing room waiting to get at its food in the basement is a later exhibit of society. The Union published a magazine in addition to giving exhibitions and enlarging the artist's sphere of society…The members were to profit, that is, the institution was to profit—by a periodic disposition of works to holders of lucky numbers…This was really a violation of the lottery laws but in those times few people seemed to think that lotteries were wicked. They became so shortly after, however, and the decline of the Art-Union dates from some expressions of disapproval that probably would have never been made if the objectors had held winning numbers. The building of the Union was of the ambitious style affected in those days— over-ornamented and ornamented without purpose. Three rather commonplace statues adorned its front, over as many windows, but not one person in a thousand noticed them in the confusion of signs. . . . The Union is almost forgotten, for the Academy more than fills the place it held and even that is no longer big enough for a town like New York and a country like the United States… No attempts are made to boom art by factitious methods. It must go upon its own merits and it must also await a better appreciation from the American people."

The American Art-Union gallery enhanced the lives of everyday people and created an an expectation that art should be a part of everyday life. The many American galleries and museums that would follow benefited from the Art-Union's goal of providing a universal opportunity to participate in the nourishing experiences offered by the visual arts.

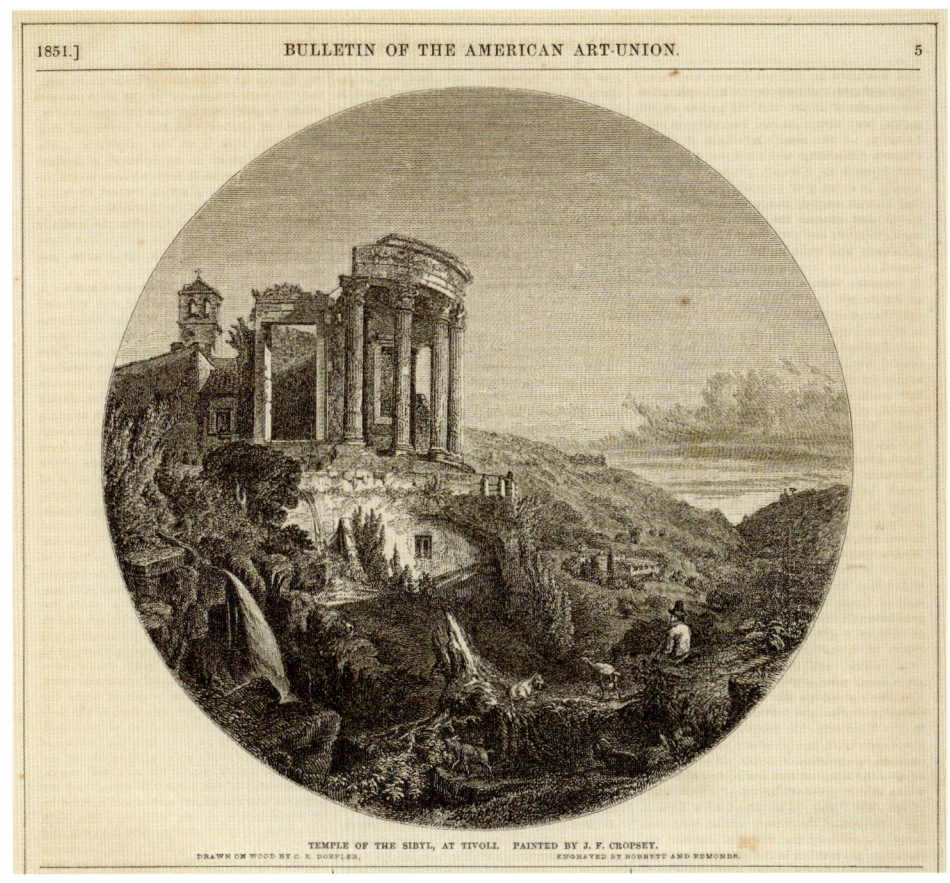

TEMPLE OF THE SIBYL, AT TIVOLI.   PAINTED BY J. F. CROPSEY.
DRAWN ON WOOD BY C. E. DOEPLER.   ENGRAVED BY BOBBETT AND EDMONDS.

Bobbett and Edmonds after Jasper Cropsey, *Temple of the Sibyl at Tivoli*, American Art-Union, engraving, 1851, GM 5126.1061.5

The following paintings and engravings in the Gilcrease collection were American Art-Union prizes or distributions. *The Thirsty Trapper*, Alfred Jacob Miller (GM136.743) and *Fort Laramie*, Alfred Jacob Miller (GM126.727). Both were part of the final year liquidation of assets sale in1852); *Indian Burial*, Seth Eastman (GM126.1122), 1848 lottery; *Sioux Playing Ball*, Charles Deas (GM126.1152), 1848 lottery; *Boone's First View of Kentucky*, William Tylee Ranney (GM126.1233), 1850 lottery; *Crossing the Ferry*, William Tylee Ranney (GM126.1234), 1846 lottery; James Smillie after Asher B. Durand, *Dover Plains* (GM15.1143); James Smillie after John F. Kensett, *Mount Washington from the Valley of Conway* (GM15.1139); Charles Burt after C. R. Leslie, *Anne Page, Slender and Shallow, A Scene from the Merry Wives of Windsor* (GM15.1146); Charles Burt after William Tylee Ranney, *Marion Crossing the Pedee* (GM15.1142); Alfred Jones, Smillie & Hinshelwood after Asher B. Durand, *The Capture of Major Andre*; Alfred Jones after Francis Edmonds,

The New Scholar (GM15.1141), and *John Trumbull Medal* (GM 08.219).

A set of ten small prints were acquired by Gilcrease Museum in 2011 incude the following: James Smillie after Thomas Cole, *Dream of Arcadia*, American Art-Union, engraving, 1850, GM15.1137; Charles Burt after Richard Caton Woodville, *The Card Players*, American Art-Union, engraving, 1850, GM15.1138; Alfred Jones after Francis Edmonds, *The New Scholar*, American Art-Union, engraving, 1850, GM15.1141; James Smillie after Asher B. Durand, *Dover Plains*, American Art-Union, engraving, 1850, GM15.1143; Alfred Jones after Emanuel Leutze, *The Image Breaker*, American Art-Union, engraving, 1850, GM15.1147; James Smillie after John F. Kensett, *Mount Washington From the Valley of Conway*, American Art-Union, engraving, 1851, GM15.1139; Charles Burt after William Sidney Mount, *Bargaining for a Horse*, American Art-Union, engraving, 1851, GM15.1140; Charles

Burt after William Tylee Ranney, *Marion Crossing the Pedee*, American Art-Union, engraving, 1851, GM15.1142; James Smillie, after Jasper Cropsey, *American Harvesting*, J. Dalton, engraving, 1851, GM15.1144; J. I. Pease after Richard Caton Woodville, *Old '76 and Young '48*, American Art-Union, engraving,1851, GM15.148.

AAU publications in the Gilcrease collection include: *Bulletin of the American Art-Union*, New York,1851, GM126.1061; *Transactions of the American Art-Union*, New York 1847, GM126.1062; *Transactions of the American Art-Union*, New York, 1848, GM126.1063; Washington Irving, Felix O. C. Darley, illus., *Rip Van Winkle*, American Art-Union, New York, 1848 (TL2010.16.05a&b); Washington Irving, Felix O. C. Darley, illus., *The Legend of Sleepy Hollow*, American Art-Union, New York, 1848 (TL2010.16.06a&b).

PHOTO CREDITS